BATTLES
OF THE
CRIMEAN WAR

BATTLES
OF THE
CRIMEAN WAR

WILLIAM H. RUSSELL

AMBERLEY

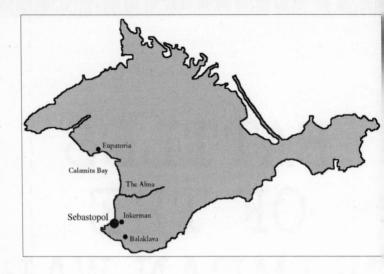

Eupatoria

Calamita Bay

The Alma

Sebastopol Inkerman

Balaklava

First published 2014

Amberley Publishing
The Hill, Stroud
Gloucestershire, GL5 4EP

www.amberley-books.com

British Library Cataloguing in Publication Data.
A catalogue record for this book is available from the British Library.

ISBN 978 1 4456 3789 1 (print)
ISBN 978 1 4456 3801 0 (ebook)

Typeset in 10pt on 12pt Sabon.
Typesetting and Origination by Amberley Publishing.
Printed in the UK.

Contents

Notice to the Reader

The interest excited by the events of the Campaign in the Crimea has not died away. Many years, indeed, must elapse ere the recital of the details of that great struggle, its glories, and its disasters, cease to revive the emotions of joy or grief with which a contemporary generation regarded the sublime efforts of their countrymen. As records on which the future history of the war must be founded, none can be more valuable than letters written from the scene, read by the light documents, such as those which will shortly be made public, can throw upon them. (The letter which appeared in *The Times* giving an account of the Battle of the Alma was written at a plank which Captain Montagu's sappers put on two barrels to form a table.) There may be misconception respecting the nature of the motives by which statesmen and leaders of armies are governed, but there can be no mistake as to what they do; and, although one cannot always ascertain the reasons which determine their outward conduct, their acts are recorded in historical memoranda not to be disputed or denied. For the first time in modern days the commanders of armies have been compelled to give to the world an exposition of the considerations by which they were actuated during a war, in which much of the sufferings of our troops was imputed to their ignorance, mismanagement, and apathy. They were not obliged to adopt that course by the orders of their superiors, but by the pressure of public opinion; and that pressure became so great that each, as he felt himself subjected to its influence, endeavoured to escape from it by throwing the blame on the shoulders of his colleagues, or on a military scapegoat, known as 'the system.' As each in self-defence flourished his pen or his tongue against his brother, he made sad rents in the mantle of official responsibility and secrecy. Even in Russia the press, to its own astonishment, was called on to expound the merits of captains and explain grand strategical operations; and the public there, read in the official organs of their Government very much the same kind of matter as our British public in the evidence given before the Chelsea Commissioners. Much of what was hidden has been revealed. We know more than we did; but we never shall know all.

I avail myself of a brief leisure to revise, for the first time, letters written under very difficult circumstances, and to re-write those portions of them which relate to the most critical actions of the war. From the day the Guards landed in Malta down to the fall of Sebastopol, and the virtual conclusion of the war, I had but one short interval of repose. I was with the first detachment of the British army which set foot on Turkish soil, and it was my good fortune to land with the first at Scutari, at Varna, and at Old Fort, to be present at Alma, Balaklava, Inkerman, to accompany the Kertch and the Kinburn expeditions, and to witness every great event of the siege – the assaults on Sebastopol, and the Battle of the Tchernaya. It was my still greater good fortune to be able to leave the Crimea with the last detachment of our army. My sincere desire is, to tell the truth, as far as I knew it, respecting all I have witnessed. I had no alternative but to write fully, freely, fearlessly, for that was my duty, and to the best of my knowledge and ability it was fulfilled. There have been many emendations, and many versions of incidents in the war, sent to me from various hands – many now cold for ever – of which I have made use, but the work is chiefly based on the letters which, by permission of the proprietors of *The Times*, I was allowed to place in a new form before the public.

W. H. RUSSELL
July, 1858

1

Arrival and Disembarkation

The causes of the last war with Russia, overwhelmed by verbiage, and wrapped up in coatings of protocols and dispatches, at the time are now patent to the world. The independence of Turkey was menaced by the Czar, but France and England would have cared little if Turkey had been a power whose fate could affect in no degree the commerce or the reputation of the allies. France, ever jealous of her prestige, was anxious to uphold the power of a nation and a name which, to the oriental, represents the force, intelligence, and civilization of Europe. England, with a growing commerce in the Levant, and with a prodigious empire nearer to the rising sun, could not permit the one to be absorbed and the other to be threatened by a most aggressive and ambitious state. With Russia, and France by her side, she had not hesitated to inflict a wound on the independence of Turkey which had been growing deeper every day. But when insatiable Russia, impatient of the slowness of the process, sought to rend the wounds of the dying man, England felt bound to stay her hands, and to prop the falling throne of the Sultan.

Although England had nothing to do with the quarrels of the Greek and Latin Churches, she could not be indifferent to the results of the struggle. If Russia had been permitted to exercise a protectorate over the Greek subjects of the Porte, and to hold as material guarantee the provinces of the Danube, she would be the mistress of the Bosphorus, the Dardanelles, and even the Mediterranean. France would have seen her moral weight in the East destroyed. England would have been severed from her Indian Empire, and menaced in the outposts of her naval power.

A council of war was held on Tuesday, July 18th, at Varna, at which Marshal St Arnaud, Lord Raglan, Admiral Hamelin, Admiral Dundas, Admiral Lyons, and Admiral Bruat were present, and it was resolved that the time had come for an active exercise of the powers of the allied forces by sea and land. The English Cabinet, urged probably by the English press, which on this occasion displayed unusual boldness in its military counsels and decision in its suggestions of hostility against the enemy, had despatched the most positive orders to Lord Raglan to make a descent in the Crimea, and to besiege Sebastopol, of which little was known except that it was the great arsenal of Russia in the Black Sea.

The arrangements for the conveyance of the troops to their destination were of the largest and most perfect character; and when all the transports were united, they constituted an armada of 600 vessels, covered by a fleet with 3,000 pieces of artillery.

Although, at first sight, this force appeared irresistible, it could not be overlooked that the enemy had a large fleet within a few hours' sail – that in using our men-of-war as transports, we lost their services in case of a naval action – that our army had suffered much from illness and death, and that the expedition had something of uncertainty, if not audacity, in its character – all that was fixed being this, that we were to descend at the Katcha, beat the Russians, and take Sebastopol.

Writing at the time, I said:

> I am firmly persuaded that the patience of people at home, who are hungering and thirsting for the news of 'the Fall of Sebastopol', will be severely tried, and that the chances are a little against the incidents of its capture being ready by Christmas for repetition at Astley's. It is late, very late, in the year for such a siege as there is before us, and I should not be surprised if we are forced to content ourselves with the occupation of a portion of the Crimea, which may become the basis of larger and more successful operations next year.

It was a vast armada. No pen could describe its effect. Ere an hour had elapsed it had extended itself over half the circumference of the horizon. Possibly no expedition so complete and so terrible in its means of destruction, with such enormous power in engines of war and such capabilities of locomotion, was ever yet sent forth. The speed was restricted to four miles and a half per hour, but with a favouring wind it was difficult to restrain the vessels to that rate, and the transports set no sail. The course lay N.E. by E., and the fleet was ordered to make for a point 40 miles due west of Cape Tarkan. On looking to the map it will be seen that the point thus indicated is about 50 miles east of Fidonisi, or Serpents' Island, off the mouth of the Danube, and that it lies about 100 miles to the north-east of Sebastopol, Cape Tarkan being a promontory of the Crimea, 63 miles north of the fortress. It was understood that this point was the rendezvous given to our French and Turkish allies. The fleet, in five irregular and straggling lines, flanked by men-of-war and war steamers, advanced slowly, filling the atmosphere with innumerable columns of smoke, which gradually flattened out into streaks and joined the clouds, adding to the sombre appearance of this well-named 'Black' Sea. The land was lost to view very speedily beneath the coal clouds and the steam clouds of the fleet, and as we advanced, not an object was visible in the half of the great circle which lay before us, save the dark waves and the cold sky.

Not a bird flew, not a fish leaped, not a sail dotted the horizon. Behind us was all life and power – vitality, force, and motion – a strange scene in this so-called Russian lake! From time to time signals were made to keep the stragglers in order, and to whip up the laggards, but the execution of the plan by no means equaled the accuracy with which it had been set forth upon paper, and the deviations from the mathematical regularity of the programme were very natural. The effect was not marred by these trifling departures from strict rectilinearity, for the fleet seemed all the greater and the more imposing as the eye rested on these huge black hulls weighing down upon the face of the waters, and the infinite diversity of rigging which covered the background with a giant network.

A few farm-houses were dimly discernible in the distance over the waste and low-lying plains, which seemed embrowned by great heats.

Little dark specks, supposed to be cattle, could also be distinguished. Shortly before six o'clock the anchor was let go in 16 fathoms of water, at the distance of 12 or 15 miles from shore. The number of vessels was prodigious – forty-four steamers could be counted, though many of the French vessels were not visible. When evening set in, the bands of the various regiments, the drums and fifes of those who had no bands, the trumpets of cavalry and horse artillery, and the infantry bugles formed a concert monstre, which must have been heard on shore in spite of the contrary breeze. Some of the ships lay closer in than we did, and they were so thick that collisions took place more than once, happily without any serious consequences.

The sunset was of singular beauty and splendour. Heavy masses of rich blue clouds hung in the west, through innumerable golden chasms of which the sun poured a flood of yellow glory over the dancing waters, laden with great merchantmen, with men-of-war staggering under press of canvas, and over line after line of black steamers, contending in vain to deface the splendour of the scene. When night came on, and all the ships' lights were hung out, it seemed as if the stars had settled down on the face of the waters. Wherever the eye turned were little constellations twinkling far and near, till they were lost in faint halos in the distance. The only idea one could give of this strange appearance is that suggested by the sight from some eminence of a huge city lighted up, street after street, on a very dark night. Flashes of the most brilliant lightning, however, from time to time lifted the veil of night from the ocean, and disclosed for an instant ships and steamers lying at anchor as far as could be seen. About eight o'clock, just as every one had turned in for the night, orders were sent on board to the deputy-quartermaster-general of each division respecting the preparations for the disembarkation of the men. The men seemed in excellent health and spirits. The number of fever and cholera cases, though greater than we could have wished, was not sufficient to cause any very great alarm. No doubt the voyage had done the army good, and they all looked forward with confidence to their landing next day.

The place off which we anchored on the night of Tuesday, September 12th, was marked on the charts as Schapan. It is 14 miles distant N.N.E. from our starting-point on Tuesday at noon, so that we only ran that length the whole of the afternoon from twelve to six o'clock. At six o'clock on the morning of the 13th, signal was given to weigh and proceed, and at eight o'clock the lines were formed and the expedition proceeded, steering towards the S.E. It was evident, from the course we had taken, that the expedition was going towards Eupatoria, a town situated on a low promontory of land about 34 miles distant from Sebastopol.

Towards noon the ships of the expedition closed in with the shore. The country was flat, but numerous herds of cattle were to be seen in the plains and salt marshes, and the farm-houses became more frequent as we proceeded southwards. We soon after saw the Cossacks in twos or threes – or at least horsemen whom every one declared to be those famous irregulars – scouring along towards the town, but there were very few of them, and they were at long intervals; now and then a farmer-looking man, in a covered cart, was visible, jogging along, as it appeared, with perfect indifference to the formidable apparition of some 400 vessels keeping company with him at the distance of some 5 or 6 miles only.

Eupatoria soon became visible. It lies on a spit of sand, and for a long time we imagined that it was defended by heavy works, for the solid stone houses close by the sea-coast were so increased by refraction and lifted up so high, that they looked like forts. We could see up the main streets of the town with our glasses very clearly. Cossacks dotted all the hills, watching us, and some of them were 'driving' the cattle across the sandy hillocks towards the interior. There seemed to be a blockhouse on shore, and a kind of earthwork, near which was a flagstaff, but no flag was exhibited.

The place thus selected for our landing was a low strip of beach and shingle, cast up by the violence of the surf, and forming a sort of causeway between the sea and a stagnant salt-water lake. The lake is about 1 mile long, and ½ mile broad, and when we first arrived, its borders and surface were frequented by vast flocks of wildfowl. The causeway was not more than 200 yards broad, leading, at the right or southern extremity of the lake, by a gentle ascent, to an irregular table-land or plateau of trifling elevation, dotted with tumuli or barrows, such as are seen in several parts of England. Towards the sea this plateau presented a precipitous face of red clay and sandstone, varying in height from 100 to 150 feet, and it terminated by a descent almost to the sea-level, at the distance of nearly 2 miles from the shores of the lake. Thence towards the south there was a low sandy beach, with a fringe of shingle raised by the action of the waves above the level of the land, and saving it from inundation. This low coast stretched along as far as the eye could reach, till it was lost beneath the base of the mountain ranges over Sebastopol. The country inland, visible from the decks of our ships, was covered with cattle, with grain in stack, with farm-houses. The stubble-fields were covered with wild lavender, southernwood, and other fragrant shrubs, which the troops collected for fuel, and which filled the air with an aromatic perfume.

Now and then some Cossacks were visible, scouring along the roads to the interior, and down south towards the menaced stronghold of the Czar; but they were not numerous, and at times it was doubtful whether the people we saw were those freebooters of the Don, or merely Crim Tartar herdsmen, armed with cattle-spears. The post carriage from Sebastopol to Odessa was also seen rolling leisurely along, and conveying, probably, news of the great armament with which the coast was menaced.

As the ships of our expedition drew up in lines parallel to the beach, the French fleet passed us under steam, and extended itself on our right, and ran in close to shore below the cliffs of the plateau. Their small war steamers went much nearer than ours were allowed to do, and a little after seven o'clock the first French boat put off from one of the men-of-war; not more than fifteen or sixteen men were on board her. She was beached quietly on shore at the southern extremity of the real cliff already mentioned. The crew leaped out; they formed into a knot on the strand, and seemed busily engaged for a few moments over one spot of ground, as though they were digging a grave. Presently a flag-staff' was visible above their heads, and in a moment more the tricolor was run up to the top, and fluttered out gaily in the wind, while the men took off their hats, and no doubt did their '*Vive l'Empereur!*' in good style. The French were thus the first to take possession and seisin of the Crimea.

There was no enemy in sight. The most scrutinizing gaze at this moment could not have detected a hostile uniform along the coast. The French Admiral fired a gun shortly after eight o'clock, and the disembarkation of their troops commenced. In little more than an hour they got 6,000 men on shore. This was very smart work, but it must be remembered that nearly all the French army were on board line-of-battle ships, and were at once carried from their decks to the land by the men-of-war's boats. The fleet of French men-of-war carried more than 20,000 men. Their whole force to be landed consisted of 23,600 men.

Our army amounted to 27,000 men, who were embarked in a vast number of transports, covering a great extent of water. But they were carried in comfort and safety; and, though there was still much sickness on board, it was as nothing compared to the mortality among the closely-packed French. Perhaps no army ever was conveyed with such luxury and security from shore to shore as ours in the whole history of war.

About nine o'clock one black ball was run up to the fore of the *Agamemnon* and a gun was fired to enforce attention to the signal. This meant, 'Divisions of boats to assemble round ships for which they are told off, to disembark infantry and artillery.' In an instant the sea was covered with a flotilla of launches, gigs, cutters, splashing through the water, some towing flats, and the large Turkish boats, others with horse-floats plunging heavily after them. They proceeded with as great regularity as could be expected to their appointed ships, and the process of landing commenced.

Up to this moment not an enemy was to be seen; but as the boats began to shove off from the ships, five horsemen slowly rose above the ridge on the elevated ground, to the right of the strip of beach which separated the salt-water lake from the sea in front of us. After awhile four of them retired to one of the tumuli inland opposite the French fleet. The other retained his position, and was soon the cynosure of all neighbouring eyes. The Russian was within about 1,100 yards of us, and through a good telescope we could watch his every action.

He rode slowly along by the edge of the cliff, apparently noting the number and disposition of the fleet, and taking notes with great calmness in a memorandum book. He wore a dark screen frock-coat, with a little silver lace, a cap of the same colour, a sash round his waist, and long leather boots. His horse, a fine bay charger, was a strange contrast to the shaggy rough little steeds of his followers. There they were, 'the Cossacks', at last! – stout, compact-looking fellows, with sheepskin caps, uncouth clothing of indiscriminate cut, high saddles, and little fiery ponies, which carried them with wonderful ease and strength. Each of these Cossacks carried a thick lance of some 15 feet in length, and a heavy sabre. At times they took rapid turns by the edge of the cliff in front of us – now to the left, now to the rear, of their officer, and occasionally they dipped out of sight, over the hill, altogether. Then they came back, flourishing their lances, and pointed to the accumulating masses of the French on their right, and more than ½ mile from them, on the shore, or scampered over the hill to report progress as to the lines of English boats advancing to the beach. Their officer behaved very well. He remained for an hour within range of a Minié rifle, and making a sketch in his portfolio of our appearance, we all expected she was going to drop a shell over himself and his little party. We were glad our expectations were not realized, if it were only on the chance of the sketch being tolerably good, so that the Czar might really see what our armada was like.

Very amusing was it to watch the loading and unloading of the boats. A gig or cutter, pulled by eight or twelve sailors, with a paddle-box boat, flat, or Turkish pinnace in tow (the latter purchased for the service), would come up alongside a steamer or transport in which troops were ready for disembarkation. The officers of each company first descended, each man in full dress. Over his shoulder was slung his havresack, containing what had been, ere it underwent the process of cooking, four pounds and a half of salt meat, and a bulky mass of biscuit of the same weight. This was his ration for three days. Besides this, each officer carried his greatcoat, rolled up and fastened in a hoop round his body, a wooden canteen to hold water, a small ration of spirits, whatever change of under-clothing he could manage to stow away, his forage-cap, and, in most instances, a revolver. Each private carried his blanket and greatcoat strapped up into a kind of knapsack, inside which was a pair of boots, a pair of socks, a shirt, and, at the request of the men themselves, a forage-cap; he also carried his water canteen, and the same rations as the officer, a portion of the mess cooking apparatus, firelock and bayonet of course, cartouch box and fifty rounds of ball-cartridge for Minié, sixty rounds for smooth-bore arms.

As each man came creeping down the ladder. Jack helped him along tenderly from rung to rung till he was safe in the boat, took his firelock and stowed it away, removed his knapsack and packed it snugly under the seat, patted him on the back, and told him 'not to be afeerd on the water'; treated 'the sojer', in fact, in a very kind and tender way, as though he were a large but not a very sagacious 'pet', who was not to be frightened or lost sight of on any account, and did it all so quickly, that the large paddle-box boats, containing 100 men, were filled in five minutes. Then the latter took the paddle-box in tow, leaving her, however, in charge of a careful coxswain, and the same attention was paid to getting the 'sojer' on shore that was evinced in getting him into the boat; the sailors (half or wholly naked in the surf) standing by at the bows, and handing each man and his accoutrement down the plank to the shingle, for fear 'he'd fall off and hurt himself'. Never did men work better than our blue-jackets; especially valuable were they with horses and artillery; and their delight at having a horse to hold and to pat all to themselves was excessive. When the gun-carriages stuck fast in the shingle, half a dozen herculean seamen rushed at the wheels, and, with a 'Give way, my lad – all together', soon spoked it out with a run, and landed it on the hard sand. No praise can do justice to the willing labour of these fine follows. They never relaxed their efforts as long as man or horse of the expedition remained to be landed, and many of them, officers as well as men, were twenty-four hours in their boats.

By twelve o'clock, that barren and desolate beach, inhabited but a short time before only by the seagull and wild-fowl, was swarming with life. From one extremity to the other, bayonets glistened, and redcoats and brass-mounted shakoes gleamed in solid masses. The air was filled with our English speech, and the hum of voices mingled with loud notes of command, cries of comrades to each other, the familiar address of 'Bill' to 'Tom', or of 'Pat' to 'Sandy', and an occasional shout of laughter.

After a short time the country people began to come in, and we found they were decidedly well inclined towards us. Of course they were rather scared at first, but before the day was over they had begun to approach the beach, and to bring cattle, sheep, and vegetables for sale. Their carts, or rather arabas, were detained, but liberally paid for; and so well satisfied were the owners, that they went home, promising increased supplies to-morrow. The men were apparently of pure Tartar race, with small eyes very wide apart, nose very much sunk, and a square substantial figure. They generally wore turbans of lambswool, and jackets of sheepskin with the wool inwards. They spoke indifferent Turkish, and were most ready with information respecting their Russian masters, by whom they had been most carefully disarmed. A deputation of them waited on Lord Raglan to beg for muskets and powder to fight the Muscovite. They told us that the ground round Sebastopol had been mined for miles, but such rumours are always current about a fortress to be defended, and Russian mines not better constructed than those at Silistria could not do much harm. They said, too, that the cholera, of which we had had such dreadful experience, had been most fatal at Sebastopol, that 20,000 of the troops and seamen were dead, and that the latter had been landed to man the forts. They estimated the force between us and Sebastopol at about 15,000 men, and the garrison at 40,000 more. They added, however, that there was an army south of Sebastopol, which had been sent to meet an expected attack on Kaffa. On the whole, the information we at first obtained was encouraging, and the favourable disposition of the people, and their willingness to furnish supplies, were advantages which had not been expected.

Few of those who were with the expedition will forget the night of the 14th of September. Seldom or never were 27,000 Englishmen more miserable. No tents had been sent on shore, partly because there had been no time to land them, partly because there was no certainty of our being able to find carriage for them in case of a move. Towards night the sky looked very black and lowering; the wind rose, and the rain fell in torrents. The showers increased in violence about midnight, and early in the morning fell in drenching sheets, which pierced through the blankets and greatcoats of the houseless and tentless soldiers.

The work was, however, to be done, and in the afternoon orders were given to land cavalry. For this purpose it was desirable to approach the beach as close as possible, and a signal to this effect was made to the cavalry steamers. The attendance of cutters, launches, paddle-box boats, and horsefloats from the navy was prompt, and the seamen of the Royal and mercantile marine rivalled each other in their efforts. Never did men work so hard, so cheerfully, or so well. The horses, too, were so acclimated to ship life – they were so accustomed to an existence of unstable equilibrium in slings, and to rapid ascents and descents from the tight ropes, that they became comparatively docile. Besides this, they were very tired from standing for fourteen days in one narrow box, were rather thin and sickly, and were glad of change of air and position.

Before the disembarkation had concluded for the day, signal was made for all ships to 'land tents'. It need not be said that this order was most gratefully received. But alas! the order was countermanded, and the tents which had been landed were sent back to the ships again. Our French allies, deficient as they had been in means of accommodation and stowage and transport, had yet managed to land their little scraps of tents the day they disembarked. Whilst our poor fellows were soaked through and through, their blankets and greatcoats saturated with wet, and without any change of raiment, the French close at hand, and the Turks, whose tents were much more bulky than our own, were lying snugly under cover. The most serious result of the wetting was, however, a great increase in illness among the troops.

On the 15th of September, signal had been made from the *Emperor* for all ships to send their sick on board the *Kangaroo*. Before evening she had about 1,500 invalids in all stages of suffering on board. When the time for sailing arrived, the *Kangaroo* hoisted, in reply to orders to proceed, this signal – 'It is a dangerous experiment.' The *Emperor* then signalled – 'What do you mean?' The reply was

– 'The ship is unmanageable.' All the day she was lying with the signal up – 'Send boats to assistance'; and at last orders were given to transfer some of her melancholy freight to other vessels also proceeding to Constantinople. Many deaths occurred on board – many miserable scenes took place which it would be useless to describe. It was clear, however, that neither afloat nor on shore was the medical staff sufficient. More surgeons were required, both in the fleet and in the army. Often – too often – medical aid could not be obtained at all; and it frequently came too late.

On the 17th the disembarkation of stores continued and was completed, and the tents were carried up to the various divisions with great labour by large fatigue parties. The siege train still remained on board ship, and it was intended to land it at the mouth of the river Belbeck, close to Sebastopol, as we could not stay to put it ashore at Old Fort. The Cossacks came round our outposts, and the sky at night was reddened by the glare of their burnings. The Tartars said the Russians had 15,000 men posted in an entrenched camp on the Alma river, about 12 miles distant, on the road to Sebastopol. A troop of the 11th Hussars, who went out reconnoitring, were pursued by a regiment of Cossacks, but retired in order without any casualty. Captain Creswell, an officer of the regiment, who was a great favourite with his comrades, died of cholera in the little village in which his troop was quartered.

At twelve o'clock on the night of Monday, September 18th, orders were given by Lord Raglan that the troops should strike tents at daybreak, and that all tents should be sent on board the ships of the fleet. M. de Bazancourt asserts that the French Marshal was ready to march on the 17th, and that he all along hoped to do so, but that the English were not prepared, as they had an immense quantity of *impedimenta*. He further says that it was arranged between the Generals to defer the march till 11 a.m. on the 18th, but that we again delayed the movement when the time came, and that Marshal St Arnaud wrote to Lord Raglan to say he would move without him if he was not ready the following morning.

At three o'clock in the morning of the 19th, the camp was roused by the *réveil*, and the 50,000 sleepers woke into active life. The boats from the ships lined the beach to receive the tents which were again returned to the ships. The English commissariat officers struggled in vain with the very deficient means at their disposal to meet the enormous requirements of an army of 26,000 men, for the transport of baggage, ammunition, and food; and a scene, which to an unpractised eye seemed one of utter confusion, began and continued for several hours, relieved only by the steadiness and order of the regiments as they paraded previous to marching. It was nine o'clock ere the whole of our army was ready. The day was warm. The country beyond the salt lake, near which we were encamped, was entirely destitute of tree or shrub, and consisted of wide plains, marked at intervals of 2 or 3 miles with hillocks and long irregular ridges of hills running down towards the sea at right angles to the beach. It was but little cultivated, except in the patches of land around the unfrequent villages built in the higher recesses of the valleys. Hares were started in abundance, and afforded great sport to the soldiers whenever they halted, and several were fairly hunted down among the lines. All oxen, horses, or cattle, had been driven off by the Cossacks. The soil was hard and elastic, and was in excellent order for artillery. The troops presented a splendid appearance. The effect of these grand masses of soldiery descending the ridges of the hills, rank after rank, with the sun playing over forests of glittering steel, can never be forgotten by those who witnessed it. Onward the torrent of war swept; wave after wave, huge stately billows of armed men, while the rumble of the artillery and tramp of cavalry accompanied their progress. Many sick men fell out, and were carried to the rear. It was a painful sight – a sad contrast to the magnificent appearance of the army in front, to behold litter after litter borne past to the carts, with the poor sufferers who had dropped from illness and fatigue. However, the march went on, grand and irresistible.

At last, the smoke of burning villages and farm-houses announced that the enemy in front were aware of our march. It was melancholy to see the white walls of the houses blackened with smoke – the flames ascending through the roofs of peaceful homesteads – and the ruined outlines of deserted hamlets.

2

The Battle of the Alma

Presently, from the top of a hill, a wide plain was visible, beyond which rose a ridge darkened here and there by masses which the practised eye recognised as cavalry. Right before us was a neat white house unburnt, though the outhouses and farm-yard were burning. This was the Imperial Post-house of Bouljanak, just 20 miles from Sebastopol, and some of our officers and myself were soon busily engaged in exploring the place.

The house was deserted and gutted. Only a picture of a saint, bunches of herbs in the kitchen, and a few household utensils, were left; and a solitary pea-hen stalked sadly about the threshold, which soon fell a victim to a revolver. A small stream ran past us, which was an object of delight to our thirsty soldiers, who had marched more than 8 miles from their late camp. After a short halt for men and horses by the stream, over which the post-road was carried by a bridge which the enemy had left unbroken for the passage of our artillery, the army pushed on again.

The cavalry (about 500 men of the 8th Hussars, the 11th Hussars, and 13th Light Dragoons) pushed on in front, and on arriving about a mile beyond the post-house, we clearly made out the Cossack Lancers on the hills in front. Lord Cardigan threw out skirmishers in line, who covered the front at intervals of 10 or 12 yards from each other. The Cossacks advanced to meet us in like order, man for man, the steel of their long lances glittering in the sun. They were rough-looking fellows, mounted on sturdy little horses; but the regularity of their order and the celerity of their movements showed that they were by no means despicable foes. As our skirmishers advanced, the Cossacks halted at the foot of the hill. From time to time a clump of lances rose over the summit of the hill and disappeared. Lord Cardigan was eager to try their strength, and permission was given to him to advance somewhat nearer; but as he did so, dark columns of cavalry appeared in the recesses of the hills. Lord Lucan therefore ordered the cavalry to halt, gather in their skirmishers, and retire slowly. When our skirmishers halted, the Cossacks commenced a fire of carabines from their line of vedettes, which was quite harmless. Few of the balls came near enough to let the whiz be heard. I was riding between the cavalry and the skirmishers, with Lieutenant-Colonel Dickson, R.A., Captain Fellowes, 12th Lancers, Dr Elliott, R.A., and we were looking out anxiously for the arrival of Maude's Troop, when the Russians, emboldened by our halt, came over the brow of the hill, and descended the slope in three columns, the centre of which advanced nearer than the others.

'Now,' said Dickson, 'we'll catch it. These fellows mean mischief.' I conceived that it would be a very pleasant thing to look at, whatever they meant. Our skirmishers, who had replied smartly to the fire of the Cossacks, but without effect, retired and joined their squadrons. At every fifty paces our cavalry faced. Fellowes rode off to quicken the advance of the artillery. Suddenly one of the Russian squares opened – a spurt of white smoke rose out of the gap, and a round shot, which first pitched close to my horse and covered me with dust, tore over the column of cavalry behind, and rolled away between the ranks of the riflemen in the rear, just as they came in view. In another instant a second shot bowled right through the 11th Hussars, and knocked over a horse, taking off his rider's leg above the ankle. Another and another followed. Meantime the C Troop followed by the I Troop, galloped over the hillock, but were halted by Lord Raglan's order at the base in rear of the cavalry on the left flank.

Our cavalry was drawn up as targets for the enemy's guns, and had they been of iron they could not have been more solid and immovable. The Russian gunners were rather slow, but their balls came bounding along, quite visible as they passed, right from the centre of the cavalry columns. After some thirty rounds from the enemy, our artillery, having cleared their front, opened fire. Captain Brandling laid the first gun, No. 5, and fired with so true an aim that the shell was seen to burst right over a Russian gun, and apparently to shut it up. All our shells were not so successful as the first, but one, better directed than the rest, burst right in the centre of a column of light infantry, which the Russians had advanced to support their cavalry. Our fire became so hot that the enemy retired in fifteen minutes after we opened on them, and manoeuvring on our left with their light cavalry, seemed to threaten us in that direction; but Captains Maude and Henry having shifted their guns so as to meet their front, the enemy finally withdrew over the hills, and seemed to fall back on the Alma.

While this affair was going on the French had crept up on the right, and surprised a body of Russian cavalry with a round from a battery of 9-pounders, which scattered them in all directions. It is impossible to form an accurate notion of the effect of our fire, but it must have caused the Russians a greater loss than they inflicted on us. There is reason to believe they lost about twelve men killed, thirty-five wounded, and thirty-two horses *hors de combat*. We lost six horses, and four men were wounded. Two men lost their legs. The others, up to yesterday, though injured severely, were not in danger. A sergeant in the 11th Hussars rode coolly to the rear with his foot dangling by a piece of skin to the bone, and told the doctor he had just come to have his leg dressed. Another trooper behaved with equal fortitude, and refused the use of a litter to carry him to the rear, though his leg was broken into splinters. When the Russians had retired beyond the heights orders were given to halt and bivouac for the night, and our tired men set to work to gather weeds for fuel. So ended the affair of the Bouljanak. Lord Cardigan was, it is said, anxious to charge, but received most positive orders from Lord Lucan not to do so. Lord Raglan was anxious not to bring on any serious affair in the position in which the army was placed, and the cavalry were ordered to retire towards the Bouljanak, their retreat being supported by the 1st Brigade Light Division, and part of the 2nd Division.

As soon as the rations of rum and meat had been served out, the casks were broken up, and the staves used to make fires for cooking, aided by nettles and long grass. All night we could see the Russian position on the Alma clearly defined by the watch-fires, which illuminated the sky.

With early morning on Tuesday, September 20th, the troops were up and stirring; but the march did not begin for some hours afterwards, and this circumstance has given rise to severe strictures by several French writers on the conduct of our generals on the occasion. It appears somewhat strange that no reconnaissance was made of the Russian position by the generals. They did not reconnoitre the Alma, nor did they procure any information respecting the strength of the enemy or of the ground they occupied. They even concerted their plan before they had seen the enemy at all, relying on the bravery of the troops, not only to force the Russians from their lines, but, if necessary, to swim, or to ford a stream of unknown depth, with steep rotten banks, the bridges across which might, for all they knew, and certainly ought, according to the practice of war, to have been effectually destroyed by the enemy, so as to make the passage of guns all but impossible.

We shall first follow the French attack. On returning to his troops, Bosquet, with the brigade of d'Autemarre, followed by its artillery, moved on the village, whilst the brigade of General Bouat was directed to march to the very mouth of the river, and to ascend by the first of the paths indicated, after having crossed the shallow bar, in single file, up to their waists on a sort of narrow rib of hard sand which had been discovered by the officers of the *Roland*. The artillery of the brigade, being unable to pass, was sent back to join that of d'Autemarre's brigade; and the soldiers of Bouat's brigade, having crossed the river, commenced to climb up the steep paths to the top of the opposite height without meeting any obstruction from the enemy, who had, indeed, been driven away from the seaside by the heavy guns of the steamers.

The brigade of d'Autemarre, which passed the Alma without any difficulty, by the bridge close to the burnt village of Almatamak, moving forward at the same time with great celerity, swarmed up the very steep cliffs on the opposite side, and gaining the heights in a few minutes, after immense exertions, crowned the summit, and dispersed a feeble troop of Cossacks who were posted there. It will be seen that the French right had thus been permitted to ascend the very difficult heights in front of them without opposition from the enemy; and although the cliffs were so precipitous as to create considerable difficulties to even the most active, hardy, and intelligent troops in scaling their rugged face, yet it would seem very bad generalship on the part of Prince Menschikoff to have permitted them to have established themselves on the plateau, if we did not know, by the angry controversy which has taken place between him, General Kiriakoff, and Prince Gortschakoff, that it was part of his plan to allow a certain number of battalions to gain the edge of the cliffs, and then, relying on the bayonet, to send heavy masses of infantry against them and hurl them down into the Alma, and the ravines which run towards its banks. General Bosquet, when he observed this success, at once spurred up the steep road of which mention has already been made; and Major Barral, who commanded the artillery, having satisfied himself that the guns could just be brought up by the most tremendous exertions, orders were given for their advance, and they were, by prodigious efforts of horses and infantry soldiers, urged up the incline, and placed on the plateau at right angles to the line of the cliffs, so as to enfilade the Russians, on whom, protected by the 3rd Zouaves, who lay down in a small ravine about a hundred yards in front, they at once opened fire.

Prince Menschikoff, surprised by the extraordinary rapidity of this advance, and apprized of its success by the roar of the French guns, ordered up three batteries of eight pieces each to silence the French fire, and to cover an advance of his infantry against the two brigades which were forming on his left; and finding that the French maintained themselves against this superior fire, in a rage despatched two field batteries to crush them utterly. These guns were badly managed, and opened in line at the distance of 900 yards, and the fire, for nearly an hour, was confined to a duel of artillery, in which the French, though suffering severely, kept their ground with great intrepidity and courage. All at once the Russians ordered some cavalry and a field battery to menace the right of the line of French guns; but Bouat's brigade having pushed on to meet them, and a few well-directed shells having burst among the horsemen, they turned round and retired with alacrity. According to the concerted plan, the Division Canrobert and the Division Napoleon were not to attack till the Division Bosquet had gained the heights, and were engaged with the enemy. The directions given by the Marshal to the Generals ere they advanced were simply, 'Keep straight before you, and follow your own inspiration for your manoeuvres. We must gain these heights. I have no other instructions to give to men on whom I rely.' On hearing the first guns of Bosquet's artillery, the French, in the centre and in the left, deployed and advanced, covered by a number of riflemen.

The 1st Zouaves, under Colonel Bourbaki, at once rushed to the front, driving before them a line of Russian riflemen and skirmishers placed among the orchard trees and rivers which skirted the deep banks of the Alma, and availing themselves of the branches of these trees to swing themselves across the narrow stream into which others plunged up to the waist. The Russian regiment of Moscow came down the opposite slopes to support their skirmishers, but were driven back with loss by the sudden fire of the batteries of the First Division, that had just come into action. Having thus cleared the way, the 1st and 9th battalions of Chasseurs, the 7th of the line, and the 1st Zouaves advanced amid a storm of grape, round shot, and musketry up the high banks before them, at the other side of which were deployed masses of the enemy, concealed from view in the ravines and by the inequalities of the ground.

At the same time, the Prince's division advancing towards Bourliouk, which was in flames, was met by a very serious fire of riflemen and skirmishing parties of infantry from the vineyards and rugged ground on the other side of the stream, and by a plunging fire of artillery, which was answered by the batteries of his division; but, after a short pause, the first line, consisting of Cler's Zouaves and the infantry of marine, supported by the second line under General Thomas, passed the Alma and drove back the enemy, who opened a masked battery upon them, which occasioned considerable loss. Canrobert's division, meantime, was compelled to attack without the aid of its artillery; for the river in their front was not practicable for guns, and they were obliged to be carried round to the right to follow the road by which Bosquet's batteries had already reached the summit; but the column pushed on energetically, and forming on the crest of the plateau by battalions, in double columns on two lines, ready to form square under the fire of the enemy's artillery, which had been engaged with that of the French second division, drove back the Russian regiments in front, which, on retiring, formed in square in front of their right flank.

It was then that the officers perceived a white stone tower, about 800 yards on their left, behind which was formed a dense mass of the enemy's infantry. These with great precision advanced, at the same time pouring in a tremendous fire, at the distance of 200 yards, upon Canrobert's division, which was, as we have seen, left without its artillery. The general, perceiving his danger, sent off a staff officer to Bosquet's division, and a battery, commanded by Captain Fievet, coming up to his assistance in all haste, opened fire with grape on the ponderous mass of the enemy, checking their fire, whilst Bosquet, by a flank movement, threatened to take its battalions in the rear.

The third division, with equal success and greater losses, attacking a mamelon occupied in force by the enemy, drove them back with great intrepidity: but it was evident by the movements of the Russians that they were about to make a great effort to save their centre, and M. St Arnaud sent off orders to General Forey, who commanded the reserve, to move one of his brigades (de Lourmel's) to General Canrobert's support, and to proceed with the other (d'Aurelle's) to the extreme right of the battle. This was a happy inspiration: d'Aurelle's brigade, with great speed, crossed the river, and arrived to the support of Canrobert's division at a most critical moment. The Russians seemed to consider the Telegraph Tower as the key of the centre of their position. Sharpshooters, within the low wall outside the work, and batteries on its flanks, directed a steady fire on the French, who were checked for a moment by its severity: but the two batteries of the reserve came up and drew off some of the enemy's fire. The Russians, however, still continued a serious fusillade, and directed volleys of grape against the French, who were lying down in the ravine till the decisive moment should arrive for them to charge the enemy. The losses of our allies were sensible; it was evident that the Russian cavalry, says, M. de Bazancourt, were preparing for a rush in upon them from the flank of the Russian square, which, partially covered by the Telegraph Tower, kept up an incessant fire from two faces upon the French.

Colonel Cler, at this critical moment, perceiving that the 1st and 2nd Zouaves, the Chasseurs, and the 39th Regiment had arrived, calling to his men to charge, dashed at the tower, which, after a short but sanguinary combat, they carried at the point of the bayonet, driving out the Russians in confusion, and at the very moment General Canrobert, with his division, advanced at the double to support the movement. Struck down for a moment by a fragment of a shell which wounded him on the chest and shoulder, the gallant officer insisted upon leading on his men to complete the success obtained against the Russian left and left-centre; and Generals Bosquet and Canrobert, wheeling round their divisions from left to right, drove back the enemy towards the rear of the troops, which were still contending with the English, or forced them to seek for safety in flight. It was at this moment that M. St Arnaud, riding up to the Generals, congratulated them on the day, and directed them to proceed to the aid of the English.

Thanks be to the valour of our soldiers – thanks be to Heaven – we required no French aid that day. We received none, except that which was rendered by one battery of French artillery of the reserve, under M. de la Boussiniere, which fired a few rounds on some broken Russian columns from a spot close to the two English guns, of which I shall have to speak hereafter. Such is the part, according to their account, which the French had in the victory of the Alma. Their masses crossed the river and crowded the plateau ere they were seriously engaged, and their activity and courage, aided by the feeble generalship of the commander of the

Russian left, and by many happy chances, enabled them to carry the position with comparatively little loss.

Having thus far given the French version of the action, let us return to our countrymen, and see what was their share in this great battle, which was not decisive, so far as the fate of Sebastopol was concerned, merely because we lacked either the means or the military genius to make it so. There is one question which has often been asked in our army and in the tents of our allies, which is supposed to decide the controversy respecting the military merits of St Arnaud and Lord Raglan: 'Would Napoleon have allowed the Russians three days' respite after such a battle?' The only reply that could be made if Napoleon commanded the victorious army, and was not hampered with a colleague of equal power, was, and is, that the notion is preposterous. 'But,' say the French, 'the English were not ready to move next day.' 'Ay, it is true,' reply the English, 'because we were far from the sea; but still we offered to assist you to pursue the very night of the battle.' 'Then,' rejoin the French, 'we were too much exhausted, and it would have been foolish to have attempted such a movement, and to have divided our army.' Posterity, which cares but little for ephemeral political cliquerie, family connexion, or personal amiability, will pass a verdict in this cause which none of us can hope to influence or evade.

The reason of the extraordinary delay in executing our plan of attack has never yet been explained. Lord Raglan's excuse, as given by M. de Bazancourt, is not worth any notice but this – it is not true. The Staff-officer says that 'the army was under arms soon after 6 a.m., and on the move'. Where? – a mile or two too much inland? What were we doing for five hours? For this same authority further on says, 'It was 11 a.m. before we came in sight of the Alma.' Now, the distance between the Bouljanak and the Alma is barely 6 miles. Were we five hours marching 6 miles? This is indeed a feeble statement; but it is not quite so weak as that which follows, namely, that it was not till after 11 o'clock 'the plan of attack was finally settled'. This statement is made to cover Lord Raglan, and to prevent there being any suspicion that a plan had been arranged the night before, for the disregard and nonperformance of which the Staff-officer's uncle was responsible. That Lord Raglan was brave as a hero of antiquity, that he was kind to his friends and to his staff, that he was unmoved under fire, and unaffected by personal danger, that he was noble in manner, gracious in demeanour, of dignified bearing, and of simple and natural habits, I am, and ever have been, ready not only to admit, but to state with pleasure; that he had many and great difficulties to contend with, *domi militiæque*, I believe; but that this brave, high-spirited, and gallant nobleman had been so long subservient to the power of a superior mind – that he had lost, if he ever possessed, the ability to conceive and execute large military plans – and that he had lost, if he ever possessed, the faculty of handling great bodies of men, I am firmly persuaded, he was a fine English gentleman – a splendid soldier – perhaps an unexceptionable lieutenant under a great chief; but that he was a great chief, or even a moderately able general, I have every reason to doubt, and I look in vain for any proof of it whilst he commanded the English army in the Crimea.

It was 10 o'clock ere the British line moved towards the Alma. A gentle rise in the plain enabled us to see the Russian position for some time after, but the distance was too great to make out details, and we got into a long low bottom between the ridge and another elevation in front. Our army advanced in columns of brigades in deploying distance, our left protected by a line of skirmishers, the brigade of cavalry, and horse artillery. The army, in case of attack on the left or rear, could form a hollow square, with the baggage in the centre. Sir De Lacy Evans's division, on the extreme right, was in contact with the French left, under Prince Napoleon, which was of course furthest from the sea. At the distance of 2 miles we halted, and then the troops steadily advanced, with our left frittered into a foam of skirmishers of the Rifle Brigade, Major Northcott covered by the 11th and 8th Hussars, 13th Light Dragoons, and 17th Lancers.

This was a sight of inexpressible grandeur, and one was struck with the splendid appearance of our infantry in line as seen from the front. The bright scarlet, the white facings, and cross belts, rendering a man conspicuous, gave him an appearance of size which other uniforms do not produce. The French columns looked small compared to our battalions, though we knew they were quite as strong; but the marching of our allies, laden as they were, was wonderful. Our staff was more showy and numerous than that of the French. Nothing strikes the eye so much as a cocked hat and bunch of white feathers; several officers doffed the latter adornment, thinking that they were quite conspicuous on horseback. When the regiments halted, I went past the Light Division, part of the 2nd Division, the Guards, and the Highlanders. Many a laugh did I hear from lips which in two hours more were closed for ever. The officers and men made the most of the delay, and ate what they had with them; but there was a want of water, and the salt pork made them so thirsty that in the passage of the Alma the men stopped to drink and fill their canteens under the heaviest fire.

The plan of attack has been already described, as well as the circumstances of our early march. As we advanced we could see the enemy very distinctly – their grey-coated masses resembling patches of wood on the hill-sides. The ravines held them occasionally, but still we could see that from within a mile of the sea coast, up to the left of the Tartar village, towards which we were advancing, a strong force of infantry was posted, and now and then, as the Russian made his last disposition to meet our advance, the sun's rays flashed brightly in diamond-like points from bright steel. The line of the river below the heights they occupied was indicated by patches of the richest verdure, and by belts of fine fruit trees and vineyards. The Alma is a tortuous little stream, which has worked its way down through a red clay soil, deepening its course as it proceeds seawards, and which drains the steppe-like lands on its right bank, making at times pools and eddies too deep to be forded, though it can generally be crossed by waders who do not fear to wet their knees. The high banks formed by the action of the stream in cutting through the rich soil vary from the right side to the left, according to the course of the stream – the corresponding bank on the opposite side being generally of a slope, more or less abrupt, as the bank is high. The drop from the edge to the water varies also from 2 to 6 or 8 feet. Along the right or north bank of the Alma there is a number of Tartar houses, at times numerous and close enough to form a cluster of habitations deserving the name of a hamlet, at times scattered wide apart amid little vineyards, surrounded by walls of mud and stone of 3 feet in height. The bridge over which the post road passes from Bouljanak to Sebastopol runs close to one of these hamlets – a village, in fact, of some fifty houses. This village is approached from the north by a road winding through a plain nearly level till it comes near to the village, where the ground dips, so that at the distance of 300 yards a man on horseback can hardly see the tops of the nearer and more elevated houses, and can only ascertain the position of the stream by the willows and verdure along its banks. At the left or south side of the Alma the ground assumes a very different character – it rises at once from the water in steep banks up to plateaux at the top of varying height and extent. The general surface is pierced here and there by the course of the winter's torrents, which have formed small ravines, commanded by the heights above. A remarkable ridge of tumuli and hillocks, varying in height from 100 to 400 feet, runs along the course of the Alma on the left side, assuming the form of clitis when close to the sea, and rising in a gentle slope a little to the left of the Tillage I have mentioned, which is called by the Tartar, and marked on the maps as Burliuk.

At its commencement on the left this ridge recedes from the course of the river for several hundred yards, the ground sloping gradually from the bank up to the knolls and tumuli into which the ridge is broken. It then strikes downwards at a sharp angle to its former course, till it sinks into the high ground over the river below the village. There is then a sort of Δ formed, of which the base is the river, and the sides the elevated terrace of the ridge. This terrace, or the succession of terraces, is commanded by higher ground in the rear, but is separated from the position on its proper left by a ravine. It is marked by deep gullies towards the river. If the reader will place himself on the top of Richmond-hill, dwarf the Thames to the size of a rivulet, and imagine the hill to be deprived of vegetation, he may form some notion of the position occupied by the Russians, the plains on the left bank of the Thames will bear some similitude to the land over which the British and French advanced, barring only the verdure. On the slope of the rising ground, to the right of the bridge, the Russians had thrown up two epaulements, armed with 32-pounder batteries and 24 pound howitzers. These twelve guns enfiladed the slopes parallel to them, or swept them to the base. The principal battery consisted of a semicircular earthwork, in which were embrasures for thirteen guns. On the right, and farther in the rear, was another breastwork with embrasures for nine guns, which played on the right of the bridge. To the left, on a low ridge in front of the village, they had placed two and a half field batteries, which threw 1,000 and 1,200 yards beyond the village.

The first battery was about 300 yards distant from the river, but the hill rose behind it for 50 feet. The second was turned more towards the right. About 12.15, when we were about 3 miles from the village, the steamers ran in close to the bluff at the south side of the Alma, commenced shelling the heights, the enemy were obliged to retire their infantry and guns, and the ships covered the advance of the French right, and never permitted the Russians to molest them till they were in force on the plateau. At one o'clock we saw the French columns struggling up the hills, covered by a cloud of skirmishers. They swarmed like bees to the face of the cliffs, tiny puffs of smoke rising from every tree, and shrub, and stone. On the right they formed their masses without opposition. At sight of a threatening mass of Russian infantry, who advanced slowly, pouring in all the time a tremendous rolling fire, the French who were forming in the centre, seemed to pause, but it was only to collect their skirmishers, for as soon as they had formed they ran up the hill at the *pas de charge*, and broke up the Russians at once, who fled in disorder, with loss, up the hill. We could see men dropping on both sides, and the wounded rolling down the steep. However, our attention was soon drawn to our own immediate share in the battle. As I had slept at the head-quarters camp, I joined the general staff, and for some time rode with them; but when they halted, just before going into action. Major Burke, who was serving on the staff as Aide-de-camp to Sir John Burgoyne, advised me to retire, 'as,' said he, 'I declare I will make Sir John himself speak to you if you do not.' There was at the time very little to be seen from the ground which the staff occupied, and there were so many officers along with Lord Raglan, that it was difficult to see in front at all; and so, observing Sir De Lacy Evans somewhat in advance on the right of Lord Raglan, on higher ground about a quarter of a mile away, I turned my horse to join him, and in an instant afterwards a round shot rushed over the heads of the staff, being fired at the Rifles in advance of them. As it turned out, Sir De Lacy's small staff suffered much more severely than Lord Raglan's large one, although the Staff-officer seems firmly persuaded that the enemy's artillery was partially directed against the body to which he belonged. One could scarcely have been in a safer place on the field, considering out of so large a body only two were wounded, whereas five of General Evans's small staff were badly hit or contused. By the time I had reached Sir De Lacy Evans, who was engaged in giving orders to Brigadier Adams, the round shot were rolling through the columns, and the men halted and lay down by order of Lord Raglan. Sir De Lacy said, 'Well, if you want to see a great battle, you're in a fair way of having your wish gratified.' At this moment the whole of the village in our front burst into flames – the hay-ricks and wooden sheds about it causing the fire to run rapidly, fanned by a gentle breeze, which carried the smoke and sparks towards our line. Sir De Lacy rode towards the left to get rid of this annoyance, and to get to his men, and as he did so, the round shot came bounding among the men lying down just before us. From the groans and stifled cries it was too plain they left dead and dying in their course. The Rifles in advance of our left were sharply engaged with the enemy in the vineyard, and, anxious to see what was going on, I rode over in that direction, and arrived at the place where were stationed the staff of the Light Division. Sir George Brown was just at the time giving some orders to one of his Aides relative to the 'Russian cavalry on our left front'. I looked across the stream, and saw, indeed, some cavalry and guns slowly moving down towards the stream from the elevated ground over its banks but my eye at the same time caught a most formidable-looking mass of burnished helmets, tipped with brass, just above the top of the hill on our left, at the other side of the river. One could plainly see through the glass that they were Russian infantry, but I believe the gallant old General thought at the time that they were cavalry, and that a similar error led to the serious mistake, later in the day, which deprived the Light Division of part of its regimental strength, and wasted it on 'preparing to receive' an imaginary 'cavalry'. Sir George looked full of fight, clean shaven, neat and compact; I could not help thinking, however, there was a little pleasant malice in his salutation to me. As he rode past he said, in a very jaunty, Hyde Park manner, 'It's a very fine day Mr Russell.' At this moment the whole of our right was almost obscured by the clouds of black smoke from the burning village on our right, and the front of the Russian line above us had burst into a volcano of flame and white smoke – the roar of the artillery became terrible – we could hear the heavy rush of the shot, those terrible dumps into the ground, and the crash of the trees, through which it tore with resistless fury and force; splinter and masses of stone flew out of the walls. It was rather provoking to be told so coolly it was a very fine day amid such circumstances; but at that very moment the men near us were ordered to advance, and they did so in quick time in open line towards the walls which bounded the vineyards before us. As I had no desire to lead my old friends of the Light Division into action, I rode towards the right to rejoin Sir De Lacy Evans, if possible; and as I got on the road I saw Lord Raglan's staff riding towards the river, and the shot came flinging close to me, one, indeed, killing one of two bandsmen who were carrying a litter close to my side, after passing over the head of my horse. It knocked away the side of his face and he fell dead – a horrible sight. The G and B batteries of the Second Division were unlimbered in front, and were firing with great steadiness on the Russians; and now and then a rocket, with a fiery tail and a huge waving mane of white smoke, rushed with a shrill shout against the enemy's massive batteries. Before me all was smoke – our men were lying down still; but the 'Rifles, led by

Major Norcott, conspicuous on a black horse, were driving back the enemy's sharpshooters with signal gallantry, and clearing the orchards and vineyards in our front by a searching fire. When I reached the spot where I had last seen Sir De Lacy Evans, he was nowhere to be found, for he had, as I afterwards heard, ridden with his staff close to the river by the burning village. My position was becoming awkward. Far away in the rear was the baggage, from which one could see nothing; but where I was placed was very much exposed. A shell burst over my head, and one of the fragments tore past my face with an angry whir-r-r, and knocked up the earth at my poor pony's feet. Close at hand, and before me, was a tolerably good stone-house, one story high, with a large court-yard, in which were several stacks of hay that had not as yet caught fire. I rode into this yard, fastened up my pony to the rope binding one of the ricks, and entered the house, which was filled with fragments of furniture, torn paper, and books, and feathers, and cushion linings, and established myself at the window, from which I could see the Russian artillerymen serving their guns; their figures, now distinctly revealed against the hill side, and again lost in a spurting whirl of smoke. I was thinking what a terrible sort of field-day this was, and combating an uneasy longing to get to the front, when a tremendous crash, as though a thunderclap had burst over my head, took place right above me, and in the same instant I was struck and covered with pieces of broken tiles, mortar, and stones, the window out of which I was looking flew into pieces, parts of the roof fell down, and the room was filled with smoke.

There was no mistaking this warning to quit. A shell had burst in the ceiling. As I ran out into the yard I found my pony had broken loose, but I easily caught him, and scarcely had I mounted when I heard a tremendous roll of musketry on my left front, and looking in the direction, I saw the lines of our red jackets in the stream, and swarming over the wooden bridge. A mass of Russians were at the other side of the stream, firing down on them from the high banks, but the advance of the men across the bridge forced these battalions to retire; and I saw, with feelings which I cannot express, the Light Division scrambling, rushing, foaming like a bloody surge up the ascent, and in a storm of fire, bright steel, and whirling smoke, charge towards the deadly epaulement, from which came roar and flash incessantly. I could distinctly see Sir George Brown and the several mounted officers above the heads of the men, and could detect the dark uniforms of the Rifles scattered here and there in front of the waving mass. On the right of this body, the 30th, 50th, and 95th were slowly winning their way towards the battery, exposed to a tremendous fire, which swallowed them up in the fiery grey mantle of battle. The rush of shot was appalling, and I recollect that I was particularly annoyed by the birds which were flying about distractedly in the smoke, as I thought they were fragments of shell. Already the wounded were passing by me. One man of the 30th was the first; he limped along with his foot dangling from the ankle, supporting himself on his firelock 'Thank you kindly, sir,' said he, as I gave him a little brandy, the only drop I had left. 'Glory be to God, I killed and wounded some of the Roosians before they crippled me, anyway.'

He halted off towards the rear. In another moment two officers approached – one leaning on the other – and both wounded, as I feared, severely. They belonged to the 30th. They went into the enclosure I had left, and having assured them I would bring them help, I rode off towards the rear, and returned with the surgeon of the Cavalry Division, who examined their wounds. All this time the roar of the battle was increasing. I went back to my old spot in doing so I had to ride gently, for wounded men came along in all directions. One was cut in two by a round shot as he approached Many of them lay down under the shelter of a wall, which was however, enfiladed by the enemy. Just at this moment I saw the Guards advancing in the most majestic and stately order up the hill while through the intervals and at their flanks poured the broken masses of the Light Division, which their officers were busy in re-forming. The Highlanders, who were beyond them, I could not see; but I never will forget the awful fury, the powerful detonation of the tremendous volleys which Guards and Highlanders poured in upon the Russian battalions, which in vain tried to defend their batteries and to check the onward march of that tide of victory. All of a sudden the round shot ceased to fly along the line; then there was a sharp roll of musketry and a heavy fire of artillery which lasted for some moments. Then one, two, three round shot pitched in line, ricochetting away to the rear. As I looked round to see what mischief they did, a regiment came rapidly towards the river. I rode towards them; they were the 50th. 'The cannon shot come right this way, and you'll suffer frightfully if you go on.' As I spoke, a shell knocked up the dust to our right, and Colonel Waddy, pushing the left, led his men across the river. I rode towards the bridge. The road wall was lined by wounded. Fitzgerald (7th), with his back against the wall, was surveying his wounded legs with wonderful equanimity. 'I wish they had left me one, at all events,' said he, as we tried to stop the bleeding. As I passed the bridge there was a spattering of musketry. The cannon were still busy on our right, and field-guns were firing on the retreating Russians, whose masses were over the brow of the hill. Then there was a thundering cheer, loud as the roar of battle, and one cannon boomed amid its uproar. This was the victory. A few paces brought me to the bloody slopes where friend and foe lay in pain, or in peace for ever.

When the columns were deploying, Northcott moved from the left and advanced to the front of the Light and First Divisions, till they came to a long low stone wall. Here they waited till the line came up. The instant they did so, the two front companies, in extended order, leaped over the wall into the vineyards, the two companies in support moving down a road to their left, on a ford, by which they crossed the stream. The Rifles were first across the river. They were under the cover of a bank which bounded the plateau, and hid them from the fire at our advancing columns. It was a second terrace; for just at this place the ground was a series of three giant steps – the first being that from the river to the top of the bank; the second, from the plateau at the top of the bank to the plateau on which the enemy were in position; and the third being from that position to the highest ground of all, on which they had their reserves. No sooner had the Rifles lined this lower ridge than the enemy pushed a column of infantry, headed by some few Cossacks, down the road which led to the ford, and threatened to take them in rear and flank and destroy them, for these gallant fellows were without support. Major Norcott, however, was not dismayed, but at once made the most skilful disposition to meet this overwhelming column of the enemy. Retiring from the ridge, he placed one of the four companies under him on the road by which they were advancing, two others he posted along the bank of a vineyard on the right of this road, and with the fourth he occupied the farm-house in the centre of the vineyard: thus availing himself of the resources of the ground with much skill and judgment. At this moment there were no supports in sight – nothing to rest on form upon in the rear – the Rifles were quite alone. The Russians advanced leisurely; but to the astonishment of our officers, just as the men were about to open fire on them, the Cossacks and the column halted, and then wheeling to the right-about, retired up the road and disappeared over the brow of the hill. On looking round however, the phenomenon was soon explained – Codrington's brigade was rushing across the river under a tremendous fire and at the same time the Russians advanced heavy columns of infantry towards the ridge over the stream. The Rifles moved towards their right to join the Light Division, and at the same time poured in a close and deadly fire upon the dense formation of the enemy, which must have caused them great loss. Having effected their junction, the Rifles moved up with the Light Division, and bringing up their left shoulders, threw themselves on the flank of the battery, bravely led by Major Norcott, till they were forced to retire with their supports. One company, under Captain Colville was separated from the left wing, and did not participate as fully as the other companies in the fight; and the right wing, under Colonel Lawrence, was kept back by a variety of impediments and had no opportunity of playing the same distinguished part as the left wing.

As soon as the line of the Light Division came up to the Rifles the latter were ordered to retire, and re-form in rear of the brigades; but some few of the men could not obey the order, and were consequently in front along with the advance – some with the Guards, others with the men of Codrington's brigade. Captain the Hon. W. Colville and Lieutenant Nixon led their men, when separated from the other Companies of the wing, in front of the red soldiers, and formed up in the rear of the broken masses sullenly retiring from the earthwork, so as to lend valuable assistance to the supports which were advancing under the Duke of Cambridge, and one of these two officers brought a horse to a colonel of the Guards when he was dismounted and enabled him to resume his place at the head of his men.

The approach of the Light Division – why should I not dwell fondly on every act of that gallant body, the first 'put at' everything, the first in suffering, in daring, in endurance throughout the campaign? – their approach, then, was in double columns of brigades; the Second Division being on their right, and the second battalion of the Rifle Brigade, divided into two wings, one under Major Norcott, the other under Colonel Lawrence, being in advance in skirmishing order. When the Light Division got within long range, they deployed; the men lay down. Again they advanced; once more they were halted to lie down; this time the shot pitched among them; the same thing was repeated again ere they reached the river, and many were wounded before they got to the vineyards. Here, indeed, they were sheltered, but when the order was given to advance, the men were thrown into disorder, not so much by the heavy fire as by the obstacles opposed by hedges, stone walls, vines, and trees. These well-drilled regiments were thus deprived of the fruits of many a day's hard marching at Gallipoli, Aladyn, and Devna; but the 1st Brigade being in rather better ground and more in hand than the 2nd Brigade, moved off, and with them the 19th Regiment, belonging to Brigadier Buller, who was lost in a hollow, and afterwards, as Lord Raglan euphemistically expressed it, moved judiciously on the left flank. The 19th, 7th, 23rd, and 33rd were led at a run right to the river, gallantly conducted by Codrington. Their course was marked by killed and wounded, but the four regiments were quickly – under the shelter of the high bank at the south side, in such a state of confusion from the temporary commingling of the men in the rush, that it was necessary to re-form. The enemy, too late to support their skirmishers, sought to overwhelm them in the stream, and three battalions of grey-coated infantry came down at the double almost to the top of the bank, and poured down a heavy fire. They were straggling, but not weak; the Brigade and the 19th made a simultaneous rush up the bank, and, as they crowned it, met their enemies with a furious fire. The dense battalions, undeployed, were smitten, and as the Light Division advanced they rapidly fell back to the left, for the renewed fire of their batteries, leaving, however, many dead and wounded men. After a momentary delay, these gallant regiments, led by Sir George Brown and Brigadier Codrington, advanced up the slope which was swept by the guns of the battery; grape, round, and shell tore through their ranks, and the infantry on the flanks, advancing at an angle, poured in a steady fire from point-blank distance. It must be confessed that the advance was disorderly – instead of the men being two deep and showing an extended front of fire, they were five, six, and seven deep, in ragged columns, with scarcely any front, and not half so extended as they should have been. Thus their fire was not as powerful or their advance as imposing as it ought to have been. The General and Brigadier made some attempts to restore order, but they were unsuccessful. The men had not only got into confusion in the river from stopping to drink, as I have related, but had disordered their ranks by attacks on the grapes in the vineyards on their way. Behind the work, on rising ground, a Russian regiment kept up a most destructive file fire on our advance; the field-pieces on the flank also played incessantly upon them. Every foot they advanced was marked by lines of slain or wounded men. The 7th Fusiliers, smitten by a storm of grape, reeling to and fro like some brave ship battling with a tempest, whose sails are gone, whose masts are toppling, and whose bulwarks are broken to pieces, but which still holds on its desperate way, impelled by unquenchable fire, within a few seconds lost a third of its men. Led by 'Old Yea', it still went on – a colour lost for the time, their officers down, their files falling fast – they closed up, and still with eye which never left the foe, pressed on to meet him. The 23rd Regiment was, however, exposed more, if that were possible, to that lethal hail. In less than two minutes from the time they crowned the bank till they neared the battery the storm had smitten down twelve of their officers, of whom eight never rose again. Diminished by one-half, the gallant companies sought, with unabated heart, to reach their terrible enemies. The 19th marched right up towards the mouths of the roaring cannon which opened incessantly and swept down their ranks; the 33rd, which had moved up with the greatest audacity over broken ground towards the flank of the epaulement, where it was exposed to a tremendous fire and heavy losses from guns and musketry from the hill above, was for the moment checked by the pitiless pelting of this iron rain. Their general at this terrible crisis seemed to have but one idea – right or wrong, it was to lead them slap at the battery, into the very teeth of its hot and fiery jaws. As he rode in front, shouting and cheering on his men, his horse fell, and down he went in a cloud of dust. He was soon up, and called out, 'I'm all right. Twenty-third, be sure I'll remember this day.' It was indeed a day for any one to remember. General Codrington in the most gallant manner rode in advance of his brigade, and rode his horse right over and into the work, as if to show his men there was nothing to fear; for by this time the enemy, intimidated by the rapid, though tumultuous advance of the brigade, were falling away from the flanks of the battery, and were perceptibly wavering in their centre. The infantry behind the breastwork were retreating up the hill. The Russians were in great dismay and confusion. They limbered up their guns, which were endangered by the retirement of their infantry from the flanks of the epaulement, and retired towards their reserves, which were posted on high ground in the rear. In this retrograde movement their artillery got among the columns of the infantry, and increased the irregular nature of their retreat; but they still continued to fire, and were at least three times as numerous as the men of the Light Division who were assailing them. When Sir George Brown went down, a rifleman, named Hugh Hannan, assisted him on his horse, and as they stood under a murderous fire, saluted as he got into his seat, and said, 'Are your stirrups the right length, sir?' Major Norcott, on his old charger, which, riddled with balls, carried his master throughout the day, and lay down and died when his work was over, got up to the redoubt, which was also entered by Brown and Codrington. (The reserve artillery horses had succeeded in drawing away all the guns except one, which was still in position, and on this gun, when the first rush was made, an officer of the 33rd, named Donovan, scratched his name.) In broken groups the 23rd, with whom were mingled men of the 19th and 33rd Regiments, rushed at the earthwork, leaped across it, bayoneted a few Russians who offered resistance, and for an instant were masters of the position. Captain Bell, of the 23rd, observed a driver in vain urging by whip and spur two black horses to carry off one of the brass 16-pounder guns which had done so much execution. Bell ran up, and, seizing the reins, held a revolver to his head. He dismounted, and ran off. Bell, with the assistance of a soldier of the 7th, named Pyle, led the horses round the shoulder of the parapet to the rear of our line, where the gun remained after the Light Division was obliged to retire, and reported the capture to Sir George Brown. The horses were put into our 'black battery'. This was but an episode. The colours of the 23rd were planted on the centre of the parapet. Both the colour officers, Butler and Anstruther, were killed. The colours were hit in seventy-five places, and the pole of one was shot in two; it had to be spliced. Meantime, the Russians, seeing what a handful of men they had to deal with, gained heart. The brigade and the 19th had held the entrenchment for nearly ten minutes, keeping the massive columns above them in check by their desperate but scattered fire. Where were the supports? They were not to be seen. The advance of the Guards, though magnificent, was somewhat slow. Two of the dark-grey masses, bristling with steel on our front, began to move towards the battery. The men fired, but some staff-officer or officers called out that we were firing upon the French. A bugler sounded the 'Cease firing'. The Russians advanced, and our men were compelled to fall back. Some of the enemy, advancing from the epaulement, proceeded in pursuit, but were checked by the apparition of the Guards.

The Duke of Cambridge, who commanded the First Division, had never seen a shot fired in anger. Of his Brigadiers, only Sir Colin Campbell – a soldier trained in many a stubborn fight, and nursed in the field – was acquainted with actual warfare; but it is nevertheless the case that the deciding move of the day on our left was made by His Royal Highness, and that the Duke, who was only considered to be a cavalry officer, showed then, as on a subsequent tremendous day, that he had the qualities of a brave and energetic leader. When the last halt took place, the Guards and Highlanders lay down a good deal to the rear of the Light Division, which they were to support; and in the advance immediately afterwards, the Brigade of Guards, being on the left behind Codrington's Brigade, lost several men ere they reached the river by the fire directed on those regiments. Between them and the river the ground was much broken, and intersected by walls and the hedges of vineyards; but on their left, opposite the Highlanders, the ground was more favourable. The men wearing their bearskins – more ponderous and more heavily weighted than the men of the line – suffered much from thirst and the heat of the day, and they displayed an evident inclination to glean in the vineyards after the soldiers of the Light Division; but the Duke led them on with such rapidity that they could not leave their ranks, and the officers and sergeants kept them in most admirable order till they came to the wall, in leaping over which they were of course a little disorganised. On crossing it they were exposed to a heavier fire, and by the time they reached the river the Light Division were advancing up the slope against the enemy's guns. The bank of the stream in front was deep and rugged, but the Duke and his staff crossed it gallantly; and placing himself in front of the Guards on the left – Sir Colin Campbell being near him at the head of his Brigade, and General Bentinck being on his right – His Royal Highness led his division into action. On reaching the other side of the river the Guards got into another large vineyard, the same in which the Rifles had been stationed for a time, and it became very difficult to get them into line again, for they had of course been disordered in passing through the river. The guards threw out their sergeants in front, as if on parade, and dressed up in line, protected in some degree from fire as they did so by the ridge in front of them, and Sir Colin Campbell formed up his Highlanders on their left, as if they were 'ruled' by machinery.

It was time they were ready for action, for at this moment the Light Division was observed to be falling back towards them in disorder, and the Russians, encouraged by the partial success, but taught by their short experience that it would be rather dangerous to come too near them, were slowly advancing after them, and endeavouring to get positions for the guns; in fact, it was probable that in a few minutes more they would run them into the epaulement once more. In front of the 42nd Highlanders was the 88th Regiment halted, and doing nothing; and Colonel Cameron, who was astonished to find them in such a position, was obliged to move out of his course a little in order to pass them. As we thus come on this gallant regiment, it may be as well to say how they came here. As the 88th were about to advance from the river, having their right on the 19th and their left on the 77th, an Aide-de-Camp – I believe the Hon. Mr Clifford – came down in haste from Sir George Brown, with the words 'Cavalry! Form square! Form square!' and the right, accordingly, in some haste corresponding with the order, which was almost at the moment reiterated by Brigadier Buller, prepared to execute the movement, but the whole of the companies did not join in it, the men who were excluded, and an officer and some few of the Rifles, struggled to obtain admission into the square, which was for some moments in a very ineffective state, and scarcely ready to receive any determined charge of cavalry.

The apprehensions, however, which were entertained by a few short-sighted people were unfounded. The enemy had made no demonstration with the cavalry. They had advanced a demi-battery of artillery towards the left flank of the 2nd Brigade, and supported the advance with a body of infantry in spiked helmets. Sir George Brown, whose sight was not good though he would not wear spectacles, and General Buller, whose vision was not good although he did wear spectacles, were deceived by the appearance of this force, and sent orders to form square. It was fortunate the Russian guns did not fire upon the 88th; just as they unlimbered Codrington's Brigade began to advance on the right, and the Rifles, part of the 88th, and the 77th, who, as they crossed the river, and endeavoured to re-form under the bank, were menaced by a column of Russians firing on the gunners, forced them to retire higher up the hill. Had the artillery held their ground, they could have inflicted great loss upon us, and seriously interfered with our advance on the right; but on this, as on other occasions, the Russians were too nervous for their guns, and withdrew them. In this general movement the 77th and 88th Regiments did not participate.

There was not in the army a more gallant or better disciplined regiment than the 77th. Colonel Egerton was not only one of the bravest but one of the most intelligent, skilled, and thorough soldiers and officers in the whole service. In the trenches – at Inkerman – throughout the siege, the regiment showed of what noble material it was composed. The 88th had a fighting reputation, which they well vindicated at Inkerman, at the Quarries, and in many encounters with the enemy. It is astonishing, therefore, that the Light Division should have been in a vital moment deprived of the co-operation of these splendid soldiers, and should have been hurled in confused masses against the enemy's bayonets and artillery, reduced by the suicidal incapacity of some one or other to four regiments. That there was no notion of keeping these regiments in reserve is shown by the fact that they were never advanced in support or used as a reserve when their comrades were involved in a most perilous and unequal struggle.

The First Division advancing, and passing this portion of the Light Division, at once became exposed to fire, and received the shot which passed through the fragments of Codrington's Brigade; but as it was imperatively necessary that they should not be marched up in rear of regiments in a state of disorder, the Duke, by the advice of Sir Colin Campbell, ordered General Bentinck to move a little to his left, but ere the movement could be effected, portions of the Light Division came in contact with the centre of the line, and passing through its files to re-open in the rear, carried disorder into the centre battalion. It may be observed that this is a casualty to which extended line formations in support must always be liable, when the attacking lines in advance of them are obliged to fall back to re-form. Formations in column are of course less likely to be subjected to this inconvenience, and the broken troops can pour through the intervals between column and column with greater facility than they can pass round the flanks of lengthy and extended lines. The Coldstreams and the Grenadiers never for an instant lost their beautiful regularity and order, although they now fell fast under the enemy's fire, and several of the mounted officers lost their horses. Among these Major Macdonald was included, his horse was killed by a round shot, and he received a severe fall, but never for a moment lost his coolness and equanimity.

As the Light Division retreated behind the Guards to re-form, the Russian battalions on the flanks and behind the work fired on them continuously, and at the same moment the guns which had been drawn out of the work to the high ground over it opened heavily. The Guards were struck in the centre by this iron shower. The fragments of Codrington's Brigade poured through them. In their front was a steel-bound wall of Russian infantry. Our own men were fast falling back, firing as they retired. After them came a glistening line of Russian bayonets, as if to clear the field. For a few seconds the Scots Fusiliers wavered and lost order; they were marching over dead and dying men. The Russians were within a few yards of them, but the officers rallied the men, and, conspicuous in their efforts, suffered heavily. The colour-bearers, Lieutenant Lindsay and Lieutenant Thistlewayte, with signal gallantry, extricated themselves from a perilous position, in which for the instant their men had left them – order was restored in the centre, and on the flanks the Grenadiers, under Colonel Hood, and Coldstreams were as steady and in as perfect order as though they were on parade. For a moment, it is said, the Duke thought of halting to dress his line, but Sir Colin Campbell, who was near at hand with his Highlanders, begged his Highness not to hesitate, but to push on at once at the enemy. The Russian artillery on the slopes above sent repeated volleys of grape, canister, round, and shell through their ranks, but at this moment, threatened on the flank by the French batteries, enfiladed by a 9-pounder and 24-pound howitzer of Turner's battery, which Lord Raglan had ordered up to a knoll on the opposite side of the river, on the slope between our attack and that of the French, the Russian guns were limbered up, and ceased their fire.

Meantime General Sir De Lacy Evans had, in the most skilful and gallant manner, executed his instructions, and, with Pennefather's Brigade, had forced the Russian centre and the right centre. The Second Division advanced on the same alignement with Prince Napoleon's Division to the burning village of Bourliouk. Sir De Lacy Evans detached the 41st and the 49th Regiments, of Adams's Brigade and Turner's battery, by the right of the village, which the flames rendered impenetrable, and ordered them to force the passage. The ford in front was very deep, and the banks were bad and high, defended by a heavy fire; the regiments lost upwards of forty men in the stream and on its banks. The General placed himself at the head of the remaining regiments, and led them by the left of the village towards the river; but, experienced in war, Sir De Lacy Evans availed himself of all means to carry the enemy's position with the smallest loss to his own men; he covered the advance of his troops by the fire of eighteen pieces. Pennefather's Brigade, the 30th, 55th, and 95th Regiments, was accompanied by Fitzmayer's battery; but the General, finding Dacre's battery and Wodehouse's battery, which belonged to the First and Light Divisions, stationed near, availed himself of the services volunteered by the officers in command of them to cover the advance of his men.

The 95th Regiment, being on the extreme left of the Brigade, came upon the bridge of Bourliouk; the 55th Regiment, in the centre, had in front of them a deep ford and high banks; and the 30th Regiment were inconvenienced in their advance by the walls of the village, and by the cooking places cut in the high banks on the opposite side of the stream. On the right of the 30th Regiment came the 47th Regiment, and in the interval between these two regiments rode Sir De Lacy Evans. As soon as the Division emerged from the smoke and the houses of the village, the enemy directed on them an extremely severe fire – 'such,' says Sir De Lacy Evans, 'as few, perhaps, of the most experienced soldiers have ever witnessed', till they came to the stream, which they passed under a storm of missiles which lashed the waters into bloody foam. The 95th, led very gallantly by Colonel Webber Smith, debouched from the bridge and narrow ford just as the 7th, under Colonel Yea, formed on the other side. They were exposed to the same tremendous fire; they advanced, with colours flying, towards the left of the Russian epaulement, which Codrington was assailing, and claim the credit of having been the temporary captors of a gun on the left of the works. The 55th and 30th, led by Colonel Warren and Colonel Hoey, exposed to the full fire of two batteries and of six battalions disposed on the sides of the ravines and of the slopes above them, behaved with conspicuous gallantry, but could make no impression on the solid masses of the enemy. In a short time the 95th lost six officers killed, the Colonel and Major and nine officers wounded, and upwards of 170 men. The 55th had 128 casualties, eight of which occurred to officers, and three of which were fatal; the 30th Regiment lost 150 officers and men.

But the steadiness of our infantry and the destructive effect of their musketry were shaking the confidence of the enemy, now broken and turned on their left by the French. The Light Division was obliged to relinquish its hold of the work it had taken; but the Guards were advancing to their support – the Highlanders were moving up on the left – and the fortune of the day was every moment inclining to the allies. The French had sent to Lord Raglan for assistance, some say twice – certainly once, before we advanced. Our attack was not to begin till they had turned the left, and it is likely that M. St Arnaud arranged to send information of that fact to Lord Raglan. But our Commander-in-chief did not receive any such intelligence. He was annoyed, uneasy, and disappointed at the delay which occurred on his right. He sent Colonel Vico to ascertain the state of affairs, to communicate, if possible, with the French Generals. Meantime, the French Generals were, if we credit authorities, annoyed, uneasy, and disappointed by the slowness of the English. Prince Napoleon sent to Lord Raglan. French staff-officers came with the piteous appeal: '*Milord, je vous prie! Pour l'amour de Dieu! Venez aux Français! Nous sommes massacres!*' At last Lord Raglan gave orders to advance, although he had not heard of the success of the French attack on which the advance was to depend. When the 1st and 3rd Divisions had deployed, and were moving towards the Alma, Lord Raglan and his staff advanced, and skirting the village of Bourliouk to the right, passed down a narrow lane which led to the ford, by which part of Adams's Brigade had crossed to the other side. They proceeded round the right of Adams's Brigade, immediately between the French and Evans's extreme right, and *en route*, his lordship observed Turner's battery, and passed close to the 41st and 49th on the other side of the river, for whose disposition he gave orders to Brigadier Adams. In crossing the ford the staff were exposed to fire from the Russian guns on the high grounds opposite Bourliouk, and the infantry in support. Two of the staff officers were hit – Lieutenant Leslie, Royal Horse Guards, who was acting as orderly officer to the Commander-in-chief, and Captain Weare, Deputy-Assistant Adjutant-General. Lord Raglan gave orders for Turner's battery to come up to enfilade the enemy's guns. The lane, which formed at the other side of the ford the continuation of that road by which the Commander-in-chief had passed round Bourliouk to the river, ran at the bottom of a sheltered, ravine, which almost divided the Russian position, and formed a boundary between the English and the French attacks.

The enemy had been driven out of this ravine by the French, and the lane was unoccupied, but here and there in its windings it was swept by guns. The ravine, as it ascended, opened out, and became shallower, and on the right it wound below a small tableland, or rather a flattened knoll, of which there were several at the edge of the general level of the plateau. On ascending this knoll, Lord Raglan saw, as he anticipated, that the Russian guns commanding the ford were on his left, in such a position that they could be enfiladed, and indeed, taken in reverse. He despatched repeated orders to Turner; but owing to the steepness of the lane, and to the loss of a gun horse in the river, there was difficulty and delay in getting the guns up, and when they did arrive the Guards and Highlanders were already advancing up the hill, and closing on the Russian columns. The guns which came up were, I believe, a 24-pounder howitzer, and a 9-pounder, and as the tumbrel attached to the former had not arrived, it was served with 9-pounder ammunition and round shot. The artillery officers and General Strangways dismounted and worked the guns, as the men had not yet come up; Lieutenant Walsham arrived with the rest of the battery, and the six guns opened – on what? One officer says, on the 'artillery' of the Russians – that two shots forced a whole line of Russian guns to retire, and that the Russian General, 'seeing he was taken in flank', limbered up. But surely he could have turned round some of his numerous guns, and could have fought Turner's two with heavier metal. In fact, it was something else besides this fire of two shots (one of which hit a tumbril) which determined the retreat of the Russian artillery. It was the advance of the First and Second Divisions. The Guards were half-way up the hill when these two guns opened, and the Russians limbered up when they saw they were turned on their left, and threatened on their right. The Russian artillery officer, after he retired, directed his guns against Turner's battery, and some riflemen were sent to cripple it, one of whom shot Lieutenant Walsham as he was in the act of loading. Lord Raglan saw the day was won by the Light Division, the Second Division, the Guards, and Highlanders; for, seeing the advance of the latter, he exclaimed, 'Let us join the Guards!' and rode into the ravine to his left in their direction.

But the enemy had not yet abandoned their position. A division of infantry in columns came from the rear of the hill, and marched straight upon the Brigade of Guards. The Guards dressed up, and advanced to meet them. Some shot struck the rear of the Russian columns, they began to melt away, and wavered; still they came on slowly, and began file-firing. One column moved towards the left flank of the Guards, facing round as if to meet the Highlanders, who were moving with rapidity up from the hollow in which they had been sheltered from the enemy's fire. The two other columns faced the Guards. The distance between them was rapidly diminishing, when suddenly the Brigade poured in a fire so destructive that it annihilated their front ranks, and left a ridge of killed and wounded men on the ground. The Highlanders almost at the same moment delivered a volley, sharp, deadly, and decisive. Pennefather's Brigade, on the right of the Guards, supported by Adams, appeared on the side of the slope. The enemy, after a vain attempt to shake off the panic occasioned by that rain of death, renewed their fire very feebly, and then, without waiting, turned as our men advanced with bayonets at the charge, over the brow of the hill to join the mass of the Russian army, who, divided into two bodies, were retreating with all possible speed. Our cavalry rode up to the crest of the hill, and looked after the enemy. They took a few prisoners, but they were ordered to let them go again. Lord Raglan expressed his intention of keeping his cavalry 'in a bandbox', and was apprehensive of getting into serious difficulty with the enemy. The Battle of the Alma was won. The men halted on the battle-field, and as the Commander-in-chief, the Duke of Cambridge, Sir De Lacy Evans, and the other popular generals rode in front of the line, the soldiers shouted, and when Lord Raglan was in front of the Guards, the whole army burst into a tremendous cheer, which made one's heart leap – the effect of that cheer can never be forgotten by those who heard it. It was near five o'clock; the men had been eleven hours under arms, and had fought a battle, and the enemy were to be – 'let alone.' The Russians fired one gun as they retreated, and made some show of covering their rear with their cavalry.

Upon the conduct of the Battle of the Alma there has been much foreign criticism, and the results and deductions have been unfavourable to the Russian General, who permitted his left to be turned without any serious resistance, although he ought to have calculated on the effect of the operations by sea on that flank. In apparent opposition to this judgment there has been at the same time great praise awarded to the French for the gallantry with which they attacked that portion of the position. They deserve every laudation for the extraordinary activity, rapidity, and bravery with which they established themselves on the centre and left-centre, but on the extreme left they had no hard fighting. The English seem to have been awarded the meed of solidity and unshaken courage, but at the same time hints are thrown out that they did not move quite quickly enough, that therefore their losses were great, and their work after all not so hazardous and difficult as that of the French, inasmuch as the English attack took place only when the Russian left was turned. In effect, however, the right of the enemy presented less physical difficulties to the establishment of a hostile force on the flank, and it was there that the greatest number of artificial obstacles in the shape of guns, cavalry, and men, was accumulated. But was the plan of battle good? In the first place, we attacked the enemy in the position of his own selection, without the least attempt to manoeuvre or to turn him. It might have been difficult, situated as we were, without cavalry, and with masses of baggage, to have attempted any complex manoeuvres; but it has been asserted that by a flank march we could, by a temporary abandonment of our seaboard, have placed the enemy between two fires, and have destroyed his army in case of defeat. It has been suggested that early on the morning of the 20th the allies should have moved obliquely from the bivouac on the Bouljanak, and, crossing the Alma to the east of the enemy's position, have obliged his left to make a harassing march, to get up and occupy new ground in a fresh alignement, have deprived him of his advantages, and have endangered his retreat to Bakshi Serai or Simpheropol, if he refused battle, and that in event of his defeat, which would have been pretty certain, considering how much weaker his new line would have been, he would have been driven towards the shore, exposed to the fire of our ships, so that his force would have been obliged to lay down their arms. Menschikoff's army utterly ruined, Sebastopol would have at once surrendered, disposed as it was to have done so with very little compression. Criticism is easy after the circumstances or conduct of which you judge have had their effect; but to this it may be remarked that criticism cannot, by its very nature, be prospective. Even civilians are as good judges as military men of the grand operations of war, although they may be ignorant of details, and of the modes by which those operations have been effected. Alexander, Caesar,

Pompey, Hannibal, may have had many club colonels in their day, who thought they made 'fatal moves'; we know that in our own time there were many military men who 'had no great opinion' of either General Wellesley or General Bonaparte; but the results carry with them the weight of an irreversible verdict, which is accepted by posterity long after the cliques and jealousies and animosities of the hour have passed away for ever. Now, without being a member of a clique, having possible jealousies, and being free from the smallest animosities, I may inquire was there any generalship shown by any of the allied generals at the Alma? We have Lord Raglan, as brave, as calm, as noble, as any gentleman who ever owned England as his mother-land – trotting in front of his army, amid a shower of balls, 'just as if he were riding down Rotten Row', with a kind nod for every one, leaving his generals and men to fight it out as best they could, riding across the stream through the French riflemen, not knowing where he was going to, or where the enemy were, till fate led him to a little knoll, from which he saw some of the Russian guns on his flank, whereupon he sent an order for guns, seemed surprised that they could not be dragged across a stream, and up a hill which presented difficulties to an unencumbered horseman – then, cantering over to join the Guards ere they made their charge, and finding it over while he was in a hollow of the ground. As to the mode in which the attack was carried on by us, there was immense gallantry, devotion, and courage, and, according to military men present, no small amount of disorder.

The Light Division was strangely handled. Sir George Brown, whose sight was so indifferent that he had to get one of his officers to lead his horse across the river, seemed not to know where his division was, and permitted Brigadier Buller to march off with two regiments of his brigade, leaving the third to join Codrington's Brigade. The men got huddled together on the other side of the river under the ridge, and lay there seven or eight instead of two deep, so that when they rose and delivered fire, their front was small, and the effect diminished. Then they were led straight up at the guns in a confused mass; when they had got into the battery they were left without supports, so that the enemy forced them to relinquish their hold, and were enabled to recover the work. The Light Division had, it is true, drawn the teeth of the battery, but still the enemy were able to tire over the heads of the columns from the hill above. However, the Alma was won.

Menschikoff was in retreat, and the world was all before us on the evening of the 20th of September. Whether our generals had any foresight of what that world was to be – what were to be the fruits of victory, or the chances of disaster – let the history of the war on some future day communicate to the world.

The Russians were very much dissatisfied with the result of this battle. They put forth the rawness of the troops, their inferiority in numbers, and many other matters; they criticised severely the conduct of their generals during the action, and the disposition of the troops on the ground; but, after all, their position ought to have been impregnable, if defended by determined infantry.

The Russians have given the following account of their own position and of some incidents of the action: The centre of their position lay on the high slopes of the left bank of the river, opposite the village of Bourliouk; the left on the still higher and less accessible hills, with perpendicularly scarped sides, which rise from the river near the sea; the right wing on the gentle ascents into which this rising ground subsides about half a mile eastward of the village. The reserves, which were posted behind the centre, consisted of the regiments of Volhynia, Minsk, and Moscow, the two former of which subsequently took an active part in the siege, and were the principal workmen and combatants in constructing and occupying the famous 'white works' on the right of our position before Sebastopol. On their right flank were two regiments of hussars and two field batteries; in the rear of the right wing was stationed a regiment of Riflemen. Oddly enough, the Russian General sent off a battalion of the Moscow regiment to occupy the village of Ulukul Akles, several miles in the rear of his left wing, as if to prevent a descent behind him from the sea. The disposition of this force will be seen on reference to the plan which accompanies the description of the Battle of the Alma. The right was commanded by Lieutenant-General Knetsinsky, of the 16th Division; the centre by Prince Gortschakoff; the left by Lieutenant-General Kiriakoff, Commander of the 17th Division; and Prince Menschikoff took the control of the whole, being generally on the left of the centre, near the telegraph station.

When the Allies came in sight, the Rifle battalion, about 650 strong, crossed to the right bank of the river, and occupied the village of Bourliouk and the vineyards near it, and the regiments in front advanced their skirmishers to the left bank, and Menschikoff rode along the front from the right to the left of the line to animate the men, most of whom had been present at a mass to the Virgin early in the morning, when prayers were offered for her aid against the enemy. Our advance seemed to the Russians rather slow; but at last, at about 12.30, the Allies came within range, and a sharp fusilade commenced between the skirmishers and riflemen. About 12.20 the steamers outside began to fire on the Russian left, and forced the regiments of Minsk and Moscow to retire with loss, and killed some horses and men of the light battery stationed on their flank. Their shells struck down four officers of Menschikoff's staff later in the day, and did most effective service in shaking the confidence of the enemy, and in searching out their battalions so as to prevent their advance towards the seaboard. As the Allies advanced, the Cossacks, according to orders, set fire to the haystacks in the Tartar village, which soon caught, and poured out a mass of black smoke, mingled with showers of sparks. The guns of the Allies, from the right of the village, now began to play on the enemy, and caused so much loss in the four reserve battalions under General Oslonovich, that they, being young soldiers, began to retire of their own accord. At the same time the French gained the heights, driving back and destroying the 2nd battalion of the Moscow regiment, and holding their ground against the Minsk regiment, the 1st, 3rd, and 4th battalions of the Moscow regiment, and a numerous artillery, which arrived too late to wrest the heights from their grasp till the demonstration in the centre rendered their position certain and secure. General Kiriakoff, who commanded the left wing, seems to have been utterly bewildered, and to have acted with great imbecility, and want of decision and judgment. The Russians with whom I have conversed have assured me that he gave no orders, left every officer to do as he liked, and retired from the field, or at least disappeared from their view, very early in the fight. As the reserve battalions retired, the battalion of the Taioutine regiment, which was placed in a ravine in front of the river, withdrew as soon as it got under fire, and left a very important part of the position undefended. The Kazan and Ouglitsky regiments, defending the epaulement in which the guns were placed, suffered severely from the fire of the English riflemen, and the two battalions of the Borodino regiment, which advanced towards the river to fire on our men as they crossed the ford, were driven back with great slaughter by the continuous flight of Minié bullets. As Pennefather's brigade advanced, two battalions of the Vladimir regiment, deploying into columns of battalions, charged them with the bayonet, but were checked by our murderous fire, and only a few men were killed and wounded in the encounter between the foremost ranks, which were much broken and confused for a few moments. The advance of the French obliquely from the right, and the success of the English on the left, threatening to envelope the whole of the enemy, they began to retreat in tolerable order; but the English and French guns soon began to open a cross fire on them, and their march became less regular. A Russian officer, who has written an account of the action, relates that Prince Menschikoff, as he rode past his regiment, then marching off the ground as fast as it could under our fire, said, 'It's a disgrace for a Russian soldier to retreat,' whereupon one of the officers exclaimed, 'If you had ordered us, we would have stood our ground.' It would appear that, on arriving at the heights of the Katcha, part of the Russian army halted for a short time, and took up their position in order of battle, in case the Allies followed. As to the propriety of such a movement on our part by a portion of our army, under the circumstances, there may be some difference of opinion. As to the pursuit of the enemy on the spot by all the allied forces there can be no diversity of sentiment; but as to the proposition which Lord Raglan's friends declare he made, to continue the pursuit with our 1,100 cavalry, some artillery, and no infantry, it seems scarcely possible that it was made in seriousness. The enemy, defeated though they were, mustered nearly 30,000 men, of whom 3,500 were cavalry, and they had with them ninety-four guns. In their rear there was a most formidable position, protected by a river of greater depth and with deeper banks than the Alma. It was getting dark – no one knew the country – the troops were exhausted by a day's marching and manoeuvring under a hot sun – and yet it is said that, under these circumstances, Lord Raglan proposed a pursuit by the portion of the French who had not been engaged, by the Turkish division, and by part of our cavalry, and a hypothetical two or three batteries. Most military men will, if that assertion be substantiated, probably think less of his lordship's military capacity than ever they did before. The grounds on which M. St Arnaud is stated to have declined acceding to the wishes of Lord Raglan are these – that he could send no infantry, and that his artillery had exhausted their ammunition. Now, unquestionably St Arnaud was quite as anxious as any one could be to complete his victory, and continue the pursuit of the enemy; and in his three despatches respecting the battle he laments repeatedly his inability, from want of cavalry, to turn the retreat of the Russians into a rout. It is also true that the artillery of the French had exhausted their ammunition; but let us calmly examine the means at the disposal of the two generals to effect an operation of a most difficult and serious kind, which is said to have been suggested by the one and rejected by the other. The English army present at the Alma, in round numbers as stated in the official returns, consisted of 27,000 men; the French, of 25,000; the Turks, of 6,000 men. Of the English were engaged with such loss as would incapacitate the regiments from action – the Guards, the 7th, 19th, 23rd, 30th, 33rd, 47th, 55th, 95th, one wing of 2nd Battalion Rifle Brigade. There remained in just as good order for marching as any of the French regiments – 1st Battalion of the Royals, 4th, 79th, 44th, 21st, 1st Battalion Rifle Brigade, 50th, 49th, 77th, 88th, 20th, 28th, 38th, 42nd – fourteen Battalions – and the cavalry; and according to the French accounts all their divisions were more or less engaged, with the exception of part of Forey's. The Staff-officer admits we had 7,000 men who had not taken a part in the action; but then he adds that these 7,000 men were 'not in fact more than sufficient for the immediate necessities of the camp'. Now, as the

French force was nearly equal to ours, the necessities of their camp would be nearly equal to ours also. He avers they had '12,000 men who had never been engaged'. Be it so. But deduct 7,000 men required for 'the immediate necessities of the camp', and you will have a disposable force of 5,000 men, who, with a force of Turks (supposed to have no camp at all, and therefore to have none of the English or French necessities for eating or drinking or camping), were, according to Lord Raglan's Staff-officer, to start off at four o'clock on a September evening to chase an army of 30,000 cavalry and infantry, and ninety-four guns! That is really the most preposterous attempt to vindicate Lord Raglan's generalship that has ever been given to the world. His lordship never says a word in his published despatches to corroborate those confidential communications, and it is to be hoped that they illustrate some of 'the many opinions and motives ascribed to Lord Raglan which the Field-Marshal never entertained', to which the writer refers. Next day St Arnaud wished to advance and follow the enemy, but Lord Raglan would not listen to it, as he had 3,000 wounded English and Russians to move. That is, if the 10,000 Turks and French, and a few field batteries, had come up with and beaten the Russians, Lord Raglan would have permitted them to pursue their career of victory without support, and to do as they pleased; and if they were beaten and allowed to fall back, he would leave their wounded in the hands of the enemy, or spend still more time in burying them. But the worst of all is that, after losing two days, the English wounded were nearly all on board ship by the afternoon of the 21st – in spite of the Marshal's protest we were obliged to leave upwards of 700 wounded Russians on the ground, with one surgeon and one servant to wait upon them. The enemy halted at the Katcha till after midnight, crossing it at Aranchi, and fell back towards Sebastopol, on the north side of which a portion of the troops arrived by four o'clock on the following afternoon. Their loss was, as stated in the official accounts, 1,762 killed, 2,315 wounded, 405 contused. Two generals prisoners. Generals Kyitzinsky, Schelkanoff', Goginoff, Kourtianoff, wounded.

3

The Siege of Sebastopol
Part 1

Lord Raglan and Staff established headquarters in a snug farmhouse, surrounded by vineyards and extensive out-offices, about 4½ miles from Balaklava, on the 5th of October. From the rising ground, about a mile and a half distant from headquarters, in front, the town of Sebastopol was plainly visible. The Russians were occupied throwing up works and fortifying the exposed portions of the town with the greatest energy.

The investment of the place on the south side was, as far as possible, during the night of the 7th, completed. Our lines were to be pushed on the right and closed in towards the north, so as to prevent supplies or reinforcements passing out or in on this side of the Black River. This measure was absolutely necessary to enable our engineers to draw the lines or measure the ground.

The Russians continued to work all the week at the White Fort, and cast up strong earthworks in front of it, and also on the extreme left, facing the French. They fired shell and shot, at intervals of ten minutes, into the camps of the Second and Light Divisions. Sir George Brown had to move his quarters more to the rear.

The silence and gloom of our camp, as compared with the activity and bustle of that of the French, were very striking. No drum, no bugle-call, no music of any kind, was ever heard within our precincts, while our neighbours close by kept up incessant rolls, fanfaronnades, and flourishes, relieved every evening by the fine performances of their military bands. The fact was, many of our instruments had been placed in store, and the regimental bands were broken up and disorganised, the men being devoted to the performance of the duties for which the ambulance corps was formed. I think, judging from one's own feelings, and from the expressions of those around, that the want of music in camp was productive of graver consequences than appeared likely to occur at first blush from such a cause. Every military man knows how regiments, when fatigued on the march, cheer up at the strains of their band, and dress up, keep step, and walk on with animation and vigour when it is playing. At camp, I always observed with pleasure the attentive auditory who gathered every evening at the first taps of the drum to listen to the music. At Aladyn and Devno the men used to wander off to the lines of the 77th, because it had the best band in the division; and when the bands were silenced because of the prevalence of cholera, out of a humane regard for the feelings of the sick, the soldiers were wont to get up singing parties in their tents in lieu of their ordinary entertainment. It seemed to be an error to deprive them of a cheering and wholesome influence at the very time they needed it most. The military band was not meant alone for the delectation of garrison towns, or for the pleasure of the officers in quarters, and the men were fairly entitled to its inspiration during the long and weary march in the enemy's country, and in the monotony of a standing camp ere the beginning of a siege.

Soon after daybreak on the morning of the 10th, the Russian batteries opened a heavy fire on the right of our position, but the distance was too great for accuracy. On the same day four battalions of French, numbering 2,400 men, broke ground at nine o'clock p.m., and before daybreak they had finished a ditch, parapet, and banquette, 1,200 metres long, at a distance of 900 metres from the enemy's line; and so little did the Russians suspect the operation, that they never fired a gun to disturb them. Each man worked and kept guard at one of the covering parties in turn till daybreak, and by that time each man had finished his half metre of work, so that the 1,200 metres were completed. From this position a considerable portion of the enemy's defences on their right was quite under control, and the French could command the heaviest fort on that side. From the top of the ditch seventy-six guns could be counted in the embrasures of this work, which was called the Bastion du Mât. The French had got forty-six guns ready to mount when the embrasures should be made and faced with gabions and fascines, and the platforms were ready. Their present line was from 200 to 300 yards nearer to the enemy's lines than ours; but the superior weight of our siege guns more than compensated for the difference of distance.

On the previous night the British, who had already thrown up some detached batteries, broke ground before Sebastopol on the left. Soon after dark, 800 men were marched out silently under the charge and direction of Captain Chapman, R.E., who has the construction of the works and engineering department of the left attack under his control. About 1,200 yards of trench were made, though the greatest difficulty was experienced in working, owing to the rocky nature of the ground. The cover was tolerably good. The Russians never ceased firing, but attempted nothing more, and those who were hoping for a sortie were disappointed. As an earthwork for a battery had been thrown up the previous day, within fire of the enemy's guns, their attention was particularly directed to our movements, and throughout the day they kept up a tremendous fire on the high grounds in front of the Light and Second Divisions. The Russians, who usually ceased firing at sunset, were on the alert all night, and continued their fire against the whole line of our approaches almost uninterruptedly. Every instant the darkness was broken by a flash which had all the effect of summer lightning – then came darkness again, and in a few seconds a fainter flash denoted the bursting of a shell. The silence in the English Camp afforded a strange contrast to the constant roar of the Russian batteries, to the music and trumpet calls and lively noises of the encampment of our allies. After nightfall the batteries on the Russian centre opened so fiercely that it was expected they were covering a sortie, and the camp was on the alert in consequence. Lord Raglan, accompanied by Quartermaster-General Airey and several officers, started at ten o'clock, and rode along the lines, minutely inspecting the state and position of the regiments and works. They returned at half-past one o'clock in the morning. The casualties on the night of the 10th were, one man, 68th, died of wounds, legs taken off; one man, 57th, killed by cannon-shot; another man, 57th, arm shot off; Lieutenant Rotherham, 20th, slightly wounded in the leg by a stone which had been 'started' by a cannon-shot.

Colonel Waddy, Captain Gray, and Lieutenant Mangles, 50th, were wounded by a shell on the evening of the 11th. It was rumoured that the Russians would attack Balaklava, while the Greeks were to aid them by setting fire to the town. The information on this point was so positive, that the authorities resorted to the extreme measure of ordering the Greeks, men, women, and children, to leave the town, and the order was rigidly carried into effect before evening. An exception was made in favour of the Tartar families who were all permitted to remain. The Greeks were consoled in their flight by a good deal of plunder in the shape of clothes which had been left with them to wash.

Capt. Gordon, R.E., commenced our right attack soon after dark. 400 men were furnished from the Second and Light Divisions or the works, and strong covering parties were sent out in front and in rear to protect them. The working party was divided into four companies of 100 men each, and they worked on during the night with such good will, that before morning No. 1 party had completed 160 yards; No. 2, 78 yards; No. 3, 95 yards; No. 4, 30 yards – in all 363 yards of trench ready for conversion into batteries. These trenches were covered very perfectly. It was intended that a party of similar strength should be employed on the left and centre; but owing to one of those accidents which unavoidably occur in night work, the sappers and miners missed their way, and got in advance towards the lines of the enemy. They were perceived by an advanced post, which opened fire on them at short distance, and, wonderful to relate, missed them all. The flashes, however, showed our men that strong battalions of Russian infantry were moving silently towards our works, and the alarm was given to the division in the rear. At twenty-five minutes past one a furious cannonade was opened by the enemy on our lines, as they had then ascertained that we had discovered their approach. The Second and Light Divisions turned out, and our field guns attached to them opened fire on the enemy who were advancing under the fire of their batteries. Owing to some misunderstanding, the covering parties received orders to retire, and fell back on their lines – all but one company of riflemen, under the command of Lieutenant Godfrey, who maintained the ground with tenacity, and fired into the columns of the enemy with effect. The Russians pushed on field-pieces to support their assault. The batteries behind them were livid with incessant flashes, and the roar of shot and shell filled the air, mingled with the constant 'ping-pinging' of rifle and musket-balls. All the camps 'roused out'. The French on our left got under arms, and the rattle of drums and the shrill blast of trumpets were heard amid the roar of cannon and small arms. For nearly half-an-hour this din lasted, till all of a sudden a ringing cheer was audible on our right, rising through the turmoil. It was the cheer of the 88th, as they were ordered to charge down the hill on their unseen enemy. It had its effect, for the Russians, already pounded by our guns and shaken by the fire of our infantry, as well as by the aspect of the whole hill-side lined with our battalions, turned and fled under the shelter of their guns. Their loss was not known; ours was very trifling. The sortie was completely foiled, and not an inch of our lines was injured, while the four-gun battery (the main object of their attack) was never closely approached at all. The alarm over, every one returned quietly to tent or bivouac. In order to understand this description of the works, it will be necessary to refer to the plan which accompanies this. It affords a good idea of the appearance presented by the lines and works on the eve of the first bombardment.

At the distance of about 700 sagenes (a sagene is 7 feet), from the south extremity of the Careening Bay, was placed a round tower, round which the Russians had thrown up extensive entrenchments, armed with heavy guns. There was a standing camp of cavalry and infantry on a rising ground, on the summit of which this tower was placed, and probably 10,000 or 12,000 men were encamped there. This round tower was provided with guns, which, equally with those in the earthworks below, threw shot and shell right over our advanced posts and working parties, and sometimes pitched them over the hills in our front into the camps below. At the distance of 1,200 yards from this round tower, in a direction nearly due south-south-east, our first batteries were to be formed, and the earthworks had been thrown up there, inclining with the slope of the hill towards the end of the Dockyard Creek, from which they were distant 930 yards. The guns of works were intended to command the Dockyard Creek, the ships placed in it, and the part of the town and its defences on the west and south of the creek.

Our left attack extended up towards the slope of the ravine which divided the French from the British attacks, and which ran south-east from the end of the Dockyard Creek up to our headquarters at Khutor. Dominating both of these entrenchments for most of their course, was a heavy battery of eight Lancaster and 10-inch naval guns, placed at a distance of 2,500 yards from the enemy's lines. The extreme of the French right was about 2½ miles from the extreme of the British left attack. South of the Cemetery, and inclining up towards Quarantine Bay and the fresh water wells, were the French lines, which were beautifully made and covered. The fire of the Russian batteries thrown up from the circular position at the end of the western wall towards the barracks, near the end of the Dockyard Harbour, was incessantly directed on them, and shells sometimes burst in the lines; but as a general rule they struck the hill in front, bounded over, and burst in the rear. Our left attack crept round towards Inkerman, and commanded the place from the influx of the Tchernaya into the head of the bay or harbour of Sebastopol, to the hills near the round tower already threatened by our right attack. The French commanded the place from the sea to the ravine at the end of the Dockyard Harbour, and when their guns were mounted, it was hoped that all the forts, intrenchments, buildings, earthworks, barracks, batteries, and shipping would be destroyed.

The front of both armies united, and the line of offensive operations covered by them, extended from the sea to the Tchernaya for 7½ or 8 miles. From our extreme right front to Balaklava our line extended for about the same distance, and the position of the army had been made so strong on the eastern, south-eastern, flank and rear, as to set all the efforts of the Russians to drive us from it utterly at defiance. In the first place, the road from Kadikoi to Kamara, and the western passes of the mountains, had been scarped in three places so effectually that it would have been difficult for infantry, and therefore impossible for artillery, to get along it to attack us. A heavy gun had, however, been placed in position on the heights to command this road, and to sweep the three scarps effectually. On the heights over the east side of Balaklava, were pitched the tents of about 1,000 marines from the various ships of the fleet, and several 24-pound and 32-pound howitzers had been dragged up into position on the same elevation. At Kadikoi, towards the north-west, was situated a sailors' camp of about 800 men, with heavy guns in support, and with a temporary park for artillery and ship-guns below them. From Kadikoi towards Traktir the ground was mountainous, or rather it was exceedingly hilly, the heights having a tumular appearance, and the ridges being intersected by wide valleys, through a series of which passed on one side Prince Woronzoff's road, the road to Inkerman, and thence to Sebastopol, by a long detour over the Bakschiserai road, and that to Traktir.

On five of these tumular ridges overlooking the road to Balaklava, a party of 2,000 Turks were busily engaged casting up earthworks or redoubts, under the direction of Captain Wagman, a Prussian engineer officer, who was under the orders of Sir John Burgoyne. In each of these forts were placed two heavy guns and 250 Turks. These poor fellows worked most willingly and indefatigably, though they had been exposed to the greatest privations. For some mysterious reason or other the Turkish government sent instead of the veterans who fought under Omar Pasha, a body of soldiers of only two years' service, the latest levies of the Porte, many belonging to the non-belligerent class of barbers, tailors, and small shopkeepers. Still they were patient, hardy, and strong – how patient I am ashamed to say. I was told, on the best authority, that these men were landed without the smallest care for their sustenance, except that some Marseilles biscuits were sent on shore for their use. These were soon exhausted – the men had nothing else. From the Alma up to the 10th of October, the whole force had only two biscuits each! The rest of their food they had to get by the roadside as best they might, and in an inhospitable and desolated country they could not get their only solace, tobacco; still they marched and worked day after day, picking up their subsistence by the way as best they might, and these proud Osmanli were actually seen walking about our camps, looking for fragments of rejected biscuit. But their sorrows were turned to joy, for the British people fed them, and such diet they never had before since Mahomet enrolled his first army of the faithful. They delighted in their coffee, sugar, rice, and biscuits, but many of the True Believers were much perturbed in spirit by the aspect of our salt beef, which they believed might be pork in disguise, and they subjected it to strange tests ere it was incorporated with Ottoman flesh and blood.

Eighteen days had elapsed since our army, by a brilliant and daring forced march on Balaklava, obtained its magnificent position on the heights which envelope Sebastopol on the south side from the sea to the Tchernaya; the delay was probably unavoidable. Any officer who has been present at great operations of this nature will understand what it is for an army to land in narrow and widely separated creeks all its munitions of war – its shells, its cannonshot its heavy guns, mortars, its powder, its gun-carriages, its platforms its fascines, gabions, sandbags, its trenching tools, and all the various matériel requisite for the siege of extensive and formidable lines of fortifications and batteries. But few ships could come in at a time to Balaklava or Kamiesch; in the former there was only one small ordnance wharf, and yet it was there that every British cannon had to be landed. The nature of our descent on the Crimea rendered it quite impossible for us to carry our siege train along with us, as is the wont of armies invading a neighbouring country only separated from their own by some imaginary line. We had to send all our matériel round by sea, and then land it as best we could. But when once it was landed the difficulties of getting it up to places where it was required seemed really to commence. All these enormous masses of metal had to be dragged by men, aided by such inadequate horse-power as was at our disposal, over a steep and hilly country on wretched broken roads, to a distance of 8 miles, and one must have witnessed the toil and labour of hauling up a Lancaster or 10 inch gun under such circumstances to form a notion of the length of time requisite to bring it to its station. It will, however, serve to give some idea of the severity of this work to state one fact – that on the 10th no less than thirty-three ammunition horses were found dead, or in such a condition as to render it necessary to kill them, after the duty of the day before. It follows from all these considerations that a great siege operation cannot be commenced in a few days when an army is compelled to bring up its guns.

Again, the nature of the ground around Sebastopol offered great impediments to the performance of the necessary work of trenching, throwing up parapets, and forming earthworks. The surface of the soil was stony and hard, and after it had been removed the labourer came to strata of rock and petrous masses of volcanic formation, which defied the best tools to make any impression on them, and our tools were far from being the best. The result was that the earth for gabions and for sand-bags had to be carried from a distance in baskets, and in some instances enough of it could not be scraped together for the most trifling parapets. This impediment was experienced to a greater extent by the British than by the French. The latter had better ground to work upon, and they found fine beds of clay beneath the first coating of stones and earth, which were of essential service to them in forming their works.

The officers commanding the batteries on the right attack were Lieutenant-Colonel Dickson, Captain D'Aguilar, and Captain Strange. The officers commanding the batteries of the left attack were Major Young, Major Freese, and Major Irving. The whole of the siege-train was commanded by Lieutenant-Colonel Gambier.

Our left attack consisted of four batteries and thirty-six guns; our right attack of twenty guns in battery. There were also two Lancaster batteries and a four-gun battery of 68-pounders on our right. The French had forty-six guns. In all 117 guns to 130 guns of the Russians. The night was one of great anxiety, and early in the morning we all turned out to see the firing. On 17th October the bombardment began. It commenced by signal at 6.30 a.m.; for thirty minutes previous the Russians fired furiously on all the batteries. The cannonade on both sides was most violent for nearly two hours.

At eight o'clock it was apparent that the French batteries in their extreme right attack, overpowered by the fire and enfiladed by the guns of the Russians, were very much weakened; their fire slackened minute after minute.

At 8.30 the fire slackened on both sides for a few minutes; but recommenced with immense energy, the whole town and the line of works being enveloped in smoke.

At 8.40 the French magazine in the extreme right battery of twelve guns blew up with a tremendous explosion, killing and wounding 100 men. The Russians cheered, fired with renewed vigour, and crushed the French fire completely, so that they were not able to fire more than a gun at intervals, and at ten o'clock they were nearly silenced on that side.

At 10.30 the fire slackened on both sides, but the Allies and Russians re-opened vigorously at 10.45. Our practice was splendid but our works were cut up by the fire from the Redan and from the works round a circular martello tower on our extreme right.

At 12.45 the French line-of-battle ships ran up in most magnificent style and engaged the batteries on the sea side. The scene was indescribable, the Russians replying vigorously to the attacks by sea and land, though suffering greatly.

At 1.25 another magazine in the French batteries blew up. The cannonade was tremendous. Our guns demolished the Round Tower but could not silence the works around it.

At 1.40 a great explosion took place in the centre of Sebastopol amid much cheering from our men, but the fire was not abated. The Lancaster guns made bad practice, and one of them burst.

At 2.55 a terrific explosion of a powder magazine took place in the Russian Redan Fort. The Russians, however, returned to their guns, and still fired from the re-entering angle of their works.

The cannonade was continuous from the ships and from our batteries, but the smoke did not permit us to discern whether the British fleet was engaged.

At 3.30 a loose powder store inside our naval battery was blown up by a Russian shell, but did no damage. The enemy's earthworks were much injured by our fire, the Redan nearly silenced, and th fire of the Round Tower entrenchments diminished, though the inner works were still vigorous.

At 3.35 the magazine inside the works of the Round Fort was blown up by our shot.

At 4.00 the ships outside were ripping up the forts and stone works and town by tremendous broadsides. Only the French flag was visible, the English fleet being on the opposite side of the harbour. Orders were given to spare the town and buildings as much as possible.

From 4.00 to 5.30 the cannonade from our batteries was very warm, the Russians replying, though our fire had evidently established its superiority over theirs, the ships pouring in broadside after broadside on Forts Nicholas and Constantino at close ranges.

Towards dusk the fire slackened greatly, and at night it ceased altogether, the Russians for the first time being silent.

The French lost about 200 men, principally by the explosions; our loss was very small – not exceeding 100 killed and wounded from the commencement of the siege.

The fire was resumed on the morning of the 18th, soon after daybreak. The French on that occasion were unable to support us, their batteries being silenced. During the night the Russians remounted their guns and brought up fresh ones, and established a great superiority of fire and weight of metal.

On the 18th, early in the morning, a vedette was seen 'circling left' most energetically – and here, in a parenthesis, I must explain that when a vedette 'circles left', the proceeding signifies that the enemy's infantry are approaching, while to 'circle right' is indicative of the approach of cavalry. On this signal was immediately heard the roll-call to 'boot and saddle'; the Scots Greys and a troop of Horse Artillery assembled with the remaining cavalry on the plain; the 93rd got under arms, and the batteries on the heights were immediately manned. The distant pickets were seen to advance, and a dragoon dashed over the plain with the intelligence that the enemy was advancing quickly. Then cavalry and infantry moved upon the plain, remaining in rear of the eminences from which the movements of the vedettes had been observed. This state of things continued for an hour, when, from the hills, about 3,000 yards in front, the Turks opened fire from their advanced entrenchments. The Moskows then halted in their onward course, and in the evening lighted their watch-fires about 2,000 yards in front of our vedettes, the blaze showing bright and high in the darkness. Of course we were on the alert all night, and before the day broke were particularly attentive to our front. If the Russians had intended to attack us at that time, they could not have had a more favourable morning, a low dense white fog covering the whole of the plain. The sun rose, and the mist disappeared, when it was found the Russians had vanished also.

The next day, the 19th, we naturally expected would be a quiet one, and that we should not be annoyed by having to remain at our arms for our final work. Not a bit of it; we had just laden ourselves with havresacks to forage among the merchant shipping in the harbour, when a vedette was seen to 'circle right' most industriously. 'Boot and saddle' again resounded through the cavalry camps, and another day was passed like its predecessor, the enemy finally once more retiring, this time without advancing near enough for a shot from the Turks.

The enemy scarcely fired during the night of the 18th. Our batteries were equally silent. The French on their side opened a few guns on their right attack, at which they worked all night to get them into position; but they did not succeed in firing many rounds before the great preponderance of the enemy's metal made itself felt, and their works were damaged seriously; in fact, their lines, though nearer to the enemy's batteries than our own in some instances, were not sufficiently close for the light brass guns with which they were armed.

At daybreak on the 19th the firing continued as usual from both sides. The Russians, having spent the night in repairing the batteries, were nearly in the same position as ourselves, and, unaided or at least unassisted to the full extent we had reason to expect by the French, we were just able to bold our own during the day. Some smart affairs of skirmishers and sharpshooters took place in front. Our riflemen annoyed the Russian gunners greatly, and prevented the tirailleurs from showing near our batteries. On one occasion the Russian riflemen and our own men came close upon each other in a quarry before the town. Our men had exhausted all their ammunition; but as soon as they saw the Russians, they seized the blocks of stone which were lying about, and opened a vigorous volley on the enemy. The latter either had empty pouches, or were so much surprised that they forgot to load, for they resorted to the same missiles. A short fight ensued, which ended in our favour, and the Russians retreated, pelted vigorously as long as the men could pursue them. The coolness of a young artillery officer, named Maxwell, who took some ammunition to the batteries through a tremendous fire along a road so exposed to the enemy's fire that it has been called 'The Valley of Death', was highly spoken of on all sides. The blue-jackets were delighted with Captain Peel, who animated the men by the exhibition of the best qualities of an officer, though his courage was sometimes marked by an excess that bordered on rashness. When the Union Jack in the sailors' battery was shot away, he seized the broken staff, and leaping up on the earthworks, waved the old bit of bunting again and again amid a storm of shot, which fortunately left him untouched.

Our ammunition began to run short, but supplies were expected every moment. Either from a want of cartridges, or from the difficulty of getting powder down to the works, our twelve-gun battery was silent for some time. The Admiral (Sir E. Lyons), on his little grey pony, was to be seen hovering about our lines indefatigably. The French fire slackened very much towards one o'clock, the enemy pitching shells right into their lines and enfilading part of their new works. Hour after hour one continuous boom of cannon was alone audible, and the smoke screened all else from view. At a quarter past three there was an explosion of powder in the tower opposite to our right attack. The Flagstaff Fort seemed much knocked about by the French. The Redan and Round Tower earthworks fired nearly as well as ever. As it was very desirable to destroy the ships anchored in the harbour below us, and to fire the dockyard buildings, our rockets were brought into play, and, though rather erratic in their flight, they did some mischief, but not so much as was expected. Wherever they fell the people could be seen flying up the streets when the smoke cleared. At three o'clock p.m. the town was on fire; but after the smoke had excited our hopes for some time, it thinned away and went out altogether. They kept smartly at work from three guns in the Round Tower works, and from some four or five in the Redan, on our batteries.

Two 68-pounders were mounted during the night of the 19th in our batteries, and the firing, which nearly ceased after dark, was renewed by daybreak. We were all getting tired of this continual 'pound-pounding', which made a great deal of noise, wasted much powder, and did very little damage. Our amateurs were quite disappointed and tired out. Rome was not built in a day, nor could Sebastopol be taken in a week. In fact, we had run away with the notion that it was a kind of pasteboard city, which would tumble down at the sound of our cannon as the walls of Jericho fell at the blast of Joshua's trumpet. The news that Sebastopol had fallen, which we received via England, excited indignation and astonishment. The army was enraged, as they felt the verity, whenever it might be realised, must fall short of the effect of that splendid figment. They thought that the laurels of the Alma would be withered in the blaze of popular delight at the imaginary capture.

People at home must have known very little about us or our position. I was amused at seeing in a journal a letter from an 'Old Indian', on the manufacture of campaign bread *more Indico*, in which he advised us to use salt, milk, and butter in the preparation of what must be most delicious food. Salt was a luxury which was very rarely to be had, except in conjunction with porky fibre; and as to milk and butter, the very taste of them was forgotten. Lord Raglan was very glad to get a little cold pig and ration rum and water the night before we entered Balaklava. However, the hardest lot of all was reserved for our poor horses. All hay rations for baggagers were rigidly refused; they only received a few pounds of indifferent barley. There was not a blade of grass to be had – the whole of these plateaux and hills were covered with thistles only, and where the other covering of the earth went I know not. The hay ration for a charger was restricted to 6 lb daily. Under these circumstances horseflesh was cheap, and friendly presents were being continually offered by one man to another of 'a deuced good pony', which were seldom accepted.

The next day, the 20th, I had a foraging expedition, and returned with a goose, butter, preserved milk, &c. – a very successful foray, and a full havresack. We were just beginning our meal of commissariat beef and pork, tempered with the contents of the aforesaid havresack, when away went the vedette again, first circling right and then reversing as suddenly to the left. Again sounded trumpet, bugle, and drum through the plain, and masses again moved into position upon it. So we remained till dark, a night attack on the Turkish position in our front being anticipated, and so we again stood all ready for some hours, during which the only amusement was in the hands of the Turks, who fired a round or two; darkness found us similarly occupied.

At 2.50 p.m. a fire broke out behind the Redan. At 3.15 p.m. a fire of less magnitude was visible to the left of the Redan, further in towards the centre of the town. Prince Edward of Saxe-Weimar was wounded in the trenches. His wound was, however, not at all serious. Our loss was three killed and thirty-two or thirty-three wounded.

On the 21st a battery was finished before Inkerman, and two 18-pounders were mounted in it, in order to silence the heavy ship gun which annoyed the Second Division. The steamer *Vladimir* came up to the head of the harbour and opened fire on the right attack. She threw her shell with beautiful accuracy, and killed two men and wounded twenty others before we could reply effectually. A large traverse was erected to resist her fire, and she hauled off. Twenty-two guns were placed in a condition to open in this attack by the exertions of the men under Major Tylden, who directed it.

Lord Dunkellin, Captain Coldstream Guards, eldest son of the Marquis of Clanricarde, was taken prisoner on the 22nd. He was out with a working party of his regiment, which had got a little out of their way, when a number of men were observed through the dawning light in front of them. 'There are the Russians,' exclaimed one of the men. 'Nonsense, they're our fellows,' said his lordship, and off he went towards them, asking in a high tone as he got near,

'Who is in command of this party?' His men saw him no more, but he was afterwards exchanged for the Russian Artillery officer captured at Mackenzie's farm.

The Russians opened a very heavy cannonade on us in the morning; they always did so on Sundays. Divine Service was performed with a continued bass of cannon rolling through the responses and liturgy. The Russians made a stealthy sortie during the night, and advanced close to the French pickets. When challenged, they replied, 'Inglis, Inglis,' which passed muster with our allies as *bona fide* English; and before they knew where they were, the Russians had got into their batteries and spiked five mortars. They were speedily repulsed; but this misadventure mortified our brave allies exceedingly.

The return of killed and wounded for the 22nd, during the greater part of which a heavy fire was directed upon our trenches, and battery attacks right and left, showed the excellent cover of our works and their great solidity. We only lost one man killed in the Light Division, and two men in the Siege Train; of wounded we had one in the First Division, two in the Second Division, two in the Third Division, six in the Fourth Division, five in the Light Division, and ten in the Siege Train. A request made to us by the French that we would direct our fire on the Barrack Battery, which annoyed them excessively, was so well attended to, that before evening we had knocked it to pieces and silenced it. But sickness continued, and the diminution of our numbers every day was enough to cause serious anxiety. Out of 35,600 men borne on the strength of the army, there were not at this period more than 16,500 rank and file fit for service. In a fortnight upwards of 700 men were sent as invalids to Balaklava. There was a steady drain of some forty or fifty men a day going out from us, which was not dried up by the numbers of the returned invalids. Even the twenty or thirty a day wounded and disabled, when multiplied by the number of the days we had been here, became a serious item in the aggregate.

We were badly off for spare gun carriages and wheels, for ammunition and forage. Whilst our siege works were languishing and the hour of assault appeared more distant, the enemy were concentrating on our flank and rear, and preparing for a great attempt to raise the siege.

4

The Battle of Balaklava

If the exhibition of the most brilliant valour, and of a daring which would have reflected lustre on the best days of chivalry, could afford full consolation for the affair of the 25th of October, we had no reason to regret the loss we sustained.

In the following account I describe, to the best of my power, what occurred under my own eyes, and I state the facts which I heard from men whose veracity was unimpeachable. A certain feeling existed in some quarters that our cavalry had not been properly handled since they landed in the Crimea, and that they had lost golden opportunities from the indecision and excessive caution of their leaders. It was said that our cavalry ought to have been manoeuvred at Bouljanak in one way or in another, according to the fancy of the critic. It was affirmed, too, that the Light Cavalry were utterly useless in the performance of one of their most important duties – the collection of supplies for the army – that they were 'above their business, and too fine gentlemen for their work'; that our horse should have pushed the flying enemy after the Battle of the Alma; and, above all, that at Mackenzie's farm first, and at the gorge near Kamara on the 7th October, they had been improperly restrained from charging, and had failed in gaining great successes, which would have entitled them to a full share of the laurels of the campaign, owing solely to the timidity of the officer in command. The existence of this feeling was known to many of our cavalry, and they were indignant and exasperated that the faintest shade of suspicion should rest upon any of their corps. With the justice of these aspersions they had nothing to do, and perhaps the prominent thought in their minds was that they would give such an example of courage to the world, if the chance offered itself, as would shame their detractors for ever.

It has been already mentioned that several battalions of Russian infantry crossed the Tchernaya, and threatened the rear of our position and our communication with Balaklava. Their bands could be heard playing at night by the travellers along the Balaklava road to the camp, but they 'showed' but little during the day, and kept among the gorges and mountain passes through which the roads to Inkerman, Simpheropol, and the south-east of the Crimea wind towards the interior. The position we occupied was supposed by most people to be very strong. Our lines were formed by natural mountain slopes in the rear, along which the French had made entrenchments. Below these entrenchments, and very nearly in a right line across the valley beneath, were four conical hillocks, one rising above the other as they reached from our lines ; the farthest, which joined the chain of mountains opposite to our ridges being named Canrobert's Hill, from the meeting there of that general with Lord Raglan after the march to Balaklava. On the top of each of these hills the Turks had thrown up redoubts, each defended by 250 men, and armed with two or three heavy ship guns – lent by us to them, with one artilleryman in each redoubt to look after them. These hills crossed the valley of Balaklava at the distance of about 2½ miles from the town. Supposing the spectator, then, to take his stand on one of the heights forming the rear of our camp before Sebastopol, he would have seen the town of Balaklava, with its scanty shipping, its narrow strip of water, and its old forts, on his right hand ; immediately below he would have beheld the valley and plain of coarse meadow land, occupied by our cavalry tents, and stretching from the base of the ridge on which he stood to the foot of the formidable heights at the other side; he would have seen the French trenches lined with Zouaves a few feet beneath, and distant from him, on the slope of the hill; a Turkish redoubt lower down, then another in the valley; then, in a line with it, some angular earthworks ; then, in succession, the other two redoubts up to Canrobert's Hill.

At the distance of 2 or 2½ miles across the valley was an abrupt rocky mountain range covered with scanty brushwood here and there, or rising into barren pinnacles and *plateaux* of rock. In outline and appearance this portion of the landscape was wonderfully like the Trosachs. A patch of blue sea was caught in between the overhanging cliffs of Balaklava as they closed in the entrance to the harbour on the right. The camp of the Marines, pitched on the hill sides more than 1,000 feet above the level of the sea, was opposite to the spectator as his back was turned to Sebastopol and his right side towards Balaklava. On the road leading up the valley, close to the entrance of the town and beneath these hills, was the encampment of the 93rd Highlanders.

The cavalry lines were nearer to him below, and were some way in advance of the Highlanders, but nearer to the town than the Turkish redoubts. The valley was crossed here and there by small waves of land. On the left the hills and rocky mountain ranges gradually closed in towards the course of the Tchernaya, till, at 3 or 4 miles' distance from Balaklava, the valley was swallowed up in a mountain gorge and deep ravines, above which rose tier after tier of desolate whitish rock, garnished now and then by bits of scanty herbage, and spreading away towards the east and south, where they attained the Alpine dimensions of the Tschatir Dagh. It was very easy for an enemy at the Belbek, or in command of the road of Mackenzie's farm, Inkerman, Simpheropol, or Bakschiserai, to debouch through these gorges at any time upon this plain from the neck of the valley, or to march from Sebastopol by the Tchernaya, and to advance along it towards Balaklava, till checked by the Turkish redoubts on the southern side, or by the fire from the French works on the northern – i.e., the side which, in relation to the valley at Balaklava, formed the rear of our position. It was evident enough that Menschikoff and Gortschakoff had been feeling their way along this route for several days past, and very probably at night the Cossacks had crept up close to our pickets which were not always as watchful as might be desired, and had observed the weakness of a position far too extended for our army to defend, and occupied by their despised enemy, the Turks.

At half-past seven o'clock on the eventful morning of the 25th, an orderly came galloping in to the head-quarters camp from Sir

Colin Campbell with the news, that at dawn a strong corps of Russian horse, supported by guns and battalions of infantry had marched into the valley, had nearly dispossessed the Turks of the redoubt No. 1 (that on Canrobert's Hill, which was farthest from our lines), and they had opened fire on the redoubts Nos. 2, 3, and 4. Lord Lucan, who was in one of the redoubts when they were discovered, brought up his guns and some of his heavy cavalry, but they were obliged to retire owing to the superior weight of the enemy's metal.

Orders were despatched to Sir George Cathcart and the Duke of Cambridge, to put the Fourth and the First in motion; and intelligence of the advance of the Russians was furnished to General Canrobert. Immediately the General commanded General Bosquet to set the Third Division under arms, and sent artillery and 200 Chasseurs d'Afrique to assist us. Sir Colin Campbell, who was in command of Balaklava, had drawn up the 93rd Highlanders a little in front of the road to the town, at the first news of the advance of the enemy. The Marines on the heights got under arms; the seamen's batteries and Marines' batteries, on the heights close to the town, were manned, and the French artillerymen and the Zouaves prepared for action along their lines. Lord Lucan s men had not had time to water their horses; they had not broken their fast from the evening of the day before, and had barely saddled at the first blast of the trumpet, when they were drawn up on the slope behind the redoubts in front of their camp, to operate on the enemy's squadrons.

When the Russians advanced, the Turks fired a few rounds, got frightened at the advance of their supports, 'bolted', and fled with an agility quite at variance with common-place notions of Oriental deportment on the battle-field.

Soon after eight o'clock, Lord Raglan and his staff turned out and cantered towards the rear of our position. The booming of artillery, the spattering roll of musketry, were heard rising from the valley, drowning the roar of the siege guns before Sebastopol. As I rode in the direction of the firing, over the undulating plain that stretches away towards Balaklava, on a level with the summit of the ridges above it, I observed a French light infantry regiment (the 27th, I think) advancing from our right towards the ridge near the telegraph-house, which was already lined by companies of French infantry. Mounted officers scampered along its broken outline in every direction.

General Bosquet followed with his staff and a small escort of Hussars at a gallop. Never did the painter's eye rest on a more beautiful scene than I beheld from the ridge. The fleecy vapours still hung around the mountain tops, and mingled with the ascending volumes of smoke; the patch of sea sparkled freshly in the rays of the morning sun, but its light was eclipsed by the flashes which gleamed from the masses of armed men.

Looking to the left towards the gorge, we beheld six masses of Russian infantry, which had just debouched from the mountain passes near the Tchernaya, and were advancing with solemn stateliness up the valley. Immediately in their front was a line of artillery. Two batteries of light guns were already a mile in advance of them, and were playing with energy on the redoubts, from which feeble puffs of smoke came at long intervals. Behind these guns, in front of the infantry, were bodies of cavalry. They were three on each flank, moving down en echelon towards us, and the valley was lit up with the blaze of their sabres, and lance points, and gay accoutrements. In their front, and extending along the intervals between each battery of guns, were clouds of mounted skirmishers, wheeling and whirling in the front of their march like autumn leaves tossed by the wind. The Zouaves close to us were lying like tigers at the spring, with ready rifles in hand, hidden chin deep by the earthworks which ran along the line of these ridges on our rear; but the quick-eyed Russians were manoeuvring on the other side of the valley, and did not expose their columns to attack. Below the Zouaves we could see the Turkish gunners in the redoubts, all in confusion as the shells burst over them. Just as I came up, the Russians had carried No. 1 redoubt, the farthest and most elevated of all, and their horsemen were chasing the Turks across the interval which lay between it and redoubt No. 2.

At that moment the cavalry, under Lord Lucan, were formed – the Light Brigade, under Lord Cardigan, in advance; the Heavy

Brigade, under Brigadier-General Scarlett, in reserve, drawn up in front of their encampment, and were concealed from the view of the enemy by a slight 'wave' in the plain. Considerably to the rear of their right, the 93rd Highlanders were in front of the approach to Balaklava. Above and behind them, on the heights, the Marines were visible through the glass, drawn up under arms, and the gunners could be seen ready in the earthworks, in which were placed the ships' heavy guns. The 93rd had originally been advanced somewhat more into the plain, but the instant the Russians got possession of the first redoubt they opened fire on them from our own guns, which inflicted some injury, and Sir Colin Campbell 'retired' his men to a better position. Meantime the enemy advanced his cavalry rapidly. The Turks in redoubt No. 2 fled in scattered groups towards redoubt No. 3, and Balaklava; but the horse-hoof of the Cossack was too quick for them, and sword and lance were busily plied among the retreating herd. The yells of the pursuers and pursued were plainly audible. As the Lancers and Light Cavalry of the Russians advanced they gathered up their skirmishers. The shifting trails of men, which played all over the valley like moonlight on the water, contracted, gathered up, and the little *peloton* in a few moments became a solid column. Up came their guns, in rushed their gunners to the abandoned redoubt, and the guns of No. 2 soon played upon the dispirited defenders of No. 3 redoubt. Two or three shots in return and all was silent. The Turks swarmed over the earthworks, and ran in confusion towards the town, firing at the enemy as they ran. Again the solid column of cavalry opened like a fan, and resolved itself into a 'long spray' of skirmishers. It lapped the flying Turks, steel flashed in the air, and down went the Moslem on the plain. In vain the naval guns on the heights fired on the Russian cavalry; the distance was too great. In vain the Turkish gunners in the batteries along the French entrenchments endeavoured to protect their flying countrymen; their shot flew wide and short of the swarming masses.

The Turks betook themselves towards the Highlanders, where they checked their flight and formed on the flanks. As the Russian cavalry on the left of their line crowned the hill across the valley, they perceived the Highlanders drawn up at the distance of some half a mile. They halted, and squadron after squadron came up from the rear. The Russians drew breath for a moment, and then in one grand line charged towards Balaklava. The ground flew beneath their horses' feet; gathering speed at every stride, they dashed on towards that *thin red line tipped with steel*. The Turks fired a volley at 800 yards and ran. As the Russians came within 600 yards, down went that line of steel in front, and out rang a rolling volley of Minié musketry. The distance was too great; the Russians were not checked, but swept onwards, here and there knocked over by the shot of our batteries; but ere they came within 250 yards, another volley flashed from the rifles. The Russians wheeled about, and fled faster than they came. 'Bravo, Highlanders! Well done!' shouted the excited spectators. But events thickened; the Highlanders and their splendid front were soon forgotten – men scarcely had a moment to think of this fact, that the 93rd never altered their formation to receive that tide of horsemen. 'No,' said Sir Colin Campbell, 'I did not think it worth while to form them even four deep!' Then they moved *en échelon*, in two bodies, with another in reserve. The cavalry who had been pursuing the Turks on the right were coming up to the ridge beneath us, which concealed our cavalry from view. The Heavy Brigade in advance was drawn up in two lines. The first line consisted of the Scots Greys, and of their old companions in glory, the Enniskillens; the second, of the 4th Royal Irish, of the 5th Dragoon Guards, and of the 1st Royal Dragoons. The Light Cavalry Brigade was on their left, in two lines also.

Lord Raglan sent orders to Lord Lucan to cover the approaches, and his heavy horse were just moving from their position near the vineyard and orchard, when he saw a body of the enemy's cavalry coming after him over the ridge. Lord Lucan rode after his cavalry, wheeled them round, and ordered them to advance against the enemy. The Russians – evidently *corps d'élite* – their light blue jackets embroidered with silver lace, were advancing at an easy gallop towards the brow of the hill. A forest of lances glistened in their rear, and several squadrons of grey-coated dragoons moved up quickly to support them as they reached the summit. The instant they came in sight, the trumpets of our cavalry gave out the warning blast which told us all that in another moment we should see the shock of battle beneath our very eyes. Lord Raglan, all his staff and escort, and groups of officers, the Zouaves, French generals and officers, and bodies of French infantry on the height, were spectators of the scene as though they were looking on the stage from the boxes of a theatre. Every one dismounted, and not a word was said. The Russians advanced down the hill at a slow canter, which they changed to a trot, and at last nearly halted.

The trumpets rang out again through the valley, and the Greys and Enniskilleners went right at the centre of the Russian cavalry. The space between them was only a few hundred yards; it was scarce enough to let the horses 'gather way', nor had the men quite space sufficient for the full play of their sword arms. The Russian line brought forward each wing as our cavalry advanced, and threatened to annihilate them as they passed on. Turning a little to the left, so as to meet the Russian right, the Greys rushed on with a cheer that thrilled to every heart – the wild shout of the Enniskilleners rose through the air at the same instant. As lightning flashes through a cloud, the Greys and Enniskilleners pierced through the dark masses of Russians. The shock was but for a moment. There was a clash of steel and a light play of sword-blades in the air, and then the Greys and the redcoats disappeared in the midst of the shaken and quivering column. The first line of Russians, which had been smashed by and had fled off at one flank and towards the centre, were coming back to swallow up our handful of men. By sheer steel and sheer courage Enniskillener and Scot were winning their way right through the enemy's squadrons, and already grey horses and red coats appeared at the rear mass, when the 4th Dragoon Guards, riding at the right flank of the Russians, and the 5th Dragoon Guards, following close after the Enniskilleners, rushed at the enemy and put them to utter rout.

A cheer burst from every lip – in the enthusiasm, officers and men took off their caps and shouted with delight; and thus keeping up the scenic character of their position, they clapped their hands again and again. Lord Raglan at once despatched Lieutenant Curzon, aide-de-camp, to convey his congratulations to Brigadier-General Scarlett, and to say 'Well done!' The Russian cavalry, followed by our shot, retired in confusion, leaving the ground covered with horses and men.

At ten o'clock the Guards and Highlanders of the First Division were seen moving towards the plains from their camp. The Duke of Cambridge came up to Lord Raglan for orders, and his lordship, ready to give the honour of the day to Sir Colin Campbell, who commanded at Balaklava, told His Royal Highness to place himself under the direction of the Brigadier. At forty minutes after ten, the Fourth Division also took up their position in advance of Balaklava. The cavalry were then on the left front of our position, facing the enemy; the Light Cavalry Brigade *en échelon* in reserve, with guns, on the right; the 4th Royal Irish, the 5th Dragoon Guards, and Greys on the left of the brigade, the Enniskillens and 1st Royals on the right. The Fourth Division took up ground in the centre; the Guards and Highlanders filed off towards the extreme right, and faced the redoubts, from which the Russians opened on them with artillery, which was silenced by the rifle skirmishers under Lieutenant Godfrey.

At fifty minutes after ten, General Canrobert, attended by his staff, and Brigadier-General Rose, rode up to Lord Raglan, and the staffs of the two Generals and their escorts mingled in praise of the magnificent charge of our cavalry, while the chiefs apart conversed over the operations of the day, which promised to be one of battle. At fifty-five minutes after ten, a body of cavalry, the Chasseurs d'Afrique, passed down to the plain, and were loudly cheered by our men. They took up ground in advance of the ridges on our left.

Soon after occurred the glorious catastrophe. The Quartermaster-General, Brigadier Airey, thinking that the Light Cavalry had not gone far enough in front, gave an order in writing to Captain Nolan, 15th Hussars, to take to Lord Lucan. A braver soldier than Captain Nolan the army did not possess. He was known for his entire devotion to his profession, and for his excellent work on our drill and system of remount and breaking horses. He entertained the most exalted opinions respecting the capabilities of the English horse soldier. The British Hussar and Dragoon could break square, take batteries, ride over columns, and pierce any other cavalry, as if they were made of straw. He thought they had missed even such chances as had been offered to them – that in fact, they were in some measure disgraced. A matchless horseman and a first-rate swordsman he held in contempt, I am afraid even grape and canister. He rode off with his orders to Lord Lucan.

When Lord Lucan received the order from Captain Nolan, and had read it, he asked, we are told, 'Where are we to advance to?' Captain Nolan pointed with his finger in the direction of the Russians, and according to the statements made after his death said, 'There are the enemy, and there are the guns,' or words to that effect.

Lord Raglan had only in the morning ordered Lord Lucan to move from the position he had taken near the centre redoubt to 'the left of the second line of redoubts occupied by the Turks'. Seeing that the 93rd and invalids were cut off from the cavalry, Lord Raglan sent another order to Lord Lucan to send his heavy horse towards Balaklava, and that officer was executing it just as the Russian horse came over the ridge. The Heavy Cavalry charge then took place, and afterwards the men dismounted on the scene. After an interval of half an hour, Lord Raglan again sent an order to Lord Lucan – 'Cavalry to advance and take advantage of any opportunity to recover the heights. They will be supported by infantry, which has been ordered to advance upon two fronts.'* Lord Raglan's reading of this order was, that the infantry had been ordered to advance on two fronts. It does not appear that the infantry had received orders to advance; the Duke of Cambridge and Sir G. Cathcart stated they were not in receipt of such instruction. Lord Lucan advanced his cavalry to the ridge, close to No. 5 redoubt, and while there received from Captain Nolan an order which as follows: 'Lord Raglan wishes the cavalry to advance rapidly to the front, follow the enemy, and try to prevent the enemy carrying away the guns; troops of Horse Artillery may accompany. French cavalry is on your left. Immediate.'

Lord Lucan gave the order to Lord Cardigan to advance upon the guns, conceiving that his orders compelled him to do so. The noble Earl saw the fearful odds against him. It is a maxim of war, that 'cavalry never act without a support'. 'Infantry should be close at hand when cavalry carry guns, as the effect is only instantaneous', and should always be placed on the flank of a line of cavalry. The only support our light cavalry had was the heavy cavalry at a great distance behind them, the infantry and guns being far in the rear. There were no squadrons in column. There was a plain to charge over, before the enemy's guns could be reached, of a mile and a half in length.

At ten minutes past eleven our Light Cavalry Brigade advanced. The whole Brigade scarcely made one effective regiment, according to the numbers of continental armies; and yet it was more than we could spare. They swept proudly past, glittering in the morning sun in all the pride and splendour of war. They advanced in two lines, quickened their pace as they closed towards the enemy. At the distance of 1,200 yards the whole line of the enemy belched forth, from thirty iron mouths, a flood of smoke and flame. The flight was marked by instant gaps in our ranks, by dead men and horses, by steeds flying wounded or riderless across the plain. In diminished ranks, with a halo of steel above their heads, and with a cheer which was many a noble fellow's death-cry, they flew into the smoke of the batteries; but ere they were lost from view the plain was strewed with their bodies.

Through the clouds of smoke we could see their sabres flashing as they rode between the guns, cutting down the gunners as they stood. We saw them riding through, returning, after breaking through a column of Russians, and scattering them like chaff, when the flank fire of the batteries on the hill swept them down. Wounded men and dismounted troopers flying towards us told the sad tale. At the very moment a regiment of Lancers was hurled upon their flank. Colonel Shewell, of the 8th Hussars, whose attention was drawn to them by Lieutenant Phillips, saw the danger, and rode his few men straight at them. It was as much as our Heavy Cavalry Brigade could do to cover the retreat of the miserable remnants of that band of heroes as they returned to the place they had so lately quitted in all the pride of life. At thirty-five minutes past eleven not a British soldier, except the dead and dying, was left in front of these Muscovite guns. The Heavy Cavalry, in columns of squadrons, moved slowly backwards, covering the retreat of the broken men. The ground was left covered with our men and with hundreds of Russians, and we could see the Cossacks busy searching the dead. Our infantry made a forward movement towards the redoubts after the cavalry came in, and the Russian infantry in advance slowly retired towards the gorge; at the same time the French cavalry pushed forward on their right, and held them in check, pushing out a line of skirmishers, and forcing them to withdraw their guns.

Captain Nolan was killed by the first shot fired, as he rode in advance of the first line. Lord Cardigan received a lance thrust through his clothes.

While the affair was going on, the French cavalry made a most brilliant charge at the battery on our left, and cut down the gunners; but they could not get off the guns, and had to retreat with the loss of two captains and fifty men killed and wounded out of their little force of 200 Chasseurs.

The Russians from the redoubt continued to harass us, and the First Division were ordered to lie down in two lines. The Fourth Division, covered by the rising ground, and two regiments of French infantry which had arrived in the valley, followed by artillery, moved onwards to operate on the Russian right, already threatened by the French cavalry. The Russians threw out skirmishers to meet the French skirmishers, and the French contented themselves with keeping their position. At 11 a.m., the Russians, feeling alarmed at our steady advance and at the symptoms of our intention to turn or cut off their right, retired from No. 1 redoubt, which was taken possession of by the allies. At fifteen minutes past eleven they abandoned redoubt No. 2, blowing up the magazine; and, as we still continued to advance, they blew up and abandoned No. 3 at forty-five minutes past eleven; but, to our great regret, we could not prevent their taking off seven out of nine guns in the works.

At forty-eight minutes past eleven, the Russian infantry began to retire, a portion crept up the hills behind the 1st redoubt, which still belonged to them. The artillery on the right of the First Division fired shot and rockets at the 1st redoubt, but could not do much good, nor could the heavy guns of the batteries near the town carry so far as to annoy the Russians. At twelve o'clock the greater portion of the French and English moved on, and an accession to the artillery was made by two French batteries, pushed on towards the front of our left. The First Division remained still in line along the route to Balaklava. From twelve to fifteen minutes passed, not a shot was fired on either side, but the Russians gathered up their forces towards the heights over the gorge, and, still keeping their cavalry on the plain, manoeuvred in front on our right. At twenty-eight minutes after twelve the allies again got into motion, with the exception of the First Division, which moved *en échelon* towards the opposite hills, keeping their right wing well before Balaklava. At forty minutes after twelve, Captain Calthorpe was sent by Lord Raglan with orders which altered the disposition of our front, for the French, at 1 p.m. showed further up on our left. As our object was solely to keep Balaklava, we had no desire to bring on a general engagement; and as the Russians would not advance, but kept their cavalry in front of the approach to the mountain passes, it became evident the action was over. The cannonade, which began again at a quarter-past twelve, and continued with very little effect, ceased altogether at a quarter-past one. The two armies retained their respective positions.

Lord Raglan continued on the hill-side all day, watching the enemy. It was dark ere he returned to his quarters. With the last gleam of day we could see the sheen of the enemy's lances in their old position in the valley; and their infantry gradually crowned the heights on their left, and occupied the road to the village which is beyond Balaklava to the southward. Our Guards were moving back, as I passed them, and the tired French and English were replaced by a French division, which marched down to the valley at five o'clock.

We had 13 officers killed or taken, 162 men killed or taken; 27 officers wounded, 224 men wounded. Total killed, wounded, and missing, 426. Horses, killed or missing, 394; horses wounded, l26; total, 520.

In the night when our guns were taken into Sebastopol, there was joy throughout the city, and it was announced that the Russians had gained a great victory. A salvo of artillery was fired, and at nine o'clock p.m. a tremendous cannonade was opened against our lines by the enemy. It did no injury. At 1 p.m. on the 26th, about 4,000 men made an attack on our right flank, but were repulsed by Sir De Lacy Evans's Division, with the loss of 600 men killed and wounded. As I was engaged in my tent and did not see the action, I think it right to give the dispatches which relate this brilliant affair.

Lieutenant-General Sir De Lacy Evans to Lord Raglan.
2nd Division, Heights of the Tchernaya, Oct. 27, 1854.

My Lord,
Yesterday the enemy attacked this division with several columns of infantry supported by artillery. Their cavalry did not come to the front. Their masses, covered by large bodies of skirmishers, advanced with much apparent confidence. The division immediately formed line in advance of our camp, the left under Major-General Pennefather, the right under Brigadier-General Adams. Lieutenant-Colonel Fitzmayer and the Captains of batteries (Turner and Yates) promptly posted their guns and opened fire upon the enemy.

Immediately on the cannonade being heard, the Duke of Cambridge brought up to our support the brigade of Guards under Major-General Bentinck, with a battery under Lieutenant-Colonel Dacres. His Royal Highness took post in advance of our right to secure that flank, and rendered me throughout the most effective and important assistance. General Bosquet, with similar promptitude and from a greater distance, approached our position with five French battalions. Sir G. Cathcart hastened to us with a regiment of Rifles, and Sir G. Brown pushed forward two guns in co-operation by our left.

The enemy came on at first rapidly, assisted by their guns on the Mound Hill. Our pickets, then chiefly of the 49th and 30th Regiments, resisted them with remarkable determination and firmness. Lieutenant Conolly, of the 49th, greatly distinguished himself, as did Captain Bayley, of the 30th, and Captain Atcherley, all of whom, I regret to say, were severely wounded. Serjeant Sullivan also displayed at this point great bravery.

In the meantime our eighteen guns in position, including those of the First Division, were served with the utmost energy. In half an hour they forced the enemy's artillery to abandon the field. Our batteries were then directed with equal accuracy and vigour upon the enemy's columns, which (exposed also to the close fire of our advanced infancy) soon fell into complete disorder and flight. They were then literally chased by the 30th and 95th Regiments over the ridges and down towards the head of the bay. So eager was the pursuit, that it was with difficulty Major-General Pennefather eventually effected the recall of our men. These regiments and the pickets were led gallantly by Major Mauleverer, Major Champion, Major Eman and Major Hume. They were similarly pursued further towards our right by four companies of the 41st, led gallantly by Lieutenant-Colonel the Honourable P. Herbert, A.Q.M.G. The 47th also contributed. The 55th were held in reserve.

Above 80 prisoners fell into our hands, and about 130 of the enemy's dead were left within or near our position. It is computed that their total loss could scarcely be less than 600.

Our loss, I am sorry to say, has been above 80, of whom 12 killed, 5 officers wounded. I am happy to say, hopes are entertained that Lieutenant Conolly will recover, but his wound is dangerous.

I will have the honour of transmitting to your Lordship a list of officers, non-commissioned officers, and privates, whose conduct attracted special notice. That of the pickets excited general admiration.

To Major-General Pennefather and Brigadier-General Adams I was, as usual, greatly indebted. To Lieutenant-Colonel Dacres, Lieutanant- Colonel Fitzmayer, Captains Turner, Yates, Woodhouse, and Hamley, and the whole of the Royal Artillery, we are under the greatest obligation.

Lieutenant-Colonel Herbert, A.Q.M.G., rendered the division, as he always does, highly distinguished and energetic services. Lieutenant-Colonel Wilbraham, A.A.G., while serving most actively, I regret to say, had a very severe fall from his horse. I beg leave also to recommend to your Lordship's favourable consideration the excellent services of Captains Glasbrook and Thompson, of the Quartermaster-General's Department, the Brigade-Majors Captains Armstrong and Thackwell, and my personal staff, Captains Allix, Gubbins, and the Honourable W. Boyle.

I have, &c.

De Lacy Evans, Lieutenant-General.

Lord Raglan to the Duke of Newcastle.
Before Sebastopol, Oct. 28, 1854.

My Lord Duke,

I have nothing particular to report to your Grace respecting the operations of the siege since I wrote to you on the 23rd instant. The fire has been somewhat less constant, and our casualties have been fewer, though I regret to say that Captain Childers, a very promising officer of the Royal Artillery, was killed on the evening of the 23rd, and I have just heard that Major Dalton, of the 49th, of whom Lieutenant-General Sir De Lacy Evans entertained a very high opinion, was killed in the trenches last night.

The enemy moved out of Sebastopol on the 26th with a large force of infantry, cavalry, and artillery, amounting, it is said, to 6,000 or 7,000 men, and attacked the left of the Second Division, commanded by Lieutenant-General Sir De Lacy Evans, who speedily and energetically repulsed them, assisted by one of the batteries of the First Division and some guns of the Light Division, and supported by a brigade of Guards, and by several regiments of the

Fourth Division, and in rear by the French Division, commanded by General Bosquet, who was most eager in his desire to give him every aid.

I have the honour to transmit a copy of Sir De Lacy Evans's report, which I am sure your Grace will read with the highest satisfaction, and I beg to recommend the officers whom he particularly mentions to your protection.

Captain Bayley of the 30th, and Captain Atcherley of the same regiment, and Lieutenant Conolly of the 49th, all of whom are severely wounded, appear to have greatly distinguished themselves.

I cannot speak in too high terms of the manner in which Lieutenant-General Sir De Lacy Evans met this very serious attack. I had not the good fortune to witness it myself, being occupied in front of Balaklava at the time it commenced, and having only reached his position as the affair ceased, but I am certain I speak the sentiments of all who witnessed the operation in saying that nothing could have been better managed, and that the greatest credit is due to the Lieutenant-General, whose services and conduct I have before had to bring under your Grace's notice.

I inclose the return of the losses the army has sustained since the 22nd.

I have, &c.

Raglan.

5

The Battle of Inkerman

It had rained almost incessantly for the greater part of the night of November 4th, and the early morning gave no promise of any cessation of the heavy showers. As dawn broke the fog and drifting rain were so thick that one could scarcely see 2 yards. At four o'clock a.m. the bells of the churches in Sebastopol were heard ringing drearily through the cold night air, but the occurrence excited no particular attention. About three o'clock a.m., a man of the 23rd regiment on outlying picket heard the sound of wheels in the valley, but supposed it arose from carts or arabas going into Sebastopol by the Inkerman road. After the battle he mentioned the circumstance to Major Bunbury, who rebuked him for neglecting to report it. No one suspected that masses of Russians were then creeping up the rugged heights over the Valley of Inkerman against the undefended flank of the Second Division, and were bringing into position an overwhelming artillery, ready to play upon their tents at the first glimpse of day.

Sir De Lacy Evans had long been aware of the insecurity of his position, and had repeatedly pointed it out. It was the only ground where we were exposed to surprise. Ravines and curves in the hill lead up to the crest against which our right flank was resting, without guns, intrenchments, abattis, or defence of any kind. Every one admitted the truth of the representations, but indolence, or a false sense of security led to indifference and procrastination. A battery was thrown up of sandbags on the slope of the hill, but Sir De Lacy Evans, thinking that two guns without any works to support them would only invite attack, caused them to be removed as soon as they had silenced the Light-house Battery, which had been firing on his camp.

Heavy responsibility rests on those whose neglect enabled the enemy to attack where we were least prepared for it, and whose indifference led them to despise precautions which might have saved many lives, and trebled the loss of the enemy. We had nothing to rejoice over, and almost everything to deplore, in the Battle of Inkerman. We defeated the enemy indeed, but did not advance one step nearer Sebastopol. We abashed, humiliated, and utterly routed an enemy strong in numbers, in fanaticism, and in dogged courage, but we suffered a fearful loss when we were not in a position to part with one man.

It was a little after five o'clock in the morning, when Codrington, in accordance with his usual habit, visited the outlying pickets of his brigade. It was reported that 'all was well' along the line. The General entered into conversation with Captain Pretyman, of the 33rd Regiment, who was on duty, and in the course of it some one remarked it would not be surprising if the Russians availed themselves of the gloom to make an attack. The Brigadier, an excellent officer, turned his pony round vigilant, and had only ridden a few yards, when a sharp rattle of musketry was heard down the hill on the left of his pickets, and where the pickets of the Second Division were stationed. Codrington at once turned in the direction of the firing, and in a few moments galloped back to camp to turn out his division. The Russians were advancing in force. The pickets of the Second Division had scarcely made out the infantry clambering up the steep hill through a drizzling rain before they were forced to retreat by a close sharp musketry, and driven up the hill, contesting every step, and firing as long as they had a round of ammunition. Their grey greatcoats rendered them almost invisible even when close at hand.

The pickets of the Light Division were soon assailed and obliged to fall back. About the time of the advance on our right flank took place a demonstration against Balaklava, but the enemy contented themselves with drawing up their cavalry in order of battle, supported by field artillery, at the neck of the valley, in readiness to sweep over the heights and cut off our retreat, should the assault on our right be successful. A steamer with very heavy guns was sent up by night to the head of the creek at Inkerman and threw enormous shells over the hill.

Everything that could be done to bind victory to their eagles was done by the Russian Generals. The presence of the Grand Dukes Nicholas and Michael, who told them that the Czar had issued orders that every Frenchman and Englishman was to be driven into the sea ere the year closed, cheered the common soldiers, who regard the son of the Emperor as an emanation of the Divine presence. Abundance of a coarser and more material stimulant was found in their flasks; and the priests 'blessed' them ere they went forth, and assured them of the aid and protection of the Most High. A mass was said. The joys of Heaven were offered those who might fall in the holy fight, and the favours of the Emperor were promised to those who might survive the bullets of the enemy.

The men in camp had just began to struggle with the rain in endeavouring to light their fires, when the alarm was sounded. Pennefather, to whom Sir De Lacy Evans had given up for the time the command of the Second Division, got the troops under arms. Adams's brigade, consisting of the 41st, 47th, and 49th Regiments, was pushed on to the brow of the hill to check the advance of the enemy by the road from the valley. Pennefather's brigade, consisting of the 30th, 55th, and 95th Regiments, was posted on their flank. The regiments met a tremendous fire from guns posted on the high grounds. Sir George Cathcart led such portions of the 20th, 21st, 46th, 57th, 63rd, and 68th Regiments as were not employed in the trenches, to the right of the ground occupied by the Second Division.

It was intended that Torrens's brigade should move in support of Goldie's, but the enemy were in such strength that the whole force of the division, which consisted of only 2,200 men, was needed to repel them. Codrington, with part of the 7th, 23rd, and 33rd, sought to cover the extreme of our right attack, and the sloping ground towards Sebastopol; Buller's brigade was brought up to support the Second Division on the left; Jeffrey's with the 88th, being pushed forward in the bushwood on the ridge of one of the principal ravines. As soon as Brown brought up his division, they were under fire from an unseen enemy. The Third Division, under Sir R. England, was in reserve. Part of the 50th, under Wilton, and 1st Battalion Royals, under Bell, were slightly engaged ere the day was over. The Duke of Cambridge turned out the Guards under Bentinck, and advanced on the right of the Second Division to the summit of the hill overlooking the valley of the Tchernaya. Between the left and the right of the Second Division there was a ravine, which lost itself on the plateau, close to the road to Sebastopol. This road was not protected; only a few scarps were made in it, and the pickets at night were only a short distance in advance. A low breastwork crossed this road at the plateau by the tents of the Second Division. On arriving at the edge of the plateau on the right ravine, the Duke of Cambridge saw two columns coming up the steep ground covered with brushwood. The enemy were already in the Sandbag Redoubt, but His Royal Highness at once led the Guards to the charge.

It has been doubted whether any enemy ever stood in conflicts with the bayonet, but here the bayonet was employed in a fight of the most obstinate character. We had been prone to believe that no foe could withstand the British soldier; but at Inkerman, not only were desperate encounters maintained with the bayonet, but we were obliged to resist the Russian infantry again and again, as they charged us.

It was six o'clock before the Head-Quarter camp was roused by the musketry, and by the report of field guns. Soon after seven o'clock a.m. Lord Raglan rode towards the scene, followed by his staff. As they approached, the steady, unceasing roll told that the engagement was serious. When a break in the fog enabled the Russian gunners to see the camp of the Second Division, the tents were sent into the air or set on fire. Gambier was ordered to get up two 18-pounders to reply to a fire which our light guns were utterly inadequate to meet. As he was exerting himself in his duty, Gambier was severely but not dangerously wounded. His place was taken by Lieutenant-Colonel Dickson, and the fire of those two pieces had the most marked effect in deciding the fate of the day.

Our Generals could not see where to go. They could not tell where the enemy were. In darkness and rain they had to lead our lines through thick bushes and thorny brakes, which broke our ranks. Every pace was marked by a man down, wounded by an enemy whose position was only indicated by the rattle of musketry and the rush of ball.

Cathcart, advancing from the centre of our position, came to the hill where the Guards were engaged, and, after a few words with the Duke, led the 63rd Regiment down on the right of the Guards into a ravine filled with brushwood, towards the valley of the Tchernaya. He perceived, as he did so, that the Russians had gained possession of the hill in rear of his men, but his stout heart never failed him for a moment. A deadly volley was poured into our scattered companies. Sir George cheered and led them back up the hill, and Cathcart fell from his horse close to the Russian columns. He rode at the head of the leading company, encouraging them. A cry arose that ammunition was failing. 'Have you not got your bayonets?' As he lead on his men another body of the enemy had gained the top of the hill behind them on the right, but it was impossible to tell whether they were friends or foes. The 63rd halted and fired. They were met by a fierce volley. Seymour, who was wounded, got down from his horse to aid his chief, but the enemy rushed down on them, and when our men had driven them back, they lay dead side by side. The 63rd suffered fearfully. They were surrounded, and won their desperate way up the hill with the loss of nearly 500 men. Sir George Cathcart's body was recovered with a bullet wound in the head and three bayonet wounds in the body. In this attack where the Russians fought with the greatest ferocity, and bayoneted the wounded, Colonel Swyny, 63rd, Major Wynne, 68th, Lieutenant Dowling, 20th, and other officers, met their death. Goldie, who was engaged with his brigade on the left of the Inkerman road, received the wounds of which he afterwards died about the same time. The fight had not long commenced before it was evident that the Russians had received orders to fire at all mounted officers. The regiments did not take their colours into the battle, but the officers, nevertheless, were picked off, and it did not require the colour to indicate their presence.

The conflict on the right was equally uncertain and equally bloody. The 88th in front were surrounded; but four companies of the 77th, under Major Straton, charged the Russians, and relieved their comrades. Further to the right, a fierce contest took place between the Guards and dense columns of Russians. The Guards twice charged them and drove the enemy out of the Sandbag Battery, when they perceived that the Russians had out-flanked them. They were out of ammunition. They had no reserve, and they were fighting against an enemy who stoutly contested every inch of ground, when another Russian column appeared in their rear. They had lost fourteen officers; one-half of their number were on the ground. The Guards retired. They were reinforced by a wing of the 20th under Major Crofton. Meanwhile the Second Division, in the centre of the line, was hardly pressed. The 41st Regiment was exposed to a terrible fire. The 95th only mustered sixty-four men when paraded at two o'clock, and the whole Division when assembled by Major Eman in rear of their camp after the fight was over numbered only 300 men.

At half-past nine o'clock, as Lord Raglan and his staff were on a knoll, a shell came and exploded on Captain Somerset's horse; a portion tore off the leather of Somerset's overalls. Gordon's horse was killed, and it then carried away General Strangeway's leg; it hung by a shred of flesh and bit of cloth from the skin. The old General never moved a muscle. He said in a quiet voice, 'Will any one be kind enough to lift me off my horse?' He was laid on the ground, and at last carried to the rear. He had not strength to undergo an operation, and died in two hours.

At one time the Russians succeeded in getting up close to the guns of Captain Wodehouse's and Captain Turner's batteries in the gloom of the morning. Uncertain whether they were friends or foes, our artillerymen hesitated to fire. The Russians charged, bore down all resistance, drove away or bayoneted the gunners, and succeeded in spiking four of the guns.

The rolling of musketry, the pounding of the guns were deafening. The Russians, as they charged up the heights, yelled like demons. The regiments of the Fourth Division and the Marines, armed with the old and much-belauded Brown Bess, could do nothing against the Muscovite infantry, but the Minié smote them like the hand of the Destroying Angel. The disproportion of numbers was however, too great – our men were exhausted – but at last came help. At last the French appeared on our right.

It was after nine o'clock when the French streamed over the brow of the hill on our right – Chasseurs d'Orleans, Tirailleurs Indigènes, Zouaves, Infantry of the Line, and Artillery – and fel upon the flank of the Russians. On visiting the spot it was curious to observe how men of all arms – English, French, and Russian – lay together, showing that the ground must have been occupied by different bodies of troops. The French were speedily engaged for the Russians had plenty of men for all comers. Their reserves in the valley and along the road to Sebastopol received the shattered columns which were driven down the hill, allowed them to re-form and attack again, or furnished fresh regiments to assault the Allies again and again. This reserve seems to have consisted of three large bodies – probably of 5,000 men each. The attacking force could not have been less than 20,000 men, and it is a very low estimate indeed of the strength of the Russians to place it at from 45,000 to 50,000 men of all arms. Some say there were from 55,000 to 60,000 men engaged on the side of the enemy; but I think that number excessive, and there certainly was not ground enough for them to show front upon. Captain Burnett, R.N., states that he saw fresh bodies of Russians marching up to the attack on three successive occasions, and that their artillery was relieved no less than four times. The Minié rifle did our work, and Lord Harding is entitled to the best thanks of the country for his perseverance in arming this expedition as far as he could with every rifle that could be got, notwithstanding the dislike with which the weapon was received by many experienced soldiers.

Three battalions of the Chasseurs d'Orleans rushed by, the light of battle on their faces. Their trumpets sounded above the din of battle, and when we watched their eager dash on the flank of the enemy we knew the day was safe. They were followed by a battalion of Chasseurs Indigènes. At twelve o'clock they wer driven pell-mell down the hill towards the valley, where pursuit was impossible, as the roads were commanded by artillery.

The day, which cleared up about eleven, again became obscured. Rain and fog set in, and we could not pursue. We formed in front of our lines, the enemy, covering his retreat by horse on the slopes, near the Careening Bay, and by artillery fire, fell back upon the works, and across the Inkerman Bridge. Our cavalry, the remnant of the Light Brigade, were moved into a position where it was hoped they might be of service, but they were too few to attempt anything, and lost several horses and men. Cornet Cleveland, was struck by a piece of shell and expired.

General Canrobert, who was wounded in the early part of the day, directed the French, ably seconded by General Bosquet, whose devotion was noble. Nearly all his escort were killed, wounded, or unhorsed.

The Russians, during the action, made a sortie on the French, and traversed two parallels before they were driven back; as they retired they fired mines inside the Flagstaff Fort, afraid that the French would enter pell-mell after them.

The last attempt of the Russians took place at about thirty-five minutes past twelve. At forty minutes past one Dickson's two guns had smashed up the last battery of their artillery which attempted to stand, and they limbered up, leaving five tumbrils and one gun-carriage on the field.

I went carefully over the position on the 6th, and as I examined it, I was amazed at the noble tenacity of our men. The tents of the Second Division were pitched on the verge of the plateau which we occupied, and from the right flank of the camp the ground rises gently for 200 or 300 yards to a ridge covered with scrubby brushwood, so thick that it was sometimes difficult to force a horse through it. The bushes grew in tufts, and were about 4 feet high. On gaining the ridge you saw below you the valley of the Tchernaya, a green tranquil slip of meadow, with a few white houses dotting it at intervals, some farm enclosures, and tufts of green trees. From the ridge the hill-side descended rapidly in a slope of at least 600 feet. The brushwood was very thick upon it, and at times almost impervious. At the base of this slope the road wound to Inkerman, and thence to Sebastopol. The sluggish stream stole quietly through it towards the head of the harbour, which was shut out from view by the projections of the ridge to the north. At the distance of a quarter of a mile across the valley the sides of the mountains opposite to the ridge of the plateau on which our camp stood rose abruptly in sheer walls of rock, slab after slab, to the height of several hundred feet. A road wound among those massive precipices up to the ruins of Inkerman – a city of the dead and gone and unknown – where houses, and pillared mansions, and temples, were hewn out of the face of the solid rock by a generation whose very name the most daring antiquaries have not guessed at. This road passed along the heights, and dipped into the valley of Inkerman, at the neck of the harbour. The Russians planted guns along it to cover the retreat of their troops, and at night the lights of their fires were seen glimmering through the window and door places from the chambers carved out from the sides of the precipice.

Looking down from the ridge, these ruins were, of course, to one's left hand. To the right the eye followed the sweep of the valley till it was closed in from view by the walls of the ridge, and by the mountains which hemmed in the valley of Balaklava, and one could just catch, on the side of the ridge, the corner of the nearest French earthwork, thrown up to defend our rear, and cover the position towards Balaklava. Below, to the right of the ridge, at the distance of 200 feet from the top towards the valley, was the Sandbag, or two-gun battery, intended for two guns, which had been withdrawn a few days before, after silencing a Russian battery at Inkerman, because Sir De Lacy Evans conceived that they would only invite attack, and would certainly be taken, unconnected as they would have been with any line of defence. On the left hand overlooking this battery, was a road from Balaklava right across our camp through the Second Division's tents on their front, which ran over the ridge and joined the upper road to Inkerman. Some of the Russian columns had climbed up by the ground along this road; others had ascended on the left, in front and to the right of the Sandbag Battery.

Litter-bearers, French and English, dotted the hillside, hunting through the bushes for the dead or dying, toiling painfully up with a burden for the grave, or some object for the doctor's care. Our men had acquired a shocking facility in their diagnosis. A body was before you; there was a shout, 'Come here, boys, I see a Russian!' (or 'a Frenchman', or 'one of our fellows!') One of the party advances, raises the eyelid, peers into the eye, shrugs his shoulders, says 'He's dead, he'll wait,' and moves back to the litter; some pall the feet, and arrive at equally correct conclusions by that process. The dead were generally stripped of all but their coats. The camp followers and blackguards from Balaklava, and seamen from the ships, anxious for trophies, carried off all they could take from the field.

Parties of men busy at work. Groups along the hill-side 40 or 50 yards apart. You find them around a yawning trench, 30 feet in length by 20 feet in breadth, and 6 feet in depth. At the bottom lie packed with exceeding art some thirty or forty corpses. The grave-diggers stand chatting, waiting for arrivals to complete the number. They speculate on the appearance of the body which is being borne towards them. 'It's Corporal—, of the —th, I think,' says one. 'No! It's my rear rank man, I can see his red hair plain enough,' and so on. They discuss the merits or demerits of dead sergeants or comrades. 'Well, he was a hard man: many's the time I was belled through him!' or 'Poor Mick! He had fifteen years' service – a better fellow never stepped.' At last the number in the trench is completed. The bodies are packed as closely as possible. Some have still upraised arms, in the attitude of taking aim; their legs stick up through the mould; others are bent and twisted like fantoccini. Inch after inch the earth rises upon them, and they are left 'alone in their glory'. No, not alone; for the hopes and affections of hundreds of human hearts lie buried with them!

For about one mile and a half in length by half a mile in depth the hill-side offered such sights as these. Upwards of 2,000 Russians were buried there.

As I was standing at the Sandbag Battery, talking to some officers of the Guards, who were describing their terrible losses,

Colonel Cunynghame and Lieutenant-Colonel Wilbraham of the Quarter-Master-General's staff rode up to superintend the burial operations. The instant their cocked hats were seen above the ridge a burst of smoke from the head of the harbour, and a shell right over us, crashed into the hill-side, where our men were burying the Russian dead! Colonel Cunynghame told me Lord Raglan had sent in a flag of truce that morning to inform the Russians that the parties on the hill-side were burying the dead. As he was speaking a second shell came close and broke up our party. It is quite evident that the society of two officers in cocked hats, on horseback, is not the safest in the world. We all three retired.

During the Battle of Inkerman the French were drawn up in three bodies of about 2,000 men each on the ridge of the hills over Balaklava, watching the movements of the Russian cavalry in the plain below. As I came up the enemy were visible, drawn out into six divisions, with the artillery and infantry ready to act, and horses saddled and bridled. It was evident they were waiting for the signal to dash up the hills in our rear and sabre our flying regiments. They had a long time to wait! The French lines below us were lined by Zouaves; the gunners in the redoubts, with matches lighted, were prepared to send their iron messengers through the ranks of the horse the moment they came within range. Behind the French 5,000 'Bono Johnnies' were drawn up in columns as a reserve, and several Turkish regiments were also stationed under the heights on the right, in a position to act in support should their services be required. The French were on their march from the sea to our assistance, and the black lines of their regiments streaked the grey plain as they marched double-quick towards the scene of action. The Chasseurs d'Afrique on their grey Arabs swept about the slopes of the hills to watch an opportunity for a dash. Our own cavalry were drawn up by their encampments, the Heavy Brigade on the left, the Light Brigade in the centre of our position. The latter were out of fire for some time, but an advance to the right exposed them to shot and shell. Mr Cleveland received a mortal wound, and several men and horses were injured late in the day. The Heavy Cavalry were employed in protecting our left and rear.

The column on the extreme Russian right, which came on our position at the nearest point to Sebastopol, was mainly resisted by the Fourth Division and the Marines. The Russian centre was opposed by the Second Division and the Light Division. The Guards were opposed to the third or left column of the Russians. The Fourth Division in a short time lost all its generals – Cathcart, Goldie and Torrens – killed or mortally wounded, and 700, or more than one quarter of its strength, put *hors de combat*. The Second Division came out of action with six field officers and twelve captains; Major Farrer, of the 47th Regiment, was senior, and took command of the Division.

Sir De Lacy Evans was unwell on board ship when the fight began, but he managed to ride up to the front, and I saw him on the battle-field in the thick of the fight. Captain Allix, one of his aides-de-camp, was killed; Captain Gubbins, another, was wounded.

The Brigade of the Guards lost fourteen officers killed; the wonder is that any escaped the murderous fire. The Alma did not present anything like the scene round the Sandbag Battery. Upwards of 1,200 dead and dying Russians laid behind and around and in front of it, and many a tall English Grenadier was there amid the frequent corpses of Chasseur and Zouave. At one time, while the Duke was rallying his men, a body of Russians came at him. Mr Wilson, surgeon, 7th Hussars, attached to the brigade, perceived the danger of His Royal Highness, and with great gallantry assembled a few Guardsmen, led them to the charge, and dispersed the Russians. The Duke's horse was killed. At the close of the day he called Mr Wilson in front and thanked him for having saved his life.

6

The Siege of Sebastopol Part 2

The end of October. All waiting for the French. I am not sure but that the French were waiting for us to '*écraser*' some of the obnoxious batteries which played upon their works from ugly enfilading positions. The Quarantine Fort was opposed to them on their extreme left. Then came a long, high, loopholed wall or curtain extending in front of the town from the back of the Quarantine Fort to the Flagstaff Battery. The Russians had thrown up a very deep and broad ditch in front of this wall, and the French artillery had made no impression on the stonework at the back. The Flagstaff Battery, however, and all the houses near it, were in ruin; but the earthworks in front of it, armed with at least twenty-six heavy guns, were untouched, and kept up a harassing fire on the French working parties, particularly at certain periods of the day, and at the interval between nine and eleven o'clock at night, when they thought the men were being relieved in the trenches. Inside the Road Battery we could see the Russians throwing up a new work, armed with six heavy ships' guns. They had also erected new batteries behind the Redan and behind the Round Tower. The latter was a mass of crumbled stone, but two guns kept obstinately blazing away at our twenty-one-gun battery from the angle of the earthwork around it, and the Redan had not been silenced, though the embrasures and angles of the work were much damaged. The heavy frigate which had been 'dodging' our batteries so cleverly again gave us a taste of her quality in the right attack. She escaped from the position in which she lay before where we had placed two 24-pounders for her, and came out again on the 29th in a great passion, firing regular broadsides at our battery and sweeping the hill up to it completely. Occasionally she varied this amusement with a round or two from 13-inch mortars. These shells did our works and guns much damage: but the sailors, who were principally treated to these agreeable missiles, got quite accustomed to them. 'Bill,' cries one fellow to another, 'look out, here comes Whistling Dick!' The 13-inch shell has been thus baptised by them in consequence of the noise it makes. They look up, and their keen, quick eyes discern the globe of iron as it describes its curve aloft. Long ere 'Whistling Dick' has reached the ground the blue-jackets are snug in their various hiding-places; but all the power of man could not keep them from peeping out now and then to see if the fusee is still burning. One of them approached a shell which he thought had 'gone out'; it burst just as he got close to it, and the concussion dashed him to the ground. He got up, and in his rage, shaking his fist at the spot where the shell had been, he exclaimed, 'You deceitful beggar, there's a trick to play me!'

Sir De Lacy Evans met with an accident on the 29th, which compelled him to resign the command to Brigadier-General Pennefather. His horse fell with him as he was going at a sharp trot; and the shock so weakened him that he was obliged to go on board the *Simoom*.

The Turks, or, as they were called, the 'Bono Johnnies', except by the sailors, who called them 'No bono Johnnies', were employed in working in the trenches. The first night in Captain Chapman's attack they worked till ten o'clock at night, when a Russian shell came over. They ran away, carrying a portion of our working and covering parties; they were re-formed and worked till eleven o'clock, when they declared it was 'the will of Heaven they should labour no more that night', and, as they had exerted themselves, it was considered advisable to let them go. They were decimated by dysentery and diarrhoea, and died in swarms. They had no medical officers, and our surgeons were not sufficient in number for our army. Nothing could exceed their kindness to their own sick. It was common to see strings of them on the road to Balaklava carrying men on their backs down to the miserable shed which served them as a hospital, or rather as a 'dead-house'.

A deserter from the Russian cavalry on the 30th said the Russians were without tents or cover; their fare was scanty and miserable, and their sufferings great.

The French batteries opened on the 1st of November. For an hour they fired with vivacity and effect; one battery which enfiladed them on the right was plied with energy, but the remainder, with the exception of the Flagstaff redoubt, were silent. The Russians had about 240 guns in their new works, reckoning those which had been subject to our fire. The French had sixty-four guns in position, most of them brass twenty-fours, the others thirty-twos and forty-eights, some ship's eighty-fours not mounted. The French might be seen like patches of moss on the rocks, and the incessant puffs of smoke with constant 'pop!' rose along our front from morning to night.

The earthworks around the town of Balaklava began to assume a formidable aspect. Trenches ran across the plains and joined the mounds to each other, so as to afford lines of defence. On the right of the approach the Highlanders, in three camps, were placed close to the town, with a sailors' battery of two heavy guns above. Higher up, on a very elevated hill-side, the Marines and Riflemen were encamped. There were four batteries bearing on this approach. The battery on the extreme right, on the road leading over the hills from Yalta, contained two 32-pounder howitzers; the second battery on the right, facing the valley, contained five guns; and the fourth battery, nearest Balaklava, contained eight brass howitzers, four 12-, two 32-, and two 24-pounders. The left approach was commanded by the heights held by the French infantry over the valley, and by the Turkish works in front. A formidable redoubt, under the command of Captain Powell, R.N., overlooked the approaches, armed with heavy ship's guns.

The Turks had cut up the ground so that it almost resembled a chess-board when viewed from one of the hills. They constructed ditches over valleys which led nowhere, and fortified passes conducting to abstruse little culs-de-sac in the hill sides.

From the road to Balaklava on the 3rd, we could see the Russians engaged in 'hutting' themselves for the winter, and on the 3rd of November I made a little reconnaissance of my own in their direction. Their advanced posts were just lighting bivouac fires for the night. A solitary English dragoon, with the last rays of the setting sun glittering on his helmet, was perched on the only redoubt in our possession, watching the motions of the enemy. Two Cossacks on similar duty on the second redoubt were leaning on their lances, while their horses browsed the scanty herbage at the distance of about 500 yards from our dragoon sentry. 200 yards in their rear were two Cossack pickets of twenty or thirty men each. A stronger body was stationed in loose order some 400 or 500 yards further back. Six pelotons of cavalry came next, with field batteries in the intervals. Behind each peloton were six strong columns of cavalry in reserve, and behind the intervals six battalions of grey-coated Russian infantry lay on their arms. They maintained this attitude day and night, it was said, and occasionally gave us an alert by pushing up the valley. On looking more closely into their position through the glass, it could be seen that they had fortified the high table-land on their right with an earthworth of quadrilateral form, in which I counted sixteen embrasures.

In their rear was the gorge of the Black River, closed up by towering rocks and mountain precipices. On their left a succession of slabs (so to speak) of table-land, each higher than the other, and attaining an elevation of 1,200 feet. The little village of Kamara, perched on the side of one of these slabs, commanded a view of our position, and was no doubt the head-quarters of the army in the valley. The Russians were stationed along these heights, and had pushed their lines to the sea on the high-peaked mountain chain to the south-east of our Marines. As the valley was connected with Sebastopol by the Inkerman road, they had thus drawn a *cordon militaire* around our position on the land side, and we were besieged in our camp, having, however, our excellent friend, the sea, open on the west.

On the 4th November the fire on the place and the return continued. The Russians fired about sixty guns per hour, and we replied. The French burrowed and turned up the earth vigorously. A quantity of 10-inch shot were landed, but, unfortunately, we had no 10-inch guns for them. Two guns were added to the batteries of the right attack, which now contained twenty-three pieces of artillery. Whenever I looked at the enemy's earthworks I thought of the Woolwich butt. What good had we done by all this expenditure of shot, and shell, and powder? A few guns, when we first came, might have saved incredible toil and labour because they would have rendered it all but impossible for the Russians to cast up entrenchments and works before the open entrance to Sebastopol.

Whilst we were yet in hopes of taking the place, and of retiring to the Bosphorus for winter quarters, the enemy, animated by the presence of two of the Imperial Grand Dukes, made a vigorous attempt to inflict on the allies a terrible punishment for their audacity in setting foot on the territory of the Czar. The Battle of Inkerman was at hand.

During this winter newspaper correspondents in the Crimea were placed in a rather difficult position. In common with generals and chiefs, and men-at-arms, they wrote home accounts of all we were doing to take Sebastopol, and they joined in the prophetic cries of the leaders of the host, that the fall of the city of the Czar – the centre and navel of his power in those remote regions – would not be deferred for many hours after our batteries had opened upon its defences. In all the inspiration of this universal hope, these poor wretches, who clung to the mantles of the military and engineering Elijahs, did not hesitate to communicate to the world, through the columns of the English press, all they knew of the grand operations which were to eventuate in the speedy fall of this doomed city. They cheered the heart of England with details of the vast armaments prepared against its towers and forts – of the position occupied by her troops – the imbecility of the enemy's fire – of the range of the guns so soon to be silenced – of the stations of our troops on commanding sites; and they described with all their power the grandiose operations which were being taken for the reduction of such a formidable place of arms. They believed, in common with the leaders, whose inspiration and whose faith were breathed through the ranks of our soldiers, that the allied forces were to reduce Sebastopol long ere the lines they penned could meet the expectant gaze of our fellow-countrymen at home; and they stated, under that faith and in accordance with those inspirations, that the operations of war of our armies were undertaken with reference to certain points and with certain hopes of results, the knowledge of which could not have proved of the smallest service to the enemy once beaten out of their stronghold.

Contrary to these hopes and inspirations, in direct opposition to our prophecies and to our belief, Sebastopol held out against the Allies; and the intelligence conveyed in newspapers which we all thought we should have read in the club-rooms of Sebastopol, was conveyed to the generals of an army which defended its walls, and were given to the leaders of an enemy whom we had considered would be impuissant and defeated, while they were still powerful and unconquered. The enemy knew that we had lost many men from sickness; that we had so many guns here and so many guns there, that our head-quarters were in one place, our principal powder magazines in another, that the camp of such a division had been annoyed by their fire, and that the tents of another had escaped injury from their shot, but it must be recollected that when these details were written it was confidently declared that, ere the news of the actual preliminaries of the siege could reach England, the Allies would have entered Sebastopol, that their batteries would have silenced the fire of their enemy, that the quarters of their generals would have been within the enceinte of the town, that our magazines would have been transferred to its storehouses, and that our divisions would have encamped within its walls.

How much knowledge of this sort the enemy gleaned through their spies, or by actual observation, it is not needful to inquire; but undoubtedly, without any largely speculative conjecture, it may be inferred that much of the information conveyed to them, or said to have been conveyed to them, by the English press, could have been ascertained through those very ordinary channels of communication, the eye and ear, long ere our letters had been forwarded to Sebastopol, and translated from English *in usum superiorum*. However, it is quite evident that it was not advisable to acquaint the enemy with our proceeding and movements during a siege which promised to assume the proportions and to emulate the length of those operations of a similar character in which hosts of men conveyed by formidable armadas from distant shores, set down to beleaguer some devoted fortress.

Although it might be dangerous to communicate facts likely to be of service to the Russians, it was certainly hazardous to conceal the truth from the English people. They must have known, sooner or later, that the siege towards the end of November had been for many days practically suspended, that our batteries were used up and silent, and that our army was much exhausted by the effects of excessive labour and watching, to which they have been so incessantly exposed. The Russians knew this soon enough, for a silent battery – to hazard a bull – speaks for itself. The relaxation of our fire was self-evident, but our army, though weakened by sickness, was still equal to hold their position, and to inflict the most signal chastisement upon any assailants who might venture to attack it. In fact, I believe nothing would have so animated our men, deprived as they were of cheering words and of the presence and exhortations of their generals and destitute of all stimulating influences beyond those of their undaunted spirits and glorious courage, as the prospect of meeting the Russians outside their intrenchments.

Rain kept pouring down, the wind howled over the staggering tents – the trenches were turned into dikes – in the tents the water was sometimes a foot deep – our men had neither warm nor waterproof clothing – they were out for twelve hours at a time in the trenches – they were plunged into the inevitable miseries of a winter campaign. These were hard truths, which sooner or later must have come to the ears of the people of England. It was right they should know that the beggar who wandered the streets of London led the life of a prince compared with the British soldiers who were fighting for their country, and who, we were complacently assured by the home authorities, were the best appointed army in Europe. They were fed, indeed, but they had no shelter. The tents, so long exposed to the blaze of a Bulgarian sun, and drenched by torrents of rain, let the wet through 'like sieves'.

On the 24th there was a brisk affair between the French and the Russians in front of the Flagstaff Battery, and the Russians dispelled all myths about their want of powder and ball by a most tremendous cannonade. Assaults and counter-assaults continued amid a furious fire, which lighted up the skies with sheets of flame from nine o'clock at night till nearly four in the morning. The French at one time actually penetrated behind the outer intrenchments, and established themselves for a time within the enceinte, but as there was no preparation made for a general assault, they eventually withdrew.

The struggle between French and Russians was renewed on the night of the 25th. The great bone of contention, in addition to the Ovens, was the mud fort at the Quarantine Battery, of which the French had got possession, though, truth to tell, it did not benefit their position very materially.

As the year waned and winter began to close in upon us, the army suffered greatly; worn out by night-work, by vigil in rain and storm, by hard labour in the trenches, they found themselves suddenly reduced to short allowance, and the excellent and ample rations they had been in the habit of receiving cut off or miserably reduced. For nine days, with very few exceptions, no issue of tea, coffee, or sugar, to the troops took place. These, however, are luxuries – not the necessaries of military life. The direct cause of this scarcity was the condition of the country, which caused a difficulty in getting food from Balaklava, and there was besides a want of supplies in the commissariat magazines. But though there was a cause, there was no excuse for the privations to which the men were exposed. We were all told that when the bad weather set in, the country roads would be impassable. The fine weather was allowed to go by, and the roads were left as the Tartar carts had made them, though the whole face of the country was covered thickly with small stones which seem expressly intended for road metal. As I understood, it was suggested by the officers of the Commissariat Department that they should be allowed to form depots of food, corn, and forage, as a kind of reserve at the head-quarters at the different divisions; but their carts were, after a few days' work in forming those depots, taken for the siege operations, and were employed in carrying ammunition to the trenches. Consequently, the magazines at headquarters were small, and were speedily exhausted when the daily supplies from Balaklava could no longer be procured. The food, corn, and hay were stowed in sailing vessels outside the harbour, where they had to ride in thirty or forty fathoms of water on a rocky bottom, with a terrible coast of cliff of 1,200 feet in height stretching around the bay: it was notorious that the place was subject to violent storms of wind.

As to the town, words could not describe its filth, its horrors, its hospitals, its burials, its dead and dying Turks, its crowded lanes, its noisome sheds, its beastly purlieus, or its decay. All the pictures ever drawn of plague and pestilence, from the work of the inspired writer who chronicled the woes of infidel Egypt, down to the narratives of Boccacio, De Foe, or Moltke, fall short of individual 'bits' of disease and death, which any one might see in half-a-dozen places during half an hour's walk in Balaklava. In spite of all our efforts the dying Turks made of every lane and street a cloaca, and the forms of human suffering which met the eye at every turn, and once were wont to shock us, ceased to attract even passing attention.

By raising up the piece of matting or coarse rug which hung across the doorway of some miserable house, from within which you heard wailings and cries of pain and prayers to the Prophet, you saw in one spot and in one instant a mass of accumulated woes that would serve you with nightmares for a lifetime. The dead, laid as they died, were side by side with the living. The commonest accessories were wanting; there was not the least attention paid to decency or cleanliness – the stench was appalling – the foetid air could barely struggle out to taint the atmosphere, through the chinks in the walls and roofs. The sick appeared to be tended by the sick, and the dying by the dying.

At the close of the year there were 3,500 sick in the British camp before Sebastopol, and it was not too much to say that their illness had, for the most part, been caused by hard work in bad weather and by exposure to wet without any adequate protection. Think of a tent pitched, as it were, at the bottom of a marsh, into which some twelve or fourteen miserable creatures, drenched to the skin had to creep for shelter after twelve hours of vigil in a trench like a canal, and then reflect what state these poor fellows must have been in at the end of a night and day spent in such shelter, huddled together without any change of clothing, and lying packed up as close as they could be stowed in saturated blankets. But why were they in tents? Where were the huts which had been sent out to them? The huts were on board ships in the harbour of Balaklava. Some of these huts, of which we heard so much, were floating about the beach; others had been landed, and now and then I met a wretched pony, knee-deep in mud, struggling on beneath the weight of two thin deal planks, a small portion of one of these huts, which were most probably converted into firewood after lying for some time in the camp, or turned into stabling for officers' horses when enough of *disjecta membra* had been collected. Had central depôts been established, as Mr Filder proposed while the fine weather lasted, much, if not all, of the misery and suffering of the men and of the loss of horses would have been averted.

It may be true that the enemy were suffering still more than our own men, but the calculation of equal losses on the part of England and on the part of Russia in the article of soldiery, cannot be regarded as an ingredient in the consideration of our position. Our force was deprived of about 100 men every twenty-four hours. There were between 7,000 and 8,000 men sick, wounded, and convalescent in the hospitals on the Bosphorus.

The 39th Regiment before it had landed was provided with some protection against the severity of the weather – not by government but by *The Times* Commissioner at Scutari: and I heard from the best authority that the bounty of the subscribers to the fund intrusted to *The Times* for distribution was not only well bestowed to the men, but that the officers of the regiments had evinced the greatest satisfaction at the comfort. When the various articles sent up by the Commissioner arrived at the camp, there was a rush made to get them by the regimental medical officers, and no false delicacy was evinced by them in availing themselves of the luxuries and necessaries placed at their disposal, and of which they had been in so much need.

Hundreds of men had to go into the trenches at night with no covering but their greatcoats, and no protection for their feet but their regimental shoes. Many when they took off their shoes were unable to get their swollen feet into them again, and they might be seen bare-footed, hopping along about the camp, with the thermometer at twenty degrees, and the snow half a foot deep upon the ground. The trenches were 2 and 3 feet deep with mud, snow, and half-frozen slush. Our patent stoves were wretched. They were made of thin sheet iron, which could not stand our fuel – charcoal. Besides, they were mere poison manufactories, and they could not be left alight in the tents at night. They answered well for drying clothes.

I do not know how the French got on, but I know that our people did not get a fair chance for their lives while wintering in the Crimea. Providence had been very good to us. With one exception, which must have done as much mischief to the enemy as to ourselves, we had wonderful weather from the day the expedition landed in the Crimea.

One day as I was passing through the camp of the 5th (French) Regiment of the line, an officer came out and invited me to dismount and take a glass of brandy which had been sent out by the Emperor as a Christmas gift. My host, who had passed through his grades in Africa, showed me with pride the case of good Bordeaux, the box of brandy, and the pile of good tobacco sent to him by Napoleon III – '*Le premier ami du soldat.*' A similar present had been sent to every officer of the French army, and a certain quantity of wine, brandy and tobacco had been forwarded to each company of every regiment in the Crimea. That very day I heard dolorous complaints that the presents sent by the Queen and Prince Albert to our army had miscarried, and that the Guards and Rifles had alone received the royal bounty in the very acceptable shape of a ton of Cavendish. Although he was living in a tent, the canvass was only a roof for a capacious and warm pit in which there was a bright wood fire sparkling cheerily in a grate of stones.

We 'trinqued' together and fraternised, as our allies will always do when our officers give them the chance.

It must not be inferred that the French were all healthy while we were all sickly. They had dysentery, fever, diarrhoea, and scurvy, as well as pulmonary complaints, but not to the same extent as ourselves, or to anything like it in proportion to their numbers. On the 8th of January, some of the Guards of Her Majesty Queen Victoria's Household Brigade were walking about in the snow without soles to their shoes. The warm clothing was going up to the front in small detachments. It was right that England should be made aware of the privations which her soldiers endured in this great winter campaign, that she might reward with her greenest laurels those gallant hearts, who deserved the highest honour – that honour which in ancient Rome was esteemed the highest that a soldier could gain – that in desperate circumstances he had not despaired of the Republic. And no man despaired. The exhausted soldier, before he sank to rest, sighed that he could not share the sure triumph – the certain glories – of the day when our flag was to float from Sebastopol! There was no doubt – no despondency. No one for an instant felt diffident of ultimate success. From his remains, in that cold Crimean soil, the British soldier knew an avenger and a conqueror would arise. If high courage, unflinching bravery – if steady charge – the bayonet thrust in the breach – the strong arm in the fight – if calm confidence, contempt of death, and love of country could have won Sebastopol, it had long been ours. Let England know her children as the descendants of the starved rabble who fought at Agincourt and Cressy; and let her know, too, that in fighting against a stubborn enemy, her armies had to maintain a struggle with foes still more terrible, and that, as they triumphed over the one, so they vanquished the other.

On the night of the 12th of January the wind changed round to the southward, and the thermometer rose to 34°. A speedy thaw followed, and the roads and camp once more suffered from the ravages of our old enemy – the mud. The Russians who had been very active inside the town during the day, and who had lighted great watchfires on the north side of the place, illuminated the heights over Tchernaya with rows of lights, which shone brilliantly through the darkness of the cold winter's night, and were evidently with all possible pomp and ostentation celebrating the opening of their new year. Lights shone from the windows of the public buildings, and our lonely sentries in the valleys and ravines, and the *enfans perdus* – the French sharpshooters lying in their lairs with watchful eye on every embrasure before them – might almost fancy that the inhabitants and garrison of the beleaguered city were tantalising them with the aspect of their gaiety. At midnight all the chapel bells of the city began ringing. On our side the sentries and pickets were warned to be on the alert, and the advanced posts were strengthened wherever it was practicable.

About a quarter past one o'clock in the morning the Russians gave a loud cheer. The French replied by opening fire, and the Russians instantly began one of the fiercest cannonades we had ever heard. It reminded one of those tremendous salvoes of artillery which the enemy delivered on two or three occasions before we opened our batteries in October. The earthworks flashed forth uninterrupted floods of flame, which revealed distinctly the outlines of the buildings in the town, and defences swarming with men. The roaring of shot, the screaming and hissing of heavy shell, and the whistling of carcases filled up the intervals between the deafening roll of cannon, which was as rapid and unbroken as quick file-firing. The iron storm passed over our lines uninterruptedly for more than half an hour, and the French, whose works to our left were less protected by the ground than ours, had to shelter themselves closely in the trenches, and could barely reply to the volleys which ploughed up the parapets of their works.

While the firing was going on a strong body of men had been pushed out of the town up the face of the hill towards our works in front, and on the flank of the left attack. As it was expected that some attempt of the kind would be made, a sergeant was posted at this spot with twelve men. Every reliance was placed upon his vigilance, and a strict attention to his duties, but, somehow or other, the enemy crept upon the little party, surprised, and took them prisoners, and then advanced on the covering parties with such rapidity and suddenness that the parties on duty in the trenches were obliged to retire. They rallied, however, and, being supported by the regiments in rear, they advanced, and the Russians were driven back close to the town. In this little affair one officer and nine men were wounded, six men were killed, and fourteen men taken. The French had to resist a strong sortie nearly at the same time; for a short time the Russians were within the parapet of one of their mortar batteries, and spiked two or three mortars with wooden plugs, but the French drove them back with loss, and in the pursuit got inside the Russian advanced batteries. The soldiers, indeed, say they could have taken the place if they had been permitted to do so. At two o'clock all was silent.

The *Adelaide* arrived in Balaklava on the 17th of January, after a splendid passage from England, and the passengers must have been a little astonished at the truly Christmas aspect presented by the Crimea; somewhat more real and less jovial they found it than the pictures which represented florid young gentlemen in gorgeous epaulettes, gloating over imaginary puddings and Christmas presents in snug tents, and ready to partake of the fare that England had sent to her dear boys in the Crimea, but which none of them had then received, and which none of them would ever eat in such comfort and with such appliances of luxury. There was a wind that would have effectually deprived, if wind could do it, any number of rats of their whiskers.

We were astounded, on reading our papers, to find that on the 22nd of December, London believed, the coffee issued to the men was roasted before it was given out! Who could have hoaxed them so cruelly? Around every tent there were to be seen green berries, which the men trampled into the mud, and could not roast. Mr Murdoch, chief engineer of the *Sanspareil* mounted some iron oil casks, and adapted them very ingeniously for roasting; and they came into play at Balaklava. I do not believe at the time the statement was made, one ounce of roasted coffee had ever been issued from any commissariat store to any soldier in the Crimea.

We gradually relinquished ground to our allies, and the front, which it had cost so much strength and so much health to maintain, was gradually abandoned to the more numerous and less exhausted army. Some of our regiments were reduced below the strength of a company. The French relieved the Guards of their outpost duties, and gradually extended themselves towards Inkerman. What a difference there was in the relative position of the two armies from that on the evening of the 17th of October, when the French fire had been completely snuffed out, and our own fire still maintained its strength.

There was a white frost on the night of the 22nd of January, the next morning the thermometer was at 42°. A large number of sick were sent into Balaklava on the 23rd on French mule litters and a few of our bât horses. They formed one of the most ghastly processions that ever poet imagined. Many were all but dead. With closed eyes, open mouths, and ghastly faces, they were borne along two and two, the thin stream of breath, visible in the frosty air, alone showing they were still alive. One figure was a horror – a corpse, stone dead, strapped upright in its seat, its legs hanging stiffly down, the eyes staring wide open, the teeth set on the protruding tongue, the head and body nodding with frightful mockery of life at each stride of the mule over the broken road. The man had died on his way down. As the apparition passed, the only remark the soldiers made was, 'There's one poor fellow out of pain, any way!' Another man I saw with the raw flesh and skin hanging from his fingers, the naked bones of which protruded into the cold air. That was a case of frost-bite. Possibly the hand had been dressed, but the bandages might have dropped off.

The French army received important reinforcements. The Eighth Division arrived at Kamiesch; it consisted of 10,000 good troops. The Ninth Division, under General Brunet was expected. Our allies then would muster upwards of 75,000 bayonets. The Turks did not seem to amount to more than 5,000 or 6,000. These unfortunate troops received supplies of new clothing and uniforms from Riza Pasha, the War Minister at Constantinople, and were assuming a respectable appearance.

There was very smart fighting in the trenches and advanced works between the French and Russians on the night of the 23rd and the morning of the 24th. On the 24th, Lord Raglan, attended by Major-

General Airey and a few staff officers, rode over to Balaklava. He went on board the *Caradoc* and had a long interview with Sir E. Lyons alone, previous to which there was a council of war. Lord Raglan did not return to head-quarters till it was nearly dusk.

I had a long reconnaissance of Sebastopol on the same day, in company with Captain Biddulph, of Artillery. It was a beautifully clear day, and at times it was almost warm. We went up to the hill in advance and on the left of the maison bruleé, and swept every inch of ground. The aspect of the place itself had changed very little, considering the hundreds of tons of shot and shell thrown into it; but whitewashed houses, roofed with tiles, and at most two stories high, in the suburbs, were in ruins. The roofs, doors, and windows were off, but puffs of smoke showed that the frames were covers for Russian riflemen. In front and left, lay a most intricate series of covered ways, traverses, zigzags, and parallels from the seaside, close to the Quarantine Battery, over the undulating land to the distance of 65 metres from the outer works of the Russians. Swarms of *Franctireurs* lined the advanced parallel, and kept up a continual pop, pop, pop, in reply to the Russian riflemen behind their advanced works.

The works from the Quarantine Fort to the crenelated wall, and thence to the Flagstaff Battery, seemed very much in the same state as the first day I saw them, with the exception, that the guns were withdrawn, and the defence left to riflemen. The Flagstaff parapets had been knocked to atoms long before, and the large buildings around it were all in ruins; but, on looking towards the ridge behind it, from which the streets descend, and which shelters that part of the place, I could see but little difference in its appearance to that which it presented on the 26th of September. People were walking about (relief coming up from the sea-side) carrying baskets. Between the rear of the Flagstaff Battery and this ridge, earthworks could be detected in the openings along the lines of streets, and immediately behind the first Russian intrenchment there was a formidable work armed which at two o'clock convinced us they had pretty good range, by thundering forth an astounding broadside in answer to fire from the French. There was a rattling fire from the *enfans perdus* at the embrasures, the Russians slackened their fire and replied to the French sharpshooters only. When the smoke cleared away, I could see the enemy and the French carrying away a few bodies on each side to the rear.

At the other side of the harbour, Fort Constantine was shining brightly in the sun, its white walls blackened here and there under the line of embrasures by the smoke of the guns on the 17th of October. Behind it were visible dark walls rising through the snow, and notched like saws by the lines of embrasures. The waters of the harbour, as smooth as glass, were covered with boats, plying from one side to the other, and one full of men came round the head of the Dockyard Creek towards Fort Alexander, with her white flag and blue St Andrew's cross. The large pile of Government buildings by the side of the Dockyard Creek was much injured. Close to there was a large two-decker, with a spring upon her cables lying so as to sweep the western slope of the town. A small steamer with her steam up was near at hand, either for the use of the garrison or to carry off the two-decker, in case heavy guns were unmasked upon her. To the right, at the other side of this creek, we could see into the rear of our left attack. The houses near the Redan and Garden Batteries as well as those in front of the Right Attack, and in the rear of Malakoff were in ruins. The part of the city beyond them seemed untouched. To the rear of Malakoff, which was split up, from top to bottom, as it was the first day of our fire, there was a perfect miracle of engineering.

It is impossible to speak too highly of the solidity and finish of the earthworks, thrown up to enfilade our attack, and to defend the key of their works. One line of battery was rivetted with tin boxes, supposed to be empty powder cases. This was the mere wantonness and surplusage of abundant labour. Behind this we could see about 2,000 soldiers and workmen labouring with the greatest zeal at a new line of batteries undisturbedly.

At the rear of Malakoff there was a camp, and another at the other side of the creek, close to the Citadel, on the north side. The men-of-war and steamers were lying with topgallantmasts and yards down, under the spit of land inside Fort Constantine.

Our third parallel, which was within a few hundred yards of the enemy's advanced works, was occupied by sharpshooters, who kept up a constant fire, but from my position I could not see so well into our approaches as upon those of the French.

Sickness clung to our troops, the soldiers who climbed the bloody steeps of the Alma in the splendour of manly strength, and who defended the heights over the Tchernaya exhausted, and 'washed out' by constant fatigue, incessant wet, insufficient food, want of clothing and of cover from the weather, died away in their tents night after night. Doctors, and hospitals, and nurses, came too late, and they sank to rest unmurmuringly, and every week some freshly-formed lines of narrow mounds indicated the formation of a new burial-place.

It must not be inferred that the French escaped sickness and mortality. On the contrary, our allies suffered to a degree which would have been considered excessive, had it not been compared with our own unfortunate standard of disease and death, and to the diminution caused by illness, must be added that from the nightly sorties of the Russians and the heavy fire from the batteries. According to what I heard from people, I was honoured by a good deal of abuse for telling the truth. I really would have put on my Claude Lorraine glass, if I could. I would have clothed skeletons with flesh, breathed life into the occupants of the charnelhouse, subverted the succession of the seasons, and restored the legions which had been lost; but I could not tell lies to 'make things pleasant'. Any statements I had made I have chapter, and book, and verse, and witness for. Many, very many, that I did not make could prove to be true with equal ease, and could make public, if the public interest required it. The only thing the partisans of misrule could allege was, that I did not 'make things pleasant' to the authorities, and that, amid the filth and starvation, and deadly stagnation of the camp, I did not go about 'babbling of green fields', of present abundance, and of prospects, of victory.

Yet people at home told us it was 'croaking' to state the facts, or even to allude to them! The man who could have sat calmly down and written home that our troops were healthy, that there was only an average mortality, that every one was confident of success, that our works were advancing, that we were nearer to the capture of Sebastopol than we were on the 17th of October, that transport was abundant, and the labours of our army light, might be an agreeable correspondent, but assuredly he would not have enabled the public to form a very accurate opinion on the real state of affairs in the camp before Sebastopol. The wretched boys sent out to us were not even fit for powder. They died ere a shot was fired against them. Sometimes a good draught was received; but they could not endure long vigil and exposure in the trenches.

January 28 was celebrated by an extremely heavy fire between the Russians and the French. The volleys were as heavy as those at the Alma or Inkerman, and from the numbers of Russian infantry thrown into the works, it was evident the enemy intended to dispute the small space of ground between the last French trench and the broken outworks of their late batteries with the greatest vigour. Possibly indeed, orders had been received to resist any nearer approaches of the French, who had burrowed up, zigzagged, paralleled, and parapetted the country from the Quarantine Fort to the Flagstaff Fort.

It was not to be expected that such an affair could take place without considerable loss on both sides. After daybreak the fire recommenced with great fury, and about eight o'clock a regular battle was raging in the trenches between the French and Russians. There could not have been less than 3,000 men on each side firing as hard as they could, and the lines were marked by thick curling banks of smoke. The fire slackened about nine o'clock.

By general orders dated 29th of January, Lord Raglan communicated that the Russian commanders had entered into an agreement to cease firing whenever a white flag was hoisted to indicate that a burying-party was engaged in front of the batteries. Admiral Boxer arrived to assume the command of the harbour of Balaklava, and by incessant exertions succeeded in carrying out many improvements, and in introducing some order in that focus of feebleness, confusion, and mismanagement.

On the 31st, a spy walked through some of our trenches. He was closely shaven, wore a blue frock-coat buttoned up to the chin, and stopped for some time to look at Mr Murdoch 'bouching' the guns.

Some said he was a Frenchman, others that he 'looked like doctor'. No one suspected he was a Russian till he bolted towards the Russian pickets, under a sharp fire of musketry, through which he had the good luck to pass unscathed. Orders were issued, in consequence, to admit no one into the trenches or works without a written permission, and all persons found loitering about the camp were arrested and sent to divisional head-quarters for examination.

The French were in the habit of sending out working parties towards the valley of Baidar, to cut wood for gabions and fuel. They frequently came across the Cossack pickets, and as it was our interest not to provoke hostilities, a kind of good-fellowship sprang up between our allies and the outposts. One day the French came upon three cavalry horses tied up to a tree, and the officer in command ordered them not to be touched. On the same day a Chasseur left his belt and accoutrements in a ruined Cossack picket-house, and gave up hope of recovering them, but on his next visit he found them on the wall untouched. To requite this act, a soldier who had taken a Cossack's lance and pistol, which he found against a tree, was ordered to return them. The next time the French went out, one of the men left a biscuit in a cleft stick, beckoning to the Cossack to come and eat it. The following day they found a loaf of excellent bread stuck on a stick in the same place, with a note in Russian to the effect that the Russians had plenty of biscuits, and that, although greatly obliged for that which had been left, they really did not want it; but if the French had bread to spare like the sample left in return, it would be acceptable. One day a Russian called out, as the French were retiring, '*Nous nous reverrons, mes amis – Français, Anglais, Russes, nous sommes tous amis.*' The cannonade before Sebastopol, the echoes of which, reached the remote glades distinctly, must have furnished a strange commentary on the assurance.

Every day strengthened the correctness of Sir John Burgoyne's homely saying about Sebastopol – 'The more you look at it, the less you will like it.' Three months before, that officer declared his opinion to be that the place ought to be assaulted. General Neil we heard, laughed at the notion of our reducing the place by the fire of our artillery.

There was an extremely hot contest on the night of the 6th between the French and Russians: the cannonade, which sounded all over the camp, lasted about an hour. The enemy, were labouring hard at the works in the rear of the Malakoff (or the Round Tower), and at three o'clock on the 6th I saw they had about 1,200 men employed on the earth slopes and parapets of the batteries. While I was examining the place there was scarcely a shot fired for two hours. The small steamers and boats were particularly active, running across the creek and to and fro in the harbour, and everything seemed to go on in the town much the same as usual. One portion of the place containing some fine buildings, and a large church with a cupola, as seen from the picket-house, put one in mind of the view of Greenwich from the Park Observatory through a diminishing glass. Lord Raglan ordered ten of our 13-inch mortars to be lent to the French from the *Firefly*. General Niel, expressed a decided opinion that the batteries were too far off. When we first sat down before the place, it was proposed that the first parallel should be at the usual distance of from 600 to 800 yards from the defences; but it was objected that there would be great loss of life in making it so near, and that the old rule of war which fixed the distance of the lines of the besiegers from those of the besieged was abrogated by recent improvements in gunnery, and by the increased power and range of siege guns. Our batteries were constructed at upwards of 1,000 and 1,200 yards from the enemy, and the steadiness of our artillerymen and the activity of our sailors were frustrated by the length of the range.

A considerable number of sick men (217) were sent down on the 10th from the camp to Balaklava. There were many bad cases of scurvy and of scorbutic dysentery among the men; and yet vegetables of all sorts, and lemons and oranges, were to be found in abundance, or could have been purchased in any quantities, all along the shores of the Black Sea and the Sea of Marmora. No one could say there were no ships to bring them. Balaklava contained ships which had been lying here for weeks – ay, for months – doing nothing. The splendid screw steamer *Jason*, fitted up especially as a horse transport, came in many days before from Ismed laden with cargo of wood for fuel. The expenses of such, a large vessel must have been enormous, and yet she had been in harbour for nearly a fortnight doing nothing.

There was a good deal of sickness in the French camp, and one regiment was said to have suffered as much from scorbutic diseases as any of our own, and to have ceased to exist, like the 63rd Regiment. But the French had no large steamers which they could send to forage in all the ports of Asia Minor; and, with their deficient transport, they had less sickness and less loss of life from disease cent. per cent. than our troops, while they were better provided with food and soldiers' luxuries. Had the French army undergone the same amount of vigil, labour, and fatigue to which our army was exposed, I am convinced it would have been in as bad a plight, and that it would have suffered very nearly the same losses. Their system of cooking was better; their system of hutting was better; instead of having twelve or fourteen miserable, gloomy fellows, sitting moodily together in one tent, where each man ate his meal, cooked or uncooked, as best he could, they had four men together in a tent, who were neither miserable nor gloomy as a general rule, because they had a good dish of soup and bouilli well made at the mess fire, and carried away 'piping hot' in the camp kettle of the tent. The canvass of the *tente* was in bad weather only a roof to a deep pit in the shape of the parallelogram formed by the flaps of the canvass. This pit was dug out of the earth; it contained a little fireplace at one end, with a mud chimney outside and was entered by a flight of two or three steps, which descended to the dry floor. Our men rarely dug out the earth, and their tents were generally pitched on the surface of the ground. They had no time to do any better.

On February 19th, preparations were made for a reconnaissance by Sir Colin Campbell and Vinoy against the enemy between the Tchernaya and Kamara. The weather had been unfavourable, but the few fine days from the 15th to the 19th had made the country in tolerable order for the movements of artillery and cavalry. The French were to furnish 11,600 men; Sir Colin Campbell's force was to consist of the 42nd, 79th, 93rd Highlanders, the 14th and 71st Regts' detachments of cavalry, and two batteries. Soon after dark the French began to get ready, and the hum of men betrayed the movement. By degrees the rumour spread from one confidant to the other, and by midnight a good number of outriders and amateurs were aware of what was going on, and strict orders were issued for early calls and saddling of horses 'tomorrow morning at dawn'.

Nothing excites such interest as a reconnaissance. Our army was deprived of the peculiar attractions of most wars in Europe. There was none of the romance of the Peninsular campaigns about it. We were all shut up in one dirty little angle of land, with Cossack barring the approaches to the heavenly valley around us. There were no pleasant marches, no halts in town or village, no strange scenes or change of position; nothing but the drudgery of the trenches and of fatigue parties, and the everlasting houses and works of Sebastopol, and the same bleak savage landscape around. The hardest-worked officer was glad, therefore, to get away on a reconnaissance, which gave him an excitement, and varied the monotony of his life; it was a sort of holiday for him – a hunt at Epping, if there be such a thing, to cockney existence.

Before midnight the wind changed, and began to blow, and the stars were overcast. About one o'clock the rain began to fall heavily and continued to descend in torrents for an hour. Then the wind chopped round to the north and became intensely cold, the rain crystallised and fell in hail, the gale rose higher and increased in severity every moment. Then came down a heavy snow fall. It was evident that no good could come of exposing the men, and that the attack would be a failure; it certainly would not have enabled us to form any accurate conception of the numbers or position of the enemy, inasmuch as it was impossible for a man to see a yard before him. Major Foley was despatched by General Canrobert to inform Sir Colin Campbell that the French would not move; the regiments under arms were ordered back to their tents, which they found with difficulty. When Major Foley arrived after many wanderings, at head-quarters, one of Lord Raglan's aides-de-camp was dispatched to Sir Colin Campbell to desire him to postpone any movement. This officer set out about six o'clock in the morning for the heights over Balaklava. On passing through the French camp he called upon General Vinoy to inform him of the change which the weather had effected in the plans agreed upon, but the General said he thought it would be better to move down his men to support Sir Colin in case the latter should have advanced before the counter-orders reached him. When our aide-de-camp, after a struggle with the darkness, readied Sir Colin's quarters, the General was gone. Another ride enabled him to overtake the General, who was waiting for the French, and had his troops drawn up near Kamara.

It may be imagined the news was not very pleasing to one who was all on fire, cold as he was, for a brush with the enemy, but Vinoy's promise put him into excellent spirits. It was four o'clock when the troops moved towards the plain, through the snowstorm, which increased in violence as the morning dawned. The Rifles preceded the advance, with the Highland Light Infantry, in skirmishing order. Strict orders had been given that there was to be no firing, it was hoped that we might surprise the enemy, but the falling snow prevented our men from seeing more than a few yards, and after daylight it was impossible to make out an object 5 feet in advance. However, the skirmishers managed to get hold of three sentries, belonging probably to the picket at Kamara, but their comrades gave the alarm. As our troops advanced, the Cossacks and vedettes fell back, firing their carbines and muskets into the darkness. The drums of the enemy were heard beating, and through rifts in the veil of snow their columns could be observed moving towards the heights over the Tchernaya. By this time our men had begun to suffer greatly. Their fingers were so cold they could not 'fix bayonets' when the word was given, and could scarcely keep their rifles in their hands. The cavalry horses almost refused to face the snow. The Highlanders, who had been ordered to take off their comfortable fur caps, and to put on their becoming but less suitable Scotch bonnets, suffered, especially, and some of them were severely frostbitten in the ears – indeed, there was not a regiment out in which cases of 'gelatio', chiefly of the ears and fingers, did not occur. Scarely had the enemy appeared in sight before the snow fell more heavily than ever, and hid them from our view. Sir Collin very unwillingly gave the order to return, and the men arrived at their quarters about ten o'clock a.m., very much fatigued.

The Russians during the night made a slight demonstration against us, thinking that the sentries and advanced posts might be caught sleeping or away from their posts. Their usual mode of conducting a sortie was to send on some thirty men in advance of a party of 500 or 800, in loose skirmishing order. These men advanced stealthily, *en tirailleur*, up to the line of our sentries and pickets, and felt their way cautiously, in order to ascertain if there was a weak and undefended point for the advance of the main body. If the firing was slack, the latter immediately pushed on, rushed into the trenches, bayoneted as many as resisted, and, dragging off all the men they could get as prisoners, returned to the town as rapidly as possible. Any man however weak, can rush across a landing into the nearest room, and do damage in it before he is kicked out. The French were so close to the Russians, they might be said to live next door to them. The latter could form in a small body, under cover of their works, at any hour in the night, and dash into the works ere our allies could get together to drive them back again. Some thirty-five men advanced upon the sentries stationed in front of Major Chapman's batteries (the left attack), but were perceived and challenged. They replied 'Ruski!' and were fired upon. The Riflemen in the pits in front of these lines gave them a volley, and the Tirailleurs retreated. It was strange they should have given such a reply to the sentries' challenge, but the men all declared that the Russians used the word, which would seem to be the Russians' notion of their own name in the English tongue.

Next day the sun came out, the aspect of the camps changed, and our French neighbours filled the air with their many-oathed dialogues and snatches of song. A cold Frenchman is rather a morose and miserable being, but his spirits always rise with sunshine, like the mercury of a thermometer. In company with two officers from the head-quarters camp, I had a long inspection of Sebastopol from the ground behind the French position, and I must say the result was by no means gratifying. We went up to the French picket-house first (*la Maison d'Eau* or *Maison Blanche* of the plans), and had a view of the left of the town, looking down towards the end of the ravine which ran down to the Dockyard creek, the buildings of the Admiralty, the north side of the harbour, and the plateaux towards the Belbek and behind Inkerman. As the day was clear one could see very well through a good glass, in spite of the dazzling effect of the snow and the bitter wind, which chilled the hands so as to render it impossible to retain the glass very long in one position. The little bridge of boats from the Admiralty buildings across to the French side of the town was covered with men, who were busily engaged passing across supplies, and rolling barrels and cases to the other side of the creek, showing that there was a centre of supply or some kind of depot in the Government stores behind the Redan, and opposite to the fire of our batteries.

Several large lighters, under sail and full of men, were standing over from side to side of the harbour, and dockyard galleys, manned with large crews of rowers all dressed in white jackets, were engaged in tugging flats laden with stores to the south-western side of the town. A tug steamer was also very active, and spluttered about in all directions, furrowing the surface of the water, which was scarcely 'crisped' by the breeze, so completely was the harbour landlocked. The men-of-war, with their large white ensigns barred by a blue St Andrew's cross flying from the peak, lay in a line at the north side, the top-gallant yards and masts of two out of four being down; a two-decker with bare topmasts lay on the south side, with her broadside towards the Ville Civile; and the white masts of three vessels peered above the buildings of the town farther away on the right towards Inkerman.

The inner part of the town itself seemed perfectly untouched, the white houses shone brightly and freshly in the sun, and the bells of a Gothic chapel were ringing out lustily in the frosty air. Its tall houses running up the hill sides, its solid look of masonry, gave Sebastopol a resemblance to parts of Bath, or at least put one in mind of that city as seen from the declivity which overhangs the river. There was, however, a remarkable change in the look of the city since I first saw it – there were no idlers and no women visible in the streets, and, indeed, there was scarcely a person to be seen who looked like a civilian. There was, however, abundance of soldiers, and to spare in the streets. They could be seen in all directions, sauntering in pairs down desolate-looking streets, chatting at the corners or running across the open space, from one battery to another; again in large parties on fatigue duty, or relieving guards, or drawn up in well-known grey masses in the barrack-squares. Among those who were working on the open space, carrying stores, I thought I could make out two French soldiers. At all events, the men wore long blue coats and red trousers, and, as we worked our prisoners and made them useful at Balaklava, where I had seen them aiding in making the railway, I suppose the Muscovite commanders adopted the same plan.

Outside the city, at the verge of the good houses, the eye rested on great walls of earth piled up some 10 or 12 feet, and 18 or 20 feet thick, indented at regular intervals with embrasures in which the black dots which are throats of cannon might be detected. These works were of tremendous strength. For the most part there was a very deep and broad ditch in front of them, and wherever the ground allowed of it, there were angles and *flèches* which admitted of flanking fires along the front, and of cross fires on centre points of each line of attack or approach. In front of most of the works on both the French and English sides of the town, a suburb of broken-down white-washed cottages, the roofs gone, the doors off, and the windows out, had been left standing in detached masses at a certain distance from the batteries, but gaps had been made in them so that they might not block the fire of the guns. The image of misery presented by these suburbs was very striking – in some instances the havoc had been committed by our shot, and the houses all round to the rear of the Flagstaff Battery, opposite the French, had been blown into rubbish and mounds of beams and mortar. The advanced works which the Russians left on the advance of our allies still remained and it was hard to say whether there were any guns in them or not, but they were commanded so completely by the works in their rear that it would have been impossible to hold them, and they would have afforded a good cover to the Russians, while the latter could fire through the embrasures of the old works with far greater ease than the enemy could get at them.

They threw up their new earthworks behind the cover of the suburb; when they were finished, they withdrew their men from the outer line, blew down and destroyed the cover of the houses, and opened fire from their second line of batteries. Their supply of gabions seemed inexhaustible – indeed, they had got all the brushwood of the hills of the South Crimea at their disposal. In front of the huge mounds thrown up by the Russians, foreshortened by the distance, so as to appear part of them, were the French trenches – mounds of earth lined with gabions which looked like fine matting. These lines ran parallel to those of the enemy. The nearest parallel was not 'armed' with cannon, but was lined with riflemen. Zigzags led down from trench to trench. The troops inside walked about securely, if not comfortably. The covering parties, with their arms piled, sat round their little fires, and smoked and enjoyed their coffee, while the working parties, spade in hand, continued the never-ending labours of the siege – filling gabions here, sloping and thickening the parapets there, repairing embrasures, and clearing out the fosses. Where we should have had a thin sergeant's guard at this work, the French could afford a strong company.

It was rather an unpleasant reflection, whenever one was discussing the range of a missile, and was perhaps in the act of exclaiming, 'There's a splendid shot,' that it might have carried misery and sorrow into some happy household. The smoke cleared away – the men got up – they gathered round one who moved not, or who was racked with mortal agony; they bore him away, a mere black speck, and a few shovelsful of mud marked for a little time the resting-place of the poor soldier, whose wife, or mother, or children, or sisters, were left destitute of all solace, save memory and the sympathy of their country. One such little speck I watched that day, and saw quietly deposited on the ground inside the trench. Who would let the inmates of that desolate cottage in Picardy, or Gascony, or Anjou, know of their bereavement?

We descended the hill slope towards Upton's house, then occupied by a strong picket of the French, under the command of a couple of officers. From the front of this position one could see the heights over Inkerman, the plateau towards the Belbek, the north side, the flank of the military town opposite the English, our own left attack, and the rear of the redoubtable Tower of Malakoff. The first thing that struck one was the enormous preparations on the north side, extending from the sea behind Fort Constantine far away to the right behind Inkerman towards the Belbek. The trenches, batteries, earthworks, and redoubts all about the citadel (the North Fort) were on an astonishing scale, and indicated an intention on the part of the Russians to fall back on the north side, in case of our occupying the south side of the place.

About three o'clock three strong bodies of cavalry came down towards the fort, as if they had been in the direction of the Alma or the Katcha. They halted for a time, and then resumed their march to the camp over Inkerman. In this direction also the enemy were busily working, and their cantonments were easily perceptible, with the men moving about in them. At the rear of the Round Tower, however, the greatest energy was displayed, and a strong party of men were at work on new batteries between it and the ruined suburb on the commanding hill on which the Malakoff stood.

Our own men in the left attack seemed snug enough, and well covered by their works; in front of them, on the slopes, were men, French and English, scattered all over the hill side, grubbing for roots for fuel; and further on, in front, little puffs of smoke marked the pits of the Riflemen on both sides, from which the ceaseless crack of the Minié and Liège smote the ear; but the great guns were all silent, and scarcely one was fired on the right during the day; even Inkerman and its spiteful batteries being voiceless for a wonder. As one of the officers began to rub his nose and ears with snow, and to swear they were frostbitten, and as we all felt very cold, we discontinued our reconnaissance, and returned to camp.

The wind blew keenly, and at night the thermometer was at 16°. There were few cases of illness in the trenches; but sickness kept on increasing. Typhus fever, thank God, nearly disappeared. Major General Jones declared the position was not so strong as he expected to find it from the accounts he had heard, but it was only to the eye of a practised engineer that any signs of weakness presented themselves. The heights over the sea bristled with low batteries, with the gun couchant and just peering over the face of the cliffs. Vast as these works were, the Russians were busy at strengthening them. Not less than 3,000 men could have been employed on the day in question on the ground about the citadel. One could see the staff-officers riding about and directing the labours of the men, or forming into groups, and warming themselves round the camp fires.

I was woke up shortly after two o'clock on the morning of the 24th of February by the commencement of one of the most furious cannonades since the siege began. The whole line of the Russian batteries from our left opened with inconceivable force and noise, and the Inkerman batteries began playing on our right: the weight of this most terrible fire, which shook the very earth, and lighted up the skies with incessant lightning flashes for an hour and a half, was directed against the French. The cannonade lasted from a 2.15 to 3.30 a.m. When first I heard it, I thought it was a sortie, and rode in the moonlight towards the fire; but ere I could get over the ground to Inkerman, the tumult ceased, and it was only next morning that we found out the cause of such a tremendous exhibition of power. It appeared that the activity of the French in making their approaches against the Malakoff had rendered the Russians so uneasy that they began to make counter approaches, and pushed out trenches to rifle-pits placed on the Mamelon and on the head of Careening Creek ravine. These were observed by the French, and General Bosquet, acting by order of General Canrobert, directed General de Monet and General de Meyran to attack these works with 1,000 of the 2nd Zouaves, a battalion of the 6th of the line, a battalion of the 10th of the line, and a strong body of Marines; that operation was effected about 2.00 a.m. The Russians offered a very vigorous resistance, the Zouaves were not properly supported by the Marines, or the troops of the line. De Monet was badly wounded; he lost one hand, and the other was much mutilated. In the conflict the Zouaves lost 3 officers killed, 13 wounded, 1 missing, 69 men killed and 159 wounded.

7

The Siege of Sebastopol
Part 3

It froze on the night of the 1st of March. The thermometer was at 24° at 2.00 a.m. next morning, the wind strong and very cold. It was scarcely to be believed that, with all our immense stores of warm clothing, boots and shoes were at that time by no means plentiful in the army. About 300 pairs of boots were served out to the 14th Regiment, which was employed in fatigue duty in and near Balaklava; but the thick heavy clay sucked the soles off, and for a week some of the men went about without any soles to their boots – ergo their feet were on the ground, with the thermometer at 30°: that was not agreeable locomotion.

About 240 sick men were sent in from the front to Balaklava on French ambulance mules, and were received and refreshed at the Caradoc restaurant. The preparations for the renewal of our fire were pressed on; and arrangements were made to send up 2,000 rounds a day to the front. About 200 mules were pressed into this service in addition to the railway, and the Highlanders and the artillery horses were employed in the carriage of heavy shell to the front, a duty which greatly distressed them. The men of the Fourth Division, the 17th and 18th Regiments, were armed with the Minié rifle.

The silence and calm were but the omens of the struggle which was about to be renewed for the possession of Sebastopol. The Russians were silent because the allies did not impede their works. The allies were silent because they were preparing for the contest, and were using every energy to bring up from Kamiesch and Balaklava the enormous mounds of projectiles and mountains of ammunition which were required for the service of the new batteries and to extend, complete, and strengthen their offensive and defensive lines and trenches.

The railway had begun to render us some service in saving the hard labour attendant on the transport of shot and shell, and enabled us to form a sort of small terminal depot at the distance of two miles and three quarters from Balaklava, which was, however, not large enough for the demands upon it, and it was emptied as soon as it was formed by parties of the Highland Brigade, who carried the ammunition to the camp depot, three miles and a half further on.

On the 4th of March the French and Russians had a severe rush about daybreak. Generals Canrobert, Niel, Bosquet, Bizot rode over to the English head-quarters in the course of the day, and were closeted with Lord Raglan, assisted by Sir George Brown, Sir John Burgoyne, and General Jones. They met to consider a proposition made by General Canrobert to attack the north side, by the aid of the Turks, as it seemed to him quite hopeless to attempt to drive the Russians from Inkerman. On the morning of the 5th of March early there was a repetition of the affair between the French and Russians, who began throwing a new redoubt towards the Victoria Redoubt. In order to strengthen our right, which the enemy menaced more evidently every day, the whole of the Ninth Division of the French army was moved over there. Our first spring meeting took place on the 5th, numerously attended. The races came off on a little piece of undulating ground, on the top of the ridges near Karanyi, and were regarded with much interest by the Cossack pickets at Kamara and on Canrobert's Hill. They thought at first that the assemblage was connected with some military demonstration, and galloped about in a state of excitement, but it is to be hoped they got a clearer notion of the real character of the proceedings ere the sport was over.

The weather became mild, the nights clear. Our defensive line over Balaklava was greatly strengthened, and its outworks and batteries were altered and amended considerably. The health of the troops was better, mortality and sickness decreased, and the spirits of the men were good. Fresh provisions were becoming abundant, and supplies of vegetables were to be had for the sick and scurvy-stricken. The siege works were in a state of completion, and were admirably made. Those on which our troops were engaged proceeded uninterruptedly. A great quantity of mules and ponies, with a staff of drivers from all parts of the world, was collected together, and lightened the toils of the troops and of the commissariat department. The public and private stores of warm clothing exceeded the demand. The mortality among the horses ceased, and, though the oxen and sheep sent over to the camps would not have found much favour in Smithfield, they were very grateful to those who had to feed so long on salt junk alone. The sick were nearly all hutted, and even some of the men in those camps which were nearest to Balaklava had been provided with similar comforts and accommodation.

Our siege works were a kind of Penelope's web. They were always approaching completion, and never (or at least very slowly) attaining it. The matter was in this wise: our engineers now and then saw a certain point to be gained by the erection of a work or battery at a particular place. The plans were made and the working parties were sent down, and after a few casualties the particular work was executed; but, as it generally happened that the enemy were quite alive to our proceedings, without waiting for their copies of *The Times*, we found that the Russians had by the time the work was finished, thrown up another work to enfilade or to meet our guns. Then it became necessary to do something to destroy the position and fresh plans were drawn up, and more trenches were dug and parapets erected. The same thing took place as before, and the process might have been almost indefinite but for the space of soil.

The front of Sebastopol, between English, French, and Russians, looked like a huge graveyard, covered with freshly made mounds of dark earth in all directions. Every week one heard some such gossip as this: 'The Russians have thrown up another battery over Inkerman.' 'Yes, the French are busy making another new battery in front of the redoubt.' 'Our fire will most positively open about the end of next week.' We were overdoing our 'positively last nights'.

It must not be forgotten, however, that the enemy derived equal advantage from the improvement in the weather. Valley and plain were now as firm as the finest road, and the whole country was open to the march of artillery, cavalry, infantry, and commissariat wagons. Each day the Russian camps on the north of Sebastopol increased and spread out. Each night new watchfires attracted the eye. We heard that a formidable army had assembled around Eupatoria, and it was certain that the country between that town and Sebastopol was constantly traversed by horse and foot, who were sometimes seen from the sea in very great numbers. The actual works of the siege made no progress to justify one in prophesying. Actual increase of lines and batteries and armament there was no doubt, but it existed on both sides, and there had been no comparative advantage gained by the allies. The impression which had long existed in the minds of many that Sebastopol could not be taken by assault, considering the position of the north forts, the fleet, and the army outside, gained ground. It was generally thought that the army outside ought to have been attacked and dispersed, or that the investment of the place should be completed, before we could hope to reduce the city and the citadel.

But coupled with this impression was the far stronger conviction that, had our army marched upon the place on the 25th of September, it would have fallen almost without resistance. A Russian officer, who was taken prisoner and who knew the state of the city well, declared that he could not account for our 'infatuation' in allowing the Russians to throw up works and regain heart, when we could have walked into the place, unless under the supposition that the hand of the Almighty was in it, and that He had blinded the vision and perverted the judgment of our generals. 'And now,' said he, 'He has saved Sebastopol, and we, with His help, will maintain it inviolate.'

However, let bygones be bygones on this and other points as well – they will be matters for history and posterity.

Several sea-service mortars, with a range of 3,500 yards, were sent up to the front, and the new batteries, now about to open, had the heaviest armament ever used in war.

Heavy firing was going on at the time, and a serious affair on our right, another struggle for the pits, which the enemy had thrown up on the right opposite the French, and which our allies carried gallantly, but did not succeed in retaining. These rifle-pits, which cost both armies such a quantity of ammunition, and led to so considerable a sacrifice on the part of our allies, were placed in front and to the right and left of the lower of Malakoff, about 600 yards from our works. They were simple excavations faced with sandbags, loopholed, and banked round with earth. Each of these pits contained about ten riflemen. Practice made these soldiers crack shots and very expert, so that if a man showed for a moment above the works in front of these pits he had instantly a small swarm of leaden hornets buzzing round his ears.

As it was made a point of honour by General Bosquet that our allies should take these pits, about 5,000 men were marched up to the base of the hills in front of our position, close to the Second and Light Divisions, before dusk on the night of the 17th, and shortly afterwards sent down to the advanced trenches on our right. At half-past six o'clock they were ordered to occupy the pits. About half-past seven o'clock the Fourth Division was turned out by Sir John Campbell, and took up its position on the bill nearly in front of its tents, Sir George Brown at the same time marched the Light Division a few hundred yards forward to the left and front of their encampment. These Divisions remained under arms for nearly four hours, and were marched back when the French finally desisted from their assault on the pits. The Second and Third Divisions were also in readiness. The Zouaves advanced with their usual dash and intrepidity, but they found that the enemy were already in possession. A fierce conflict commenced, but the French could not drive the Russians out. Some misapprehension led the men in the trenches to fire before their comrades reached the pits, and the enemy dispatched a large force to the assistance of the troops already engaged with the French, so that the latter were at last forced back. The contest was carried on incessantly for four hours and a half, and roused up the whole camp. From the almost ceaseless roll and flashing lines of light in front one would have imagined that a general action between considerable armies was going on, and the character of the fight had something unusual about it owing to the absence of any fire of artillery. The Zouaves bore the brunt of the fight. Through the night air, in the lulls of the musketry, the voices of the officers could be distinctly heard cheering on the men, and encouraging them: '*En avant, mes enfans!*' '*En avant, Zouaves!*' the tramp of feet and the rush of men followed; then a roll of musketry was heard diminishing to rapid file-firing – then a Russian cheer – then more musketry – dropping shots – and the voices of the officers once more. The French retired, with the loss of about 150 men killed and wounded, and a few prisoners.

On the 18th a force, computed to number about 15,000 men, entered Sebastopol from the north side. Large trains of carts and waggons were seen moving round towards the Belbck, and a considerable force bivouacked by the waterside below the citadel. About the same time a portion of the army of Inkerman, numbering, according to the best calculations, 15,000, marched down towards Mackenzie's Farm, and was reported to have crossed the Tchernaya and to have gone towards Baidar.

The Engineer officers alleged there was great difficulty in finding men to execute the necessary works, notwithstanding the improved condition of our army and the diminution of work and labour which had taken place since the co-operation of the French on our right. We frequently had not more than 900 men for duty in the trenches of the left attack, although it was considered that they ought to be defended by at least 1,200 men, and that 1,500 men would be by no means too many for the duty. I saw one parallel in which the officer on duty was told to cover the whole line of work. He had about 340 men with him, and when he had extended his line they were each nearly thirty paces apart. This was in a work exposed to attack at any moment. Notwithstanding the ground taken by the French, we were obliged to let the men stay for twenty-four hours at a time in the trenches. On an average the men had not more than three nights out of seven in bed. The French had five nights out of seven in bed. With reference to the observations which were made at home on the distribution of labour between the two armies, it must be borne in mind that when the French and English first broke ground before Balaklava we were as strong as our allies, and that it was some time after the siege began ere the relative proportions of the two armies were considerably altered to the advantage of the French by the arrival of their reinforcements.

On the 22nd a furious fight raged along our front. About nine o'clock 8,000 Russians disposed themselves in the hollows of the ground, and waited patiently till nightfall. Between eleven and twelve o'clock they rushed on the French works in front of the Mamelon, and made a dash at the trenches connecting our right with the French left. Their columns came upon the men in our advanced trenches on the right attack, with the bayonet, before we were quite prepared to receive them. When they were first discerned, they were close, and, on being challenged, replied with their universal shibboleth, 'Bono Franciz.' Taken at a great disadvantage, and pressed by superior numbers, the 7th and 97th guarding the trenches made a vigorous resistance, and drove the Russians out at the point of the bayonet, but not until they had inflicted on us serious loss, not the least being that of Captain Vicars of the 97th.

The 7th Fusileers had to run the gauntlet of a large body of the enemy, whom they drove back *à la fourchette*. The 34th Regiment were attacked by great numbers, and their Colonel, Kelly, was taken prisoner, and carried off by the enemy. In the midst of the fight, on our right, where the trench guards were at first repulsed, Major Gordon, of the Royal Engineers, displayed that cool courage and presence of mind which never forsook him. With a little switch in his hand, standing up on the top of the parapet, he encouraged the men to defend the trenches, and hurl down stones upon the Russians. He was struck by a ball which passed through the lower part of his arm, and received a bullet through the shoulder. After an hour's fight the enemy were driven back; but three officers and fourteen rank and file were killed, two officers and forty-four rank and file wounded, and two officers taken prisoners.

The French lost 13 officers and 171 men killed, 12 officers and 359 men wounded, and 4 officers and 83 men missing. Prince

Gortschakoff admitted a loss of 8 officers and 379 men killed, and 21 officers and 982 men wounded. The hill-sides below the Round Tower and the Mamelon were covered with their dead, mingled with the bodies of the French. The dead were lying about among the gabions which had been knocked down in front of the French sap in great numbers.

When the Mortar Battery was carried, the enemy held it for about fifteen minutes. At the time the heavy fire between the French and Russians was going on, a portion of the 90th Regiment were employed on fatigue duty on the right of the new advanced works on our right attack. They were in the act of returning to their posts in the Gordon Battery just at the moment the heavy firing on the right had ceased, when a scattered irregular fusillade commenced in the dark on the left of their position close to the Mortar Battery. Captain Vaughton, who commanded the party of the 90th, ordered his men to advance along the covered way to the works. They moved at the double time, and found the Russians in complete possession of the Mortar Battery. The 90th at once opened a heavy fire of musketry, when an alarm was given that they were firing upon the French; but the enemy's fire being poured in with deadly effect, the small party of the 90th were thrown into great confusion. With a loud 'hurrah', however, the gallant band sprang with the bayonet upon the enemy, who precipitately retired over the parapet. In order to keep up the fire, the men groped about among the dead Russians, and exhausted the cartridges in the enemy's pouches.

Early on Saturday morning a flag of truce was sent in by the allies with a proposition to the Russians for an armistice to bury the dead, lying in numbers – five or six Russians to every Frenchman and Englishman – in front of the Round Tower and Mamelon, and after some delay, an answer in the affirmative was returned, and it was arranged that two hours should be granted for collecting and carrying away the dead on both sides. The day was beautifully bright and warm. White flags waved gently in the faint spring breeze above the embrasures of our batteries, and from the Round Tower and Mamelon. Not a soul had been visible in front of the lines an instant before the emblems of peace were run up to the flagstaffs, and a sullen gun from the Mamelon and a burst of smoke from Gordon's batteries had but a short time previously heralded the armistice. The instant the flags were hoisted, friend and foe swarmed out of the embrasures. The sight was strange beyond description. French, English, and Russian officers were walking about saluting each other courteously as they passed, and occasionally entered into conversation, and a constant interchange of little civilities, such as offering and receiving cigar-lights, was going on. Some of the Russian officers were evidently men of high rank and breeding, their polished manners contrasted remarkably with their plain, and rather coarse clothing. While this civility was going on, we were walking over bloodstained ground, covered with evidences of recent fight, among the dead. Broken muskets, bayonets, cartouch-boxes, caps, fragments of clothing, straps and belts, pieces of shell, little pools of clotted blood, shot – round and grape – shattered gabions and sand-bags, were visible on every side. Through the midst of the crowd stalked solemn processions of soldiers bearing their departed comrades to their long home. I counted seventy-seven litters borne past me in fifteen minutes – each filled with a dead enemy.

The Russians now frequently amused themselves by shelling the camp. On the 4th, when there was a large crowd of French and English, including some of the staff, in front of the pickethouse, near the Mortar Battery, suddenly a shell fell right into the midst of the group. The greater part of the assembly threw themselves down and rolled away on the ground. At last the shell burst, and one of the fragments struck and wounded a French sentry about 50 yards off. Led horses broke loose or were let go and scampered off in all directions, and as the few officers who had nerve to remain and enjoy the discomfiture of the runaways were enjoying the joke, down came another shell into the very centre of them. The boldest could not stand this, and in a few minutes not a soul was to be seen near the ground. The Military Secretary lost his cap, owing to the eccentric evolutions of his frightened quadruped, but he speedily recovered it, and that was the only loss caused by the two shells, excepting the poor fellow put hors de combat for the time.

'Cathcart's Hill', in front of the Fourth Division camp, was the favourite resort of sight-seers. The place derived its name from General Cathcart using it as a look-out station, and as his resort of a morning. The General's marquee and the tents of his staff were close at hand. It commanded a view of the extreme French left towards Kamiesch, and of their approaches to the Flagstaff Battery and the crenellated wall. Taking up the view from this point on the left, the eye rested upon the mass of ruins in front of the French lines, seamed here and there with banks of earth or by walls of gabions, dotted with embrasures. This part of Sebastopol, between the sea at Artillery Bay and the Dockyard Creek, was exceedingly like portions of old London after the first burst of the Wide-Street Commissioners upon it. There was a strip of ruin the combined work of French and Russians, about 2 miles long and 300 or 400 yards broad, and it swept round the town like a zone. The houses inside were injured, but the tall white store-houses, the domes of churches, the porticoes of palaces, and the public buildings, shone pleasantly in the sunshine. Tier after tier of roofs rose up the crest of the hill. In front of this portion of the town the dun steppes were scarred all over by the lines of the French approaches, from which at intervals arose the smokewreaths of cannon or the puffs of the rifle, answered from the darker lines of the Russians in front of the city. At night this space was lighted up incessantly by the twinkling flashes of musketry.

Cathcart's Hill commanded a view of the whole position, with the exception of a portion of the left attack. The ground in rear of the dark lines, serrated with black iron teeth which marked our batteries, seemed almost deserted. The soldiers sauntered about in groups just below the cover of the parapets, and a deep greyish blue line denoted the artillerymen and covering parties. In front were the Russian entrenchments and batteries with the black muzzles of the guns peering through the embrasures. The grey-coated Russians stalked about the inner parapets, busily carrying gabions and repairing the damaged works. Suddenly a thick spirt of white smoke bursts from the face of the Mamelon, the shot bounds into Gordon's Battery, knocks up a pillar of earth, and then darts forward, throwing up a cloud of dust at each ricochet. Scarcely has it struck the parapet before another burst of smoke rushes out of one of the embrasures of the Naval Battery, and a mass of whitish earth is dashed up into the air from the Mamelon. Then comes a puff from one of the French batteries on the right, and a shell bursts right in the devoted work. 'Bravo the sailors!' 'Well done, French!' cry the spectators. As the words leave their lips two or three guns from the Round Tower, and as many from the Mamelon, hurl shot and shell in reply. A duel of this kind, with the occasional divertissement of a shell or round shot at working or covering parties, sometimes lasted all day. Now and then our sea-service mortars spoke out with a dull roar that shook the earth. After what seems nearly a minute of expectation a cloud of smoke and dust at the rear of the Round Tower denoted the effect of the terrible missiles. About twelve o'clock in the day the Russians left off work to go to dinner, and our men followed their example; silence reigned almost uninterruptedly for two hours or more, and then towards four o'clock the firing began again.

Meantime our officers walked about or lounged on the hillside, and smoked and chatted away the interval between breakfast and the hasty dinner which preceded the turn-out for twenty-four hours' vigil in the trenches. Many a hospitable cigar and invitation to lunch were given, the latter with the surer confidence, and with a greater chance of a ready acceptance, after the Crimean Army Fund had been established, and one was tolerably sure of a slice of a giant game-pie, to be washed down by a temperate draught of that glorious Welbeck ale which made the Duke of Portland's name a household word in our army.

On Easter Monday, April 9, the allied batteries simultaneously opened fire. The English works were armed with twenty 13-inch mortars, sixteen 10-inch mortars, twenty 24-pounders, forty-two 32-pounders, fifteen 8-inch guns, four 10-inch guns, and six 68-pounders. Although it was early dawn, it was not possible to see a man 20 yards off. A profound silence reigned. Suddenly three guns were heard on the left towards the French lines, and then the whole line of batteries opened. The Garden and Redan Batteries came into play soon after we opened fire, but some time elapsed before the Round Tower or the Mamelon answered. The enemy were taken completely by surprise, and for half an hour their guns were weakly handled. The Inkerman and Careening Bay Batteries were almost silent for three-quarters of an hour before they replied to the French batteries on our right.

A driving rain and a Black Sea fog whirled over the whole camp, which resumed the miserable aspect so well known to us during the winter. Early in the morning they were firing from seventy to eighty shots per minute, but they reduced the rate of fire. On the extreme left the French batteries were firing with energy on the loopholed wall, and on the Flagstaff and Garden Batteries, which were replying very feebly. Our left attack (Greenhill or Chapman's Batteries), directed its fire principally against the Redan, which only answered by five or six guns. Our right attack (Gordon's) aided by the advanced battery and by the French redoubts, had silenced the Mamelon and fired three or four shots for every one from the Round Tower. The Russian batteries to the right of the Mamelon were voiceless. So much could be seen, when rain and mist set in once more, and shut out all, save one faint blear of yellowish haze to the west.

About five o'clock in the evening the sun descended into a rift in the dark grey pall which covered the sky, and cast a slice of pale yellow light, barred here and there by columns of rain and masses of curling vapour, across the line of batteries. The eye of painter never rested on a more extraordinary effect, as the sickly sun, flattened between bars of cloud, seemed to force its way through the leaden sky to cast one look on the plateau, lighted up by incessant flashes of light; and long trails of white smoke, ringed with fire, whirled away by the wind. The outlines of the town, faintly rendered through the mists of smoke and rain, seemed quivering inside the circling lines of fire around the familiar outlines – the green cupola and roofs, long streets and ruined suburbs, the dockyard buildings, trenches and batteries. The only image calculated to convey an idea of the actual effect is a vision of the Potteries seen at night, all fervid with fire, out of the windows of an express train.

The practice from the left of the left attack and from the right of the right attack, which was more under observation than other parts of our works, was admirable. Our shell practice was not so good as it might have been, on account of bad fuzes. A large proportion burst in the air. Some of our fuzes were made in 1802. I have heard of some belonging to the last century, but some recent manufacture turned out the worst.

The French silenced eight or nine guns of the Bastion du Mât (Flagstaff), and almost shut up the Inkerman Batteries. On our side we had silenced half the guns in the Redan and Malakoff, and had in conjunction with the French left the Mamelon only one out of seven guns, but the Garden, the Road, and the Barrack Batteries were comparatively uninjured, and kept up a brisk fire all day. General Bizot received a fatal wound in our right attack just as he was lamenting the thinness of our parapets. He was struck by a rifle-ball under the ear, and died shortly after, much regretted by our allies and by ourselves.

The Russians, with great *sangfroid*, repaired the batteries, and appeared to have acquired confidence, but their fire was by no means so brisk as it was when the siege commenced. Omar Pasha visited Lord Raglan again on Wednesday, the 11th, and there was another council of war, at which General Canrobert and General Bosquet were present.

At dawn on Thursday, the 12th, the allied batteries and the Russians recommenced. The enemy exerted themselves to repair damages during the night, replaced damaged guns, mended embrasures and parapets, and were, in fact, nearly as ready to meet our fire as they had been at any time for six months. On our side, four of the guns for the advanced parallel, which for the previous two nights we had failed to get into position, were brought down after dark, and it was expected that material results would be produced by their fire when they were in position. Orders were sent to restrict the firing to 120 rounds per gun each day. The 13-inch mortar battery fired parsimoniously one round per mortar every thirty minutes, as it requires a long time to cool the great mass of iron heated by the explosion of 16 lb of powder. The bombardment did not cease during the day, but it was not so heavy on the whole as it had been on the three previous days. At fifty minutes past four the batteries relaxed firing, renewed it at six, and the fire was very severe till nightfall. Then the bombardment commenced and lasted till daybreak. The Sailors' Brigade suffered very severely. They lost more men than all our siegetrain working and covering parties put together. Up to half-past three o'clock on Friday, they had had seventy-three men killed and wounded, two officers killed, one wounded, and two or three contused.

At four o'clock on Friday morning, April 13, the Russians opened a destructive fire on our six-gun battery, which was in a very imperfect state, and by concentrating the fire of twenty guns upon it, dismounted some of the pieces and injured the works severely, so as to render the battery useless. One of our 24-pounders was burst by a shot which entered right at the muzzle as the gun was being discharged. Another gun, struck by a shot in the muzzle, was split up to the trunnions, the ball then sprang up into the air, and, falling at the breech, knocked off the button, in the very heat of the fire on the 12th, a Russian walked through one of the embrasures of the Round Tower, coolly descended the parapet, took a view of the profile of the work, and sauntered back again – a piece of bravado which very nearly cost him his life, as a round shot struck within a yard of him, and a shell burst near the embrasure as he re-entered.

At a council of war on the 13th, the question of assaulting the place was discussed, but Lord Raglan and the other English generals who were in favour of doing so were overruled by General Canrobert and General Niel.

On Saturday night (14th), there was a severe and protracted conflict on the left, for the French rifle-pits in front of the Quarantine Works. At first, the weight of the columns which swept out of the enemy's lines bore back the French in the advanced works, where the covering parties were necessarily thin, and many lost their lives by the bayonet. Our allies, having received aid, charged the Russians into their own lines, to which they fled with such precipitation that the French entered along with them, and could have spiked their advanced guns had the men been provided with the means. As they were retiring, the enemy made a sortie in greater strength than before. A sanguinary fight took place, in which the bayonet, the musket-stock, and the bullet were used in a pell-mell struggle, but the French asserted their supremacy, and in defiance of the stubborn resistance of the Russians, evoked by the cries and example of the officers, forced them battling back across their trenches once more, and took possession of the rifle-pits, which they held all night. The loss of our allies was considerable in this brilliant affair. The energy and spirit with which the French fought were beyond all praise.

The next morning our advanced batteries were armed with fourteen guns. They opened at daybreak, and directed so severe a fire against the Russian batteries throughout the day, that they concentrated a number of guns upon the two batteries. We nevertheless maintained our fire.

At half-past eight o'clock in the evening (15th), three mines, containing 50,000 pounds of powder, were exploded with an appalling crash, in front of the batteries of the French, 70 yards in front of the third parallel. The fourth and principal mine was not exploded, as it was found to be close to the gallery of a Russian mine, and the French were unable to make such a lodgment as was anticipated; but they established themselves in the course of the night in a portion of the outer work. The *etonnoirs* were, after several days' hard labour and nights of incessant combat, connected with the siege works. The Russians, believing the explosion to be the signal for a general assault, ran to their guns, and for an hour their batteries vomited forth prodigious volumes of fire against our lines from one extremity to the other. The force and fury of their cannonade was astonishing, but notwithstanding the length and strength of the fire, it caused but little damage to the works or to their defenders. Next day the magazine of our eight-gun battery in the right attack was blown up by a shell, and seven of our guns were silenced, but the eighth was worked with great energy by Captain Dixon, R.A., who commanded in the battery.

On the same night a very gallant feat of arms was performed by the 77th Regiment. In front of the Redan, opposite our right attack, the Russians had established capacious pits, from which they annoyed us considerably, particularly from the two nearest to us on the left-hand side. Round shot and shell had several times forced the Russians to bolt across the open ground to their batteries, but at night they repaired damages, and were back again as busy as ever in the morning. Our advanced battery would have been greatly harassed by this fire when it opened, and it was resolved to take the two pits, to hold that which was found most tenable, and to destroy the other. The pits were complete little batteries for riflemen, constructed with great skill and daring, and defended with vigour and resolution, and the fire from one well established within 300 or 400 yards of a battery was sufficient to silence the guns and keep the gunners from going near the embrasures. At eight o'clock the 77th, under Lieutenant-Colonel Egerton, with a wing of the 33rd in support in the rear, moved down the traverses towards these rifle-pits. The night was dark and windy, but the Russian sentries perceived the approach of our men, and a brisk fire was at once opened, to which our troops scarcely replied, for they rushed upon the enemy with the bayonet, and, after a short struggle, drove them out of the two pits and up the slope behind them. It was while setting an example of conspicuous bravery to his men that Colonel Egerton fell mortally wounded. Once in the pits, the engineers set to work, threw up a gabionnade in front, and proceeded to connect the nearest rifle-pit with our advanced sap. The enemy opened an exceedingly heavy fire on them, and sharpshooters from the parapets and from the broken ground kept up a very severe fusillade; but the working party continued in defiance of the storm of shot which tore over them; and remained in possession of the larger of the pits. The General of the day of the right attack telegraphed to head-quarters that our troops had gained the pits, and received directions to keep them at all hazards. At two o'clock in the morning a strong column of Russians advanced against the pits, and the combat was renewed. The enemy were met by the bayonet, they were thrust back again and again, and driven up to their batteries. The pit was most serviceable, not only against the embrasures of the Redan, but in reducing the fire of the rifle-pits on its flank. A drummer boy of the 77th engaged in the *mêlée* with a bugler of the enemy, made him prisoner and took his bugle – a little piece of juvenile gallantry for which he was well rewarded.

Next night the Russians sought to reoccupy the pits, but were speedily repulsed; the 41st Regiment had fifteen men killed and wounded. The pit was finally filled in with earth, and re-abandoned. On the 24th a council of war was held at head-quarters, and it was resolved to make the assault at 1 p.m. on the 28th. The English were to attack the Redan; the French the Ouvrages Blancs, Bastion du Mât, Bastion Centrale, and Bastion de la Quarantaine. In the course of the evening General Canrobert, however, was informed by the French admiral, that the French army of Reserve would arrive from Constantinople in a week – it was said, indeed, the Emperor would come out to take the command in person, and the assault was deferred.

During the night of the 24th the Russians came out of the Bastion du Mât (Flagstaff battery) soon after dark, and began excavating rifle-pits close to the French. Our allies drove them back at the point of the bayonet. The enemy, stronger than before, returned to their labour, and, covered by their guns, succeeded in making some progress in the work, finally, after a struggle which lasted from eight o'clock till three o'clock in the morning, and prodigious expenditure of ammunition. The French loss was estimated at 200. The Russians must have lost three times that number, judging from the heavy rolling fire of musketry incessantly directed upon them. In the morning it was discovered that the enemy were in possession of several pits, which they had succeeded in throwing up in spite of the strenuous attempts made to dislodge them.

On the 25th General Canrobert sent to inform Lord Raglan that in consequence of the information he had received of the probable arrival of the Emperor, and of the Imperial Guard and reinforcements to the strength of 20,000 men, he resolved not to make the assault on the 28th.

Up to the 27th there was no material change in the position of the allied armies before Sebastopol, or in the attitude of the enemy within and outside the city. Every night there was the usual expenditure of ammunition. Nothing, indeed, was more difficult to ascertain than the particulars of these nocturnal encounters. I need not say that all minute descriptions of charges or of the general operations of war conducted at night are not trustworthy. Each man fancies that the little party he is with bear the whole brunt of the work, and does all the duty of repulsing the enemy; and any one who takes his narrative from such sources will be sure to fall into innumerable errors.

The May-day of 1854 in the Crimea was worthy of the sweetest and brightest May Queen ever feigned by the poets in merry England! A blue sky, dotted with milk-white clouds, a warm, but not too hot a sun, and a gentle breeze fanning the fluttering canvas of the widespread streets of tents, here pitched on swelling mounds covered with fresh grass, there sunk in valleys of black mould, trodden up by innumerable feet and hoofs, and scattered broadcast over the vast plateau of the Chersonese. It was enough to make one credulous of peace, and to listen to the pleasant whispers of home, notwithstanding the rude interruption of the cannon before Sebastopol. This bright sun, however, developed fever and malaria. The reeking earth, saturated with dew and rain, poured forth poisonous vapours, and the sad rows of mounds, covered with long lank grass, which rose above the soil, impregnated the air with disease. As the atmosphere was purged of clouds and vapour, the reports of the cannon and of the rifles became more distinct. The white houses, green roofs, the domes and cupolas of Sebastopol stood out with tantalizing distinctness against the sky, and the ruined suburbs and masses of rubbish inside the Russian batteries seemed almost incorporated with the French intrenchments.

A very brilliant exploit was performed by seven battalions of French infantry, in which the 46th Regiment were particularly distinguished, during the night and morning of the 1st and 2nd of May. The enemy, alarmed by the rapid approaches of the French, had commenced a system of counter approaches in front of the

Bastion of the Quarantine, Central Bastion, and Bastion du Mât, which were assuming enormous proportions. General Pelissier demanded permission to take them. General Canrobert, whose indecision increased every day, at last gave orders for the assault. Three columns rushed out of the works shortly before seven o'clock p.m. The Russians came out to meet them – a tremendous conflict ensued, in which the French, at last, forced the Russians back into the works, followed them, stormed the outworks of the Batterie Centrale, and took off nine cohorns. In this affair, which lasted till two o'clock a.m., the French had nine officers put hors de combat, sixty-three men killed, and 210 wounded.

On the 2nd of May at 2.30 p.m., Russian troops, in three divisions, each about 2,500 strong, were seen marching into Sebastopol from the camp over the Tchernaja. A very large convoy of carts and pack animals also entered the town in the course of the day, and an equally numerous string of carts and horses left for the interior. The day was so clear that one could almost see the men's faces through the glass. The officers were well mounted, and the men marched solidly and well. Numbers of dogs preceded and played about the line of march, and as they passed by the numerous new batteries, at which the Russians were then working night and day, the labourers saluted the officers and stood gazing on the sight, just as our own artisans would stare at a body of troops in some quiet English town.

About four o'clock p.m., it was observed by us that the enemy was forming in column in the rear of the Bastion du Mât. A few moments afterwards, about 2,000 men made a rush out of the Batterie Centrale, and with a loud cheer flung themselves on the trenches. For a moment their numbers and impetuosity enabled them to drive the French out of the works as far as the parallel, but not without a desperate resistance. The smoke soon obscured the scene of the conflict from sight, but the French could be seen advancing rapidly along the traverses and covered ways to the front, their bayonets flashing through the murky air in the sun. In a few moments the Russians were driven back behind their entrenchments, which instantly opened a heavy cannonade. Several

Russian officers were taken prisoners. The enemy did not succeed in their object. Next day there was a truce; 121 French were found on the ground, and 156 Russians were delivered to their burial parties. While this affair was taking place our horseraces were going on behind Cathcart's Hill. The monotony of the siege operations was now broken.

On the 3rd of May, the 42nd, 71st, and 93rd, part of the 2nd Battalion Rifle Brigade, two companies of Sappers and Miners, 700 of the 71st Highland Light Infantry, one battery of Artillery, 50 of the 8th Hussars, and the First Division of the First Corps of the French army under D'Autemarre, sailed from Karaiesch and Balaklava; the whole force being under the command of Sir George Brown. The fleet, consisting of about forty sail, with these 12,000 men on board, arrived at the rendezvous, lat. 44.54, long. 36.28, on Saturday morning. There an express steamer, which left Kamiesch on Friday night with orders from General Canrobert, directed the immediate return of the French, in consequence of a communication from the Emperor at Paris, which rendered it incumbent on him to concentrate the forces under his command in the Chersonese. Admiral Bruat could not venture to take upon himself the responsibility of disregarding orders so imperative and so clear, and Admiral Lyons was not in a position to imitate the glorious disobedience of Nelson. Lord Raglan gave permission to Sir George Brown to go on without the French, if he thought proper, but that gallant officer did not consider his force large enough, and would not avail himself of such a proof of his General's confidence. This abrupt termination of an expedition which was intended to effect important services, excited feelings of annoyance and regret among those who expected to win honour, glory, and position.

The expedition returned on the 6th, and the troops were landed, and we began to hear further rumours of dissensions in our councils, and of differences between Lord Raglan and General Canrobert. The Emperor Napoleon had sent out a sketch of operations, to which General Canrobert naturally attached great importance, and from which Lord Raglan dissented. General Canrobert proposed that Lord Raglan should take the command of the allied armies. His lordship, after some hesitation, accepted the offer, and then proposed changes in the disposition of the two armies, to which General Canrobert would not accede. Finding himself thus compromised, Canrobert demanded permission from the Emperor to resign the command of the French army, and to take charge of a division. The Emperor acceded to the request, and General Canrobert was succeeded by General Pelissier, in command of the French army.

On the 8th of May, General Della Marmora and 5,000 Sardinians arrived in the Crimea, and were attached to the English army. Two or three steamers arrived every four-and-twenty hours laden with those excellent and soldier-like troops. They landed all ready for the field, with horses, carts, &c. Their transport cars were simple, strongly made, covered vehicles, not unlike a London bread-cart, painted blue, with the words '*Armata Sarda*' in black letters, and the name of the regiment to the service of which it belonged. The officers were well mounted, and every one admired the air and carriage of the troops, more especially the melodramatic headdress – a bandit-looking hat, with a large plume of black cock's feathers at the side – of the 'Bersaglieri'.

About one o'clock in the morning of the 10th of May, the camp was roused by an extremely heavy fire of musketry and repeated cheering along our right attack. The elevated ground and ridges in front of the Third and Fourth Divisions were soon crowded with groups of men from the tents in the rear. It was a very dark night, for the moon had not risen, and the sky was overcast with clouds, but the flashing of small arms, which lighted up the front of the trenches, the yell of the Russians (which our soldiers christened 'the Inkerman screech'), the cheers of our men, and the volume of fire, showed that a contest of no ordinary severity was taking place. For a mile and a half the darkness was broken by outbursts of ruddy flame and bright glittering sparks, which advanced, receded, died out altogether, broke out fiercely in patches in innumerable twinkles, flickered in long lines like the electric flash along a chain, and formed for an instant craters of fire. By the time I reached the front – about five minutes after the firing began – the fight was raging all along the right of our position. The wind was favourable for hearing, and the cheers of the men, their shouts, the voices of the officers, the Russian bugles and our own, were distinctly audible. The bugles of the Light Division and of the Second Division were sounding the 'turn out' on our right as we reached the high ground, and soon afterwards the alarm sounded through the French camp.

The musketry, having rolled incessantly for a quarter of an hour, began to relax. Here and there it stopped for a moment; again it burst forth. Then came a British cheer, 'Our fellows have driven them back; bravo!' A Russian yell, a fresh burst of musketry, more cheering, a rolling volley subsiding into spattering flashes and broken fire, a ringing hurrah from the front followed; and then the Russian bugles sounding 'the retreat', and our own bugles the 'cease firing', and the attack was over.

The enemy were beaten, and were retiring to their earthworks; and the batteries opened to cover their retreat. The Redan, Round Tower, Garden and Road Batteries, aided by the ships, lighted up the air from the muzzles of their guns. The batteries at Careening Bay and at the north side of the harbour contributed their fire. The sky was seamed by the red track of innumerable shells. The French, on our right, opened from the batteries over Inkerman and from the redoubts; our own batteries sent shot and shell in the direction of the retreating enemy. The effect of this combined fire was very formidable to look at, but was probably not nearly so destructive as that of the musketry. From half-past one till three o'clock the cannonade continued, but the spectators had retired before two o'clock, and tried to sleep as well as they might in the midst of the thunders of the infernal turmoil. Soon after three o'clock a.m. it began to blow and rain with great violence, and on getting up next morning I really imagined that one of our terrible winter days had interpolated itself into the Crimean May.

Whilst I was away with the Kertch expedition, the siege was pressed on by the French with great vigour, and our army was actively employed in preparing for the bombardment which was to precede the fall of the place, as all fondly hoped and believed.

There were intervals in the day when you might suppose that 'villanous saltpetre' had no more to do with a modern siege than an ancient one, and that all this demonstration of a state of conflict was merely an amicable suit upon an extensive scale. There were times at night when angry and sudden explosions sprang up as if by some unaccountable impulse or conjuration, and continued with an impetuosity which seemed as if it intended to finish the whole business in a moment. There were times when the red fusees turned and tumbled in the air like hot coals belched out of a volcano, and danced successive hornpipes upon nothing; then the clatter of small arms broke upon the ear in distant imitation of the heavy artillery, like a little dog yelping in gratuitous rivalry of a big one. The fighting was done by jerks and starts, and the combatants, like Homer's heroes, stood at ease the best part of the time, and took it coolly, meaning deadly mischief all the while.

The sharpest onset was generally on the side of our allies, about the Flagstaff or the Quarantine Battery, where they were sedulously advancing their endless mileage of trench and parallel, and promising themselves a result before long. For the third time our fire was opened along the whole range of positions on the 6th of June. At half-past two o'clock on that day 157 guns and mortars on our side, and above 300 on that of the French, awoke from silence to tumult.

The two armies – one might say the four armies, but that the Turks and Sardinians were not expected to take a very prominent part in the trench-work and assault – were in strength equal to any achievement, and in spirits ever chiding the delay, and urging that one touch of the bayonet which made all the world scamper. If the strategic necessity pointed to some more decisive action this time, so, on the other hand, the intention of going beyond a vain cannonade was tolerably plain. Our fire was kept up for the first three hours with excessive rapidity, the Russians answering by no means on an equal scale, though with considerable warmth. On our side the predominance of shells was very manifest, and distinguished the present cannonade in some degree even from the last. The superiority of our fire over the enemy became apparent at various points before nightfall, especially in the Redan, which was under the especial attention of the Naval Brigade. The Russians displayed, however, plenty of determination and bravado. They fired frequent salvos at intervals of four or six guns, and also, by way of reprisals, threw heavy shot up to our Light Division and on to the Picquet-house-hill. After dark the animosity on both sides gave signs of relaxing, but the same relative advantage was maintained by our artillery. It was a sultry day, with the dull mist of extreme heat closing down upon the valleys, and with no air to rend away the curtain of smoke which swayed between the town and our batteries; and at night flashes of lightning in the north-east made a counter-illumination on the rear of our position.

A still and sluggish atmosphere, half mist, half gunpowder, hung about the town in the early morning of June the 7th, and the sun enfilading the points of view from the horizon, telescopes were put out of joint. The Redan, however, which rose up boldly in front of the hills that sloped from Cathcart's Mound, gave some evidence of having yielded to rough treatment, the jaws of its embrasures gaping, and its fire being irregular and interrupted. At nine a cool, strong breeze sprang up, and continued throughout the day. The whole range of fire from right to left became visible in a bright sun, that for once was not scorching. The enemy either could not or would not keep up a very vigorous reply. All the early part of the day we had the work very much to ourselves. About eleven o'clock a shell from the Russians exploded a magazine in our eight-gun battery, and a yell of delight followed. Very slight harm resulted – one man was killed, one wounded, and a few scorched a little. As the day wore on, it leaked out that the double attack would probably commence at 5 or 6 p.m. An immense concourse of officers and men was gathered on Cathcart's Hill, and along the spines of the heights which wind towards Sebastopol.

The fire on our side assumed a sudden fury about three o'clock. Between five and six o'clock Lord Raglan and his staff took up a position on the edge of the hill below the Limekiln, where it commanded our four-gun battery, and looked straight into the teeth of the Redan. About half-past six the head of the French column came into view, as it climbed to the Mamelon. A rocket was thrown up, and instantly our men made a rush at the Quarries. After one slight check they drove out the Russians, and, turning round the gabions, commenced making themselves snug; but the interest was so entirely concentrated upon the more exciting scene, full in view upon the right, that they had to wait a good while before attention was directed to their conflict.

The French went up the steep to the Mamelon in loose order, and in most beautiful style. Every straining eye was upon their movements, which the declining daylight did not throw out into bold relief. Still their figures, like light shadows flitting across the dun barrier of earthworks, were seen to mount up unfailingly – running, climbing, scrambling up the slopes on to the body of the work, amid a plunging fire from the guns, which did them as yet little damage.

As an officer, who saw Bosquet wave them on, said, 'They went in like a clever pack of hounds.' In a moment some of these dim wraiths shone out clear against the sky. The Zouaves were upon the parapet, the next moment a flag was hoisted up as a rallying point and defiance, and was seen to sway hither and thither, now up, now down, as the tide of battle raged. It was seven minutes and a half from the commencement. Then there came a rush of the French through the angle, where they had entered, and momentary confusion outside. Groups were collected on the hither side in shelter. But hardly had the need of support become manifest, and a gun or two again flashed from the embrasure, than there was another run in, another sharp fight, and this time the Russians went out spiking their guns. Twice the Russians made head against the current, for they had a large mass of troops in reserve, covered by the guns of the Round Tower; twice they were forced back by the onsweeping flood of French. For ten minutes or so the quick flash and roll of small arms declared how the uncertain fight waxed and waned inside the enclosure. Then the back door, if one may use an humble metaphor, was burst open. The noise of the conflict went away down the descent on the side towards the town, and the arena grew larger.

It was apparent by the space over which the battle spread, that the Russians had been reinforced. When the higher ground again became the seat of action – when there came the second rush of the French back upon their supports, for the former one was a mere reflux or eddy of the stream – when rocket after rocket went up ominously from the French General's position, and seemed to emphasise by their repetition some very plain command, we began to get nervous. It was growing darker and darker, too, so that with our glasses we could with difficulty distinguish the actual state of affairs. There was even a dispute for some time as to whether our allies were going in or out of the work, and the staff themselves were by no means clear as to what was going on. At last, through the twilight, we discerned that the French were pouring in. After the interval of doubt, our ears could gather that the swell and babble of the fight was once more rolling down the inner face of the hill, and that the Russians were conclusively beaten. 'They are well into it this time,' says one to another, handing over the glass.

The musket flashes were no more to be seen within it. There was no more lightning of the heavy guns from the embrasures. A shapeless hump upon a hull, the Mamelon was an extinct volcano, until such time as it should please our allies to call it again into action. Then, at last, the more hidden struggle of our own men in the hollow on the left came uppermost. 'How are our fellows getting on?' says one. 'Oh! take my word for it, they're all right,' says another. And they were, so far as taking the Quarries was concerned, but they had nevertheless to fight all night.

As it grew dark our advanced battery under the Green-hill made very pretty practice by flipping shells over our men's heads at the Russians. From the misshapen outline of the Quarries a fringe of fire kept blazing and sparkling in a waving sort of curve, just like a ring of gas illuminating on a windy night; the attempt to retake them out of hand was desperately pushed, the Russians pouring in musketry, which caused us no small loss, and as it came up the gorge, contending with the fresh wind, sounded in the distance like water gulped simultaneously from a thousand bottles.

Meanwhile the fall of the Mamelon did not by any means bring the combat to an end on the side of our allies. The Zouaves, emboldened by their success, carried their prowess too far, and dreamt of getting into the Round Tower by a coup de main. A new crop of battle grew up over all the intervening hollow between it and the Mamelon, and the ripple of musket shots plashed and leaped over the broad hill-side. The combatants were not enough for victory there too, but they were enough for a sanguinary and prolonged contest, a contest to the eye far more violent than that which preceded it. The tower itself or rather the inglorious stump of what was once the Round Tower took and gave shot and shell and musketry with the most savage ardour and rapidity. The fire of its musketry was like one sheet of flame, rolling backwards and forwards with a dancing movement and, dwarfed as it was by the distance, and seen by us in profile could scarcely be compared to anything, small or large, except the notes of a piano flashed into fire throughout some rapid tune. Our gunners, observing the duration and aim of the skirmish, redoubled their exertions, and pitched their shells into the Round Tower with admirable precision, doing immense mischief to the defenders. It was dark, and every one of them came out against the heavens as it rose or swooped. From Gordon's Battery and the second parallel they streamed and plunged one after another into the enceinte up to which the Zouaves had won their way unsupported, heralded every now and then by the prompt and decisive ring of a round shot. The Russian defence, rather than their defences, crumbled away before this tremendous fire, but, on the other hand, the attack not being fed, as it was not designed, began to languish, and died gradually away.

During the night repeated attacks, six in all, were made upon our men in the Quarries, who defended their new acquisition with the utmost courage and pertinacity, and at a great sacrifice of life against superior numbers, continually replenished. The strength of the party told off for the attack was in all only 1,000, of whom 600 were in support. At the commencement 200 only went in, and another 200 followed. More than once there was a fierce hand-to-hand fight in the position itself, and our fellows had frequently to dash out in front and take their assailants in flank. The most murderous sortie of the enemy took place about three in the morning; then the whole ravine was lighted up with a blaze of fire, and a storm of shot was thrown in from the Strand Battery, and every other spot within range. With a larger body in reserve, it was not doubtful that our men could have been into the Redan. This was asserted freely both by officers and privates, and the latter expressed their opinion in no complimentary manner. They were near enough up to it to see that it was scarcely defended, and one officer lost his life almost within its limits. On our side 365 rank and file, and 35 officers, had been killed and wounded. Our loss in officers killed was great. The 88th were the severest sufferers, having three officers killed, one missing and conjectured to be killed, and four wounded – all indeed who were engaged. The four senior officers of the 62nd were put hors de combat. On the French side nearly double the number of officers, and a total of not less than 1,500 men, probably more. It was stated as high as 3,700. When morning dawned, with the wind blowing even stronger than the day before, the position held by both parties was one of expectation. The French were in great force within and on the outer slopes of the Mamelon, and also in possession of two out of the three offsets attached to the Mamelon on the Sapoune-hill. Their dead were seen lying mixed with Russians upon the broken ground outside the Malakoff Tower, and were being carried up to camp in no slack succession. In the rear of the Mamelon their efforts to intrench themselves were occasionally interrupted by shells from the ships in the harbour, and from a battery not previously known to exist further down the hill, while, on their left front, the Round Tower, showing still its formidable platforms of defence and its ragged embrasures above, fired upon their working parties, in the western face, and upon their reserves in the background.

The ammunition waggons, the ambulance carts, the French mules, with their panniers full freighted, thronged the ravine below our Light Division, which is the straight or rather the crooked road down to the attack on the right. Troops of wounded men came slowly up, some English, the greater portion French, begrimed with the soil of battle. On the left a party of Zouaves had stopped a while to rest their burden, it being the dead bodies of three of their officers. A little lower an English soldier was down on the grass exhausted and well nigh unconscious from some sudden seizure. A party of French were gathered round him, supporting him on the bank, and offering water from their canteens, which he wildly motioned aside. On the right, lining a deep bay in the gorge, was dotted over half a mile of ground a French reserve, with their muskets piled, attending the signal to move forward. They were partially within view of the Malakoff, and the round shot and shell came plumping down in the hollow, producing every minute or so little commotions of the *sauve qui peut* order, replaced the next moment by the accustomed nonchalance, and the crack of stale charges, fired off by way of precaution.

A lively and even pretty vivandière came striding up the ascent, without a symptom of acknowledgment to the racing masses of iron, and smiling as if the honour of her corps had been properly maintained. At ten o'clock the little incidents of the halting war perceptible through the telescope from the crown of the hill below the Picket-house were these: at the head of the harbour the Russians were busily engaged burying their dead; outside the abattis of the Round Tower several corpses of Zouaves were to be distinguished; about the Mamelon the French troops were hard at work, some of them stripped for coolness to their drawers, and were seen creeping down the declivity on the side towards the Malakoff, and making themselves a deep shelter from its fire. Our people, meanwhile, on the right attack were calmly shelling the Malakoff in a cool matter-of-business sort of way, but the eternal gun on its right, which has been endowed with nine months of strange vitality, launched an indirect response into the Mamelon. From and after eleven o'clock the Russians, as usual, slackened fire, nor was there any duel of artillery on a great scale until after dark.

On the 9th a white flag from the Round Tower and another on the left announced that the Russians had a petition to make. It was a grave one to make in the middle of a fierce bombardment with events hanging in the balance, and success, perhaps, depending upon the passing moments; but made it was, and granted. From one o'clock until six in the evening no shot was fired on either side, while the dead bodies which strewed the hill between the Mamelon and the Round Tower, or remained in front of the Quarries, were removed from the field. Both of the French and of the Russians large numbers were scattered over the ground of the chief conflict; among the former a large proportion were swarthy *indigenes* of Arab blood, or, as they were popularly termed by the French soldiers, Turcos, and to their contingent of the killed some were added from the very inside of the Malakoff, showing how near the impromptu attack was delivering the place into our hands. Of the Russians there lay still upon the spot some 200, a sufficient testimony to the severity of their losses in the struggle. The third battery on the Sapoune-hill was abandoned the night before, and its guns either withdrawn or tumbled down the hill.

In the early part of the day there had been a popular impulse to believe that an end of the affair would be made at night by a combined assault upon the Malakoff and the Redan. That both were within scope of capture was considered in camp as proved to demonstration. But the news of the suspension of arms dissipated the hope, and when the divisions got their orders for the night, it was no longer thought that aggression was likely, though defence might be. The enemy, with their wonted perseverance, had been making very comfortable use of their time, and when the firing recommenced, which it did instantly on the flags being lowered, a few minutes before six o'clock, it was plain that the Malakoff and Redan had both received a reinforcement of guns. Six and eleven were the numbers of remounted *bouches de feu* – exactness in such a calculation was not easy, for the Russians were laboriously artful in disguising the strength of their artillery, and frequently by moving guns from one embrasure to another make a single one play dummy for two or three. From six until nine o'clock the duel continued without special incidents; then there came a sudden splash of musketry, which lasted some few minutes and died away as unexpectedly. Another trifling musketry diversion took place about three in the morning, to relieve the monotony of the great artillery, which kept up its savagery throughout the night – ten guns for one of the enemy's – but slacked a little towards morning. We had a great number of casualties during the night in our new position on the left, into which the Russians kept firing grape and canister from the batteries which protect the rear of the Redan. They also occupied the dismantled houses above the ravine, and leisurely took shot at our people from the windows. Not unnaturally, it was a subject of the bitterest anger and complaint among the soldiers that they had to stand still and be riddled, losing day by day a number which was swollen in a week to the dimensions of a battle-roll of killed and wounded.

Through the occupation and arming of the White Batteries, situated on the edge of the ridge of Mount Sapoune, the head of the harbour was more or less in our power. The Russians themselves seemed to acknowledge this by taking outside the boom the vessels which had before been lying in that direction, and would have been commanded from the works which the French were then constructing on the site of the White Batteries of the Russians. But this was not all. These new works were to act against the two Strand batteries which the Russians had behind the Mamelon, and which, not being much commanded by any of our works, could do a good deal of harm without being exposed to much danger. The construction of French works on the Mamelon brought us to about 500 yards from the Malakoff works; it gave us a footing on the plateau on which these works lie; it furnished us with the means of approaching the rear of them, and at the same time of operating successfully on the annoying batteries in the rear of the Mamelon, which, taken thus in a cross fire, could not long resist.

The Quarry was scarcely more than 200 yards from the Redan. The battery which it contained worked successfully on the six-gun battery in the rear between the Redan and the Malakoff Tower works; and from the advanced posts our riflemen were able to prevent a good number of the guns in the Redan from working. But, for all this, the keeping of the Quarry was, especially in the beginning, not at all an easy thing; not so much, perhaps, from the attempts of the Russians to retake a point of such vital importance to them, but rather on account of the fire to which it was exposed from other Russian batteries besides the Redan. The Garden Battery on our flank, the six-gun battery in the rear, and the Malakoff works could touch it on nearly all sides. Moreover, the work, when it was taken being directed against us, offered very little protection against the riflemen of the Redan, until its face could be converted. On the 16th of June it was decided at a council of war that, after three hours' cannonade from the whole of the allied batteries, the assault should take place on the morning of the 18th of June.

Our armament consisted of thirty 13-inch mortars, twenty-four 10-inch mortars, seven 8-inch mortars, forty-nine 32-pounders, forty-six 8-inch guns, eight 10-inch guns, eight 68-pounders: total, one hundred and sixty-six guns. The French had about 280 *bouches-à-feu*. The despatch of Lord Raglan, dated 19th June, states that it was decided that the fire should be kept up for two hours after dawn; but, on the evening of the 17th, Marshal Pelissier sent over a despatch to our head-quarters, to the effect that, as the French infantry could not be placed in the trenches in the morning without the enemy seeing them, he had decided on attacking the place at daybreak, without any preliminary cannonade in the morning. Lord Raglan accepted this change of the plan of attack, although it was opposed to his private judgment, and sent orders to the divisional generals to carry it out. Sir George Brown, who was understood to be of opinion that an assault against the Redan was very doubtful, was ordered to make the arrangements.

The assaulting force, which consisted of detachments of the Light, Second, and Third Divisions, was divided into three columns. Sir John Campbell had charge of the left, Colonel Shadforth, of the 57th Regiment, of the right, and Colonel Lacy Yea, of the 7th Fusileers, of the centre column. Brigadier (afterwards Sir Henry) Barnard was directed to take his brigade of the Third Division down the Woronzoff Ravine, whilst Major-General Eyre moved down his brigade of the same Division still further to the left, with orders to threaten the works on the proper right of the Redan and in front of the Dockyard Creek, and, in case of the assault being successful, to convert the demonstration of his brigade into a serious attack on the place. The right column was destined to attack the left face of the Redan between the flanks of the batteries; the centre column was to assault the salient of the Redan; and the left column was to assault the re-entering angle formed by the right face and flank of the work; the centre column was not to advance till the other columns had well developed their attack.

On the French left, assaults under General de Salles were to be directed against the Quarantine Bastion, the Central Bastion, and the Bastion du Mât, each by a division 6,000 strong. On the French right, General d'Autemarre, with a column of 6,000 men, was to assault the Gervais Battery and the right flank of the Malakoff. General Brunet, with a similar force, from the Mamelon, was to attack the left flank of the Malakoff and the little Redan; General Mayran, from the extreme of the French right, was to fall upon the Russian batteries near Careening Creek, and the works connecting No. 1 Bastion with the Little Redan. In order to give greater completeness to the arrangements, it was decided that the French should make a demonstration against the Mackenzie Heights; and General Bosquet, who commanded the 2nd Corps d'Armée, because it was known that he was unfavourable to an assault, and preferred operations in the field, was displaced from his command by General Regnault de St Jean d'Angely. It will thus be seen that the French were to assault in six columns, constituting a force of not less than 36,000 men, with reserves of 25,000. Our assaulting columns were only 1,200 men, although there was a force in reserve of nearly 10,000 men.

The fire which opened on Sunday morning (the 17th) was marked by great energy and destructiveness. In the first relief the Quarry Battery, commanded by Major Strange, threw no less than 300 8-inch shells into the Redan, which was only 400 yards distant. Throughout Sunday 12,000 rounds, and on the following day 11,946 rounds of shot and shell were fired against Sebastopol from the British lines.

Early on Monday morning (18th of June), the troops, who had been under arms soon after midnight, moved down to the trenches. Lord Raglan and his staff were stationed in the trench in rear of the Quarries Battery. Marshal Pelissier took up his post in a battery to the rear of the Mamelon and on our right front, a considerable way from Lord Raglan. Just as some faint tinge of light in the east announced the approach of dawn, we heard a very irregular but sharp fire of musketry on our right, close to the Malakoff. In an instant all the Russian works on the right woke up into life, and the roar of artillery, mingled with musketry, became incessant. The column under General Mayran had made a premature attack! A rocket fired unintentionally misled the French general, who fell mortally wounded. In a few minutes the column was driven back with great loss. The musketry ceased. Then three rockets flew up into the gloomy sky. This was the signal for the assault, which Mayran had anticipated with such unfortunate results. General d'Autemarre's column, at the double, made a dash up the ravine which separated the Redan from the Malakoff. General Brunet led his men to attack the left of the work. The Russians received them with a tremendous fire, for the grey dawn just gave light sufficient to indicate the advance of these large masses. General Brunet fell dead, and his column was obliged to retreat, with great loss. The other column on the right of the Malakoff was somewhat more fortunate. They dashed across the ditch and over the parapet of the Gervais Battery, and drove the enemy before them. Some few get into the Malakoff itself; certainly, unless my eyes deceived me, I saw a tricolor flag waving in the centre of the work, and a few French actually reached the dockyard wall. Although it was understood that the English were not to attack until the French had carried the Malakoff, Lord Raglan resolved to assist the French at this stage of the assault, and the two rockets which was the signal for the advance were sent up. At the moment, the French were fighting outside the Malakoff, but were in possession of the Gervais battery on the right flank. Brunet's column had been driven back. A second attack on the extreme right by Mayran's column, though aided by 4,000 of the Imperial Guard under

General Mellinet, had completely failed. The Russians, warned by the assault on their left, were prepared; in the Redan, they held a great force in reserve. Their guns, loaded with grape, were manned, and the parapets were thickly lined with infantry.

The party to assault the left face of the Redan consisted of 11 officers and 400 men of the 34th Regiment, under Major Gwilt, preceded by a covering party of the Rifle Brigade and a ladder party from the Sailors' Brigade. When the signal was given, the men carrying the ladders and wool-bags rushed out of the trench; they were swept down at once by the tremendous fire. Major Gwilt ordered the 34th to lie down; but on the extreme right the men who did not receive the order advanced in sections at the double, and the whole of the storming party made a run at the re-entering angle of the left face of the Redan. On crossing the trench, our men, instead of coming upon the open in a firm body, were broken into twos and threes. This arose from the want of a temporary step above the berm, which would have enabled the troops to cross the parapet with regularity; instead of which they had to scramble over it as well as they could; and, as the top of the trench was of unequal height and form, their line was quite broken. The moment they came out from the trench the enemy began to direct on their whole front a deliberate and well-aimed *mitraille*, which increased the want of order and unsteadiness caused by the mode of their advance. Yea saw the consequences.

Having in vain tried to obviate the evil caused by the broken formation and confusion of his men, who were falling fast around him, he exclaimed, 'This will never do! Where's the bugler to call them back?' But, at that critical moment, no bugler was to be found. The gallant officer, by voice and gesture, tried to form and compose his men, but the thunder of the enemy's guns close at hand and the gloom frustrated his efforts; and as he rushed along the troubled mass of troops, endeavouring to get them into order for a rush at the batteries, a charge of their deadly missiles passed, and the noble soldier fell dead in advance of his men, struck at once in head and stomach by grape shot. A fine young officer, Hobson, the adjutant of the 7th, fell along with his chief, mortally wounded. They were thrown into confusion on getting up to the abattis, by finding a formidable barrier before them. When the 34th came up, there was only one ladder at the abattis. Major Gwilt, who was about 60 yards from the abattis, was soon severely wounded and obliged to retire. Colonel Lysons, who now took the command, ordered the men to retire. But ere the 34th regained the trenches, Captain Shiffner, Captain Robinson, and Lieutenant Hurt, were killed; Captain Jordan, Major Gwilt, Lieutenant Harman, Lieutenant Clayton, and Lieutenant Alt, were severely wounded, the last two dying of their injuries.

The column on the left told off for the attack of the re-entering angle and flank of the right of the Redan, was exposed to the same fire. There were no scaling ladders at the abattis, much less at the ditch of the Redan, nor could the Rifles keep down the enemy's artillery. Colonel Shadforth was killed whilst leading on his men most gallantly. Sir John Campbell fell dead close to the abattis. In a few moments the assaulting columns had disappeared. On our extreme left, the brigade under Major-General Eyre, consisting of the 18th on the left of the line, of the 9th Regiment and 28th Regiment in reserve, the 38th Regiment and 44th Regiment on the right, advanced to threaten the Dockyard Creek and the Barrack Batteries. Four volunteers from each company, under Major Fielden, of the 44th Regiment, covered the advance. The brigade was turned out before dawn, and marched down the road on the left of the Greenhill Battery to the Cemetery, while the necessary dispositions were being made for the attack. General Eyre, addressing the 18th, said, 'I hope, my men, that this morning you will do something that will make every cabin in Ireland ring again!' The reply was a loud cheer, which instantly drew a shower of grape. Just as the general attack began, they rushed at the Cemetery, which was very feebly defended; but the moment the enemy retreated their batteries opened a heavy fire upon it from the left of the Redan and from the Barrack Battery. They also kept up a heavy fire of musketry from a suburb close to the Dockyard Creek, by the side of the Woronzoff Road, and from a number of houses at the other side of the Creek, below the Barrack Battery. The 18th charged and carried the houses. The Russians could not depress their guns sufficiently to fire down upon our men; they directed a severe flanking fire upon them from an angle of the Redan. The 44th made a dash at the houses under the Barrack Battery, and the 38th seized hold of the suburb over the Creek Battery, so that the Russians were obliged to abandon it.

While portions of the 9th, 18th, 28th and 44th were in the houses, the 38th kept up a hot fire from the Cemetery on the Russians in the battery. One part of the brigade was exposed to a destructive fire in houses, the upper portion of which crumbled into pieces or fell in, and it was only by keeping in the lower stories, which were vaulted, that they were enabled to hold their own. The rest of the brigade, far advanced from our batteries, were almost unprotected, and were under a constant *mitraille* and bombardment from guns which our batteries failed to touch.

A sergeant and a handful of men actually got possession of a small work, in which there were twelve or fourteen artillerymen; but the Russians, seeing that they were alone, came down upon them and drove them out. An officer and half-a-dozen men got up close to the Flagstaff Battery, and were advancing into it when they saw that they were by themselves, and retreated. About fifteen French soldiers on their left aided them, but they were unsupported and they all had to retire. Another officer with twelve men took one of the Russian rifle-pits, and held possession of it throughout the day.

This partial success, however, did not change the fortunes of the day. The French were driven out of the Gervais Battery because they received no reinforcements, though not till they had held it for upwards of forty minutes. Marshal Pelissier made proposals to Lord Raglan to renew the assault. Lord Raglan, though agreeing with the French General in the practicability of a renewed assault, was of opinion that it ought not to be attempted till a heavy bombardment bad been continued for some hours. As there was a considerable distance between them, Lord Raglan had to ride over to Marshal Pelissier, to confer with him on the arrangements for the proposed assault. During the interval, the French, who were suffering heavily from the enemy's fire, became dispirited by their losses and by the inaction which followed the check they had sustained. The Russians were evidently in great force at the Malakoff; and General d'Autemarre was so convinced that the assault would not succeed, that he sent a pressing message to Marshal Pelissier to beg that he would not expose the men in a fruitless assault. Marslial Pelissier was obliged to yield to such an expression of opinion, and, Lord Raglan coinciding with him, the renewal of the assault did not take place. Although the attack upon the Redan had been discussed at a council of war, and the Engineer officers of both our attacks (Colonel Chapman and Colonel Gordon) had been called upon to assist the Generals with their advice, the result proved that the arrangements were defective and inadequate. Our officers were outwitted by the subtlety of the Russians, who had for some time masked their guns, or withdrawn them from the embrasures, as if they were overpowered and silenced by our fire.

No more decisive proof of the inefficiency of our force could be afforded than this fact – that in no case did the troops destined to assault and carry the Redan reach the outer part of the work; that no ladders were placed in the ditch; and that a very small portion indeed of the storming party reached the abattis, which was placed many yards in front of the ditch of the Redan. It cannot be said that on this occasion our men exhibited any want of courage; but so abortive and so weak was the attack, that the Russians actually got outside the parapet of the Redan, jeered and laughed at our soldiers as they fired upon them at the abattis, and mockingly invited the 'Inglisky' to come nearer. A few dilettanti have since started a theory, which has not even ingenuity to recommend it, and which, if well founded, would convey the weightiest accusation ever yet made against our commanders – and that is, that our assault against the Redan was never meant to be successful, and that it was, in fact, a mere diversion, to assist the French in getting into the Malakoff. To any one acquainted with the facts, or to those who were present, this theory must appear, not only not ingenious, but ludicrous and contemptible. Indeed, the truth is, that an assault was not merely intended to be successful, but that it was looked upon as certain to succeed. No one hinted a doubt of the carrying of the Redan, though there was a general expression of opinion, among those who knew the case, that the force detailed for the storm was perilously small, and some few, as I heard, also found fault with the position of the reserves, and thought they were placed too far in the rear to be of service in case of a check.

Our losses were severe, and they were not alleviated by the consolations of victory. No less than 22 officers and 247 men were killed, 78 officers and 1,207 men were wounded. The French lost 39 officers killed and 93 wounded; 1,600 rank and file killed or taken prisoners, and about the same number wounded – so that the loss of the Allies, on the 18th of June, amounted to nearly 5,000 officers and men. The Russians admitted a loss of 5,800; but it is remarkable in their return that the proportion of their officers killed is very much less than ours. In our army one officer was killed to every eleven men – one was wounded to every fifteen. In the French army one officer was killed to thirty men, and one was wounded to every sixteen men. In the Russian army the proportion of killed was about one officer to forty-nine men – of wounded, one officer to thirty-one men. General Jones was wounded over the trench. General Eyre was disabled by a severe cut on the head, but kept with his men till they were established in the Cemetery.

All the advantage we gained was the capture of the Cemetery, and the small Mamelon near it. The French sent over an engineer to examine the ground, and as that officer expressed an opinion that it was desirable to hold the place with a view to ulterior defensive works being erected upon it, General Eyre was assured that a strong body of men would be marched into it at night. As these troops never arrived, Colonel Adams retired from the Cemetery at night, leaving only a picket, which was also withdrawn in compliance with the instructions General Eyre received from headquarters, which were to the effect that if the French did not occupy the work our troops were to withdraw. On the following morning, Lieutenant Donnelly of the Engineers heard that the position for which we had paid so dearly was not in our possession. He appreciated its value – he saw that the Russians had not yet advanced to reoccupy it, begged and borrowed some thirty men, with whom he crept into the Cemetery. As soon as the armistice began, the Russians flocked down to the Cemetery, which they supposed to be undefended, but to their great surprise they found our men posted there, and in the evening the party was strengthened, and the Allies constructed most valuable works and batteries there.

We were close to the Mamelon, and the frequent reports of rifles and the pinging of the balls proved that the flag of truce had not been hoisted by the enemy. We were in the zigzag, a ditch about 6 feet broad and 6 feet deep, with the earth knocked about by shot at the sides, and we met Frenchmen laden with water canteens or carrying large tin cans full of coffee, and tins of meat and soup, cooked in the ravine close at hand, up to the Mamelon.

I entered along with them. The parapets were high inside the work, and were of a prodigious thickness. It was evident the Mamelon was overdone. It was filled with traverses and excavations, so that it was impossible to put a large body of men into it, or to get them in order in case of an assault. The stench from the dead, who had been buried as they fell, was fearful; and bones, and arms, and legs stuck out from the piles of rubbish on which you were treading. Many guns were also buried, but they did not decompose. Outside were plenty of those fougasses, which the Russians planted thickly. A strong case containing powder was sunk in the ground, and to it was attached a thin tube of tin or lead, several feet in length; in the upper end of the tube was enclosed a thin glass tube containing sulphuric or nitric acid. This portion of the tube was just laid above the earth, where it could be readily hid by a few blades of grass or a stone. If a person stepped upon it he bent the tin tube and broke the glass tube inside. The acid immediately escaped down the tin tube till it met a few grains of chlorate of potash. The mine exploded, and not only destroyed everything near it, but threw out a quantity of bitumen, with which it was coated, in a state of ignition. I very nearly had a practical experience of the working of these mines, for an English sentry, who kindly warned me off, did not indicate the exact direction till he found he was in danger of my firing it, when he became very communicative upon the subject. They made it disagreeable walking in the space between the works.

A line of sentries was formed by the Russians so far in front of the abattis, that General Airey was obliged to remonstrate with an aide-de-camp of General Osten-Sacken, who ordered them to retire. These men were remarkably fine, tall, muscular fellows, and one could not but contrast them with the poor weakly-looking boys in our regiments, or with the undergrown men of the French line. They were in clean new uniforms. Many of them wore medals. Their officers turned out with white kid gloves and patent leather boots.

One stout elderly Russian of rank asked one of our officers, 'How are you off for food?'

'Oh! We get everything we want; our fleet secures that.'

'Yes,' remarked the Russian, with a knowing wink, 'yes; but there's one thing you're not so well off for, and that your fleet can't supply you with, and that's sleep.'

'We're at least as well off for that as you are,' was the rejoinder. Another officer asked if we really thought, after our experience of the defence they could make, that we could take Sebastopol.

'We must; France and England are determined to take it.'

'Ah! Well,' said the other, 'Russia is determined France and England shall not have it; and we'll see who has the strongest will, and can lose most men.'

The time is not yet come for the disclosure of all the truth; but it may even now be asked, how it was that on the 6th of February, 1855, we abandoned our ground opposite the Malakoff to the French, if we really knew it to be the key of the Russian position? A change was indeed necessary, and it was evident that the English army was much too weak to occupy the space from the Dockyard Creek ravine on the left, to the valley of the Tchernaya on the right. But why, instead of allowing the French (I use that word 'allowing', inasmuch as we are given to understand that Sir John Burgoyne objected to the change) – why, instead of allowing the French to take from us the favourable ground upon our right attack, did we not move to our right, and leave the French to occupy the spot held by our left, which we maintained to the end of the siege? It seems but natural that as we had defended the right of the Allied Army at Inkerman, with so much loss, and so much courage, we should have continued to occupy a position we had rendered glorious for ever. A cession of it to the French appears to be a tacit reproach. By concentrating our left on our right attack, we could have readily carried on the siege works, and have preserved to ourselves the attack against the Malakoff, which was originally opened by us on the 17th of October, 1854. It was said that the French objected to take Chapman's attack, on the plea that they could not serve our artillery. Sir John Burgoyne then offered that our artillerymen should be left to work the English guns; but the objection, if ever it was made, was futile, inasmuch as at a subsequent period of the siege the French demanded and received the loan of more than twenty-four 32-pounders, which they used with great vigour at the final bombardment. The compliance of Sir John Burgoyne upon this point is the more to be wondered at, inasmuch as it was he who discovered the great importance of the position we so readily yielded, and it was he who announced that the Malakoff, of which he relinquished the attack to our Allies, was the veritable key of the whole of the defences of Sebastopol.

Between the death of Lord Raglan and the middle of July, no decided progress was made in the siege approaches, and the Russians contented themselves with strenuous preparations to meet another assault. But as sickness diminished, and reinforcements and fresh supplies of material were poured into the Crimea later in the month, the Allies set to work with renewed energy, and not only gained ground before Sebastopol, but began to feel their way towards the left of the enemy's position on the Belbek.

After the 18th of June, 1855, it became quite evident that our left attack was utterly useless for the purposes of an assault, and accordingly one would have thought that the whole energy of the chiefs of the British Army and of the Engineers would have been directed to push on our saps in the direction of the only point of attack the British Army had to deal with; but in effect the Redan was not approached much more closely by our Engineers subsequently to the 18th than it had been previously, and most of our efforts were directed to the augmentation of the weight and vigour of our fire from batteries already established, or to the strengthening of the Quarries Battery, which we took on the 7th of June. In fact, we seemed determined to take the place by the fire of artillery alone; and yet, when the time came we combined with it an assault, which was of course an interference with, and an abandonment of, that determination. Although our officers had the Mamelon before their eyes, they overlooked the fact that the Russians could screen a very large body of men inside their casemates and bomb-proofs, and that the garrison would suffer very little from our fire so long as it failed to search out and destroy those retreats. When the garrison of these casemates was warned, by the cessation of our fire, of the coming assault, they swarmed out in masses more numerous than the assailants, who were besides broken, and almost breathless, owing to their run from the trenches, and repulsed them ere they reached the abattis. Whenever the Russians felt our energy was overpowering them at any one particular point they withdrew their guns behind the traverse or parapet, and trusted to the strength of their earthworks, so that it was difficult to say what was the exact effect of our cannonade upon their guns. Thus, on the 18th of June, our soldiers were raked with grape and canister from points where we had imagined the guns were dismounted and silenced, and it was evident that our artillery had not gained that mastery over the enemies' pieces which was requisite to ensure success. We subsequently endeavoured to secure a better chance for our troops, at the next assault, by establishing batteries to crush the flanking tire of the angles of the Redan, and of the curtains in the direction of the salient; but the tackles broke in raising the guns, and these batteries were never armed.

From the attack of the 18th of June to the 10th of July, the enemy were employed in strengthening their works; they made such progress at the Redan, that it was judged expedient to open a heavy fire upon them. This commenced at five o'clock on the morning of the 10th of July, and lasted for four hours. Several embrasures were destroyed, and the enemy's reply was feeble; but they did not cease from their labours, and we were obliged to reserve our ammunition for general bombardment.

It will be observed that all this while the Turks never took part in the siege. The justice of the following remarks, which was apparent enough in July, 1855, seems still more evident at the present moment:

It is a singular thing, that while the French and British troops consider their most harassing work to be the duty in the trenches, the Turks, who are equally interested in the event of the war, and will be the most benefited by its success, do not take any share in actual siege operations, and amuse themselves with the mere pastime of foraging, or actually sitting in indolence for hours together, following the shadows of their tents as they move from west to east, smoking stolidly, or grinning at the antics of some mountebank comrade. Omar Pasha goes hither and thither without object, merely that his army may seem to be employed; its actual services are of little importance. It is said that an agreement was made between the allied Generals and the Porte that the Turks were not to assist in the siege. But why not? And can such an arrangement be binding when the public good demands a different course? If the Ottoman troops be so excellent behind fortifications, there can be no objection to their relieving their hard-worked allies in some of the less important positions; or they might at least be employed in some more active manner than merely moving to and fro occasionally, as if for the purpose of impressing the mind of Europe with a false idea of activity.

The first great phase in the siege had been passed – we found that the Russians could resist the Allied forces with vigour, and that they were capable of acting upon the defensive with greater energy than we gave them credit for, from their conduct at the Alma. The constant passage up the Bosphorus of vessels with troops on board from France, and artillery and material from England, evinced the preparations made by the Allies for the renewal of the struggle; but there were many who thought that the siege would not be over till the following year, and that the Allies would have to undergo the miseries of another winter in the open trenches.

Writing on the 12th of July, I said:

> Of the reduction of Sebastopol proper before the winter I have no kind of doubt. The Russian generals, though brave and determined on an obstinate defence, deserve credit for prudence and forethought. As long as a place can be held with a chance of success, or even of damaging the enemy, they will hold it; but all their proceedings induce the belief that they will not allow their troops to be cut to pieces merely for the credit of having made a desperate resistance, and of having maintained, without advantage, for a short time longer, a position which, in a military sense, is untenable. When they perceive that their retreat is seriously endangered, it is not improbable that they will altogether abandon the southern side, which they can hardly hope to hold should the Allies be able to command the harbour. They, no doubt, count at least on being able to prolong their resistance until the winter sets in; if that be impossible, they will most likely withdraw to the northern side, to which it may be impracticable to lay siege before the spring of 1856.

On the night of the 22nd, the Russians, who were either under the impression that the Allies were about to make an assault, or wished to stop our working parties, opened a heavy fire of musketry along their line, and after a great expenditure of ammunition, they retired from the parapets. The casualties in the trenches became so heavy, that the Commander-in-Chief, in several despatches, expressed his regret at the loss, which he attributed to the proximity of the works, the lightness of the nights, and the rocky nature of the ground. From the 27th to the 29th July, thirteen men were killed, and five officers and 108 men were wounded, in addition to casualties in the Naval Brigade. However, some little progress was made – our advanced parallels were strengthened, and our unlucky fifth parallel was deepened.

The French engineers were pressing on with indefatigable energy on the right and left of our position, and were close to the Malakoff on the right, and the Central and Flagstaff Bastion on the left; and it was evident that, at the next bombardment, it would scarcely be possible to preserve the town from destruction. The Russians prepared to strike a blow, the influence of which would be felt in the councils of Vienna, and in the Cabinets of every State in Europe.

Late in the evening of the 13th of August orders were given for the troops to be under arms by three in the morning. Of course, Malakoff was immediately the word, and most persons supposed that the long-talked-of assault was to be made. This, however, was soon found not to be the case. Without tap of drum or sound of bugle, the camp was afoot at the prescribed hour, the troops forming up in profound silence. The entire army was out, including the cavalry and artillery from Balaklava. The first grey of morning found a number of officers and amateurs assembled on Cathcart's Hill, the best point of observation. There was unusually little firing the day before and during the night, and all expected that this tranquillity was quickly to be broken by the din of an engagement. The interest of the situation grew stronger as the morning advanced, and as the scarlet columns became visible, massed along the lines, motionless and expectant. Superior officers, with their staff, moved to and fro; aides-de-camp traversed the heights with orders; here and there, through the still imperfect light, which began to be tinged with the first red flush of sunrise, waved the pennons of a Lancer escort. With broad day, the brief excitement ended. Before the upper edge of the sun's disc rose above the hills, the troops were marching briskly back to their tents. The morning was beautifully clear, and the spectacle was striking. In fine order, in serried columns, looking hardy, active, and cheerful, and up to any work, the Crimean army regained its canvas quarters. For the day, the danger was over – to commence again, it was believed, at night.

From certain orders that were given with respect to ammunition, mules, &c., I inferred that the army would again be under arms early the next morning. The officers were warned to be ready at a moment's notice. It was believed that reinforcements had reached Sebastopol. They had been expected for some time previously. Four divisions were talked of, two of them Imperial Guards. Word was sent up from the fleet to head-quarters that large bodies of troops had been seen collecting behind the Redan, and others behind the Tchernaya, and there were grounds for expecting a general attack along our lines. The report in camp was, that the Archduke Michael was in Sebastopol. We learned from deserters that he had been expected. General Pelissier held 40,000 men in readiness to operate on the line of the Tchernaya, which, from its extent, was perhaps the most attackable part of our position; but it was vigilantly guarded.

The fire, which opened at daybreak on Friday, continued the whole of Saturday and Sunday, but slackened on Monday. The progress of the French works was considerable, and the French seemed duly sensible of the service of our cannonade. I heard a French officer say on Saturday evening that it had enabled them to do in four hours what they previously could not have done in fifteen days. Their foremost parallel, which had been begun at the two ends, could not be completed, owing to its near proximity to the Malakoff. As soon as a gabion was put up, a storm of projectiles was hurled against it and the working party; afterwards the extremities were connected under the cover of our fire. The distance was indeed so greatly reduced between the French trenches and the Russian defences, that a vigorous assault seemed certain to succeed. The Russians always considered it a point of honour to go off in great style on the first day of a bombardment; after which they ran their guns behind the parapets, covered them with sandbags, and allowed us to blaze away without making frequent reply. Although earthworks take a deal of hammering before they show its marks, both the Redan and Malakoff began to present a very battered appearance. We had, of course, no means of ascertaining the Russian loss of men. Every night our people kept up the musketry against the proper right and the curtain of the Malakoff to protect the French workmen, and shells and bouquets of shells flew all along the lines right and left – very pretty to look at, but unpleasant to meet.

On the afternoon of the 20th, between five and six o'clock, the French batteries on the left opened a furious fire, to which the Russians warmly replied. General Pelissier, in his open carriage, with his aides-de-camp and usual hussar escort, passed through the English camp and went up to Cathcart's Hill. The fire lasted until nightfall, and then diminished. At midnight it had almost ceased, and one saw but an occasional shell in the air. At 2 a.m. orders came for the army to turn out. This was rapidly done; the troops moved to the front, and remained there until daylight. A line of telegraphic lights had been observed, commencing at Sebastopol, and running along the Inkerman heights, and it was supposed that an attack was intended. These 'turns-outs' were frequent and harassing during this period of the siege.

The Turks, who occupied the extreme right of our position, and who had to guard the two roads leading from the valley of Varnutka, did nothing in the *tabia* line. In vain did the Sardinian engineers throw out gentle hints about the propriety of erecting a couple of *epaulements*, and point out divers hills and heights peculiarly suited for a redoubt; they turned a deaf ear to all these suggestions, and, except the works which had been previously thrown up by the Piedmontese, when they held some of the positions guarded by the Turks, not a shovelful of earth, was turned up. This would have seemed so much the more surprising, as the Turks had become notorious by their fortification, at Kalafat, Giurgevo, Silistria, and Eupatoria.

8

The Battle of the Chernaya

On the 16th of August the long-threatened attack of the Russians took place, and ended in their complete defeat. Movements of large numbers of troops in the neighbourhood of Sebastopol, the unanimous reports of the deserters, of whom several came in every day, and information gained from Tartars, had given intimation that the Russians intended to try their luck once more in an offensive operation. Although, at first, the line of the Tchernaya suggested itself as the point which the Russians would most probably attack, a supposition which was moreover confirmed by all the deserters, yet, as large numbers of newly arrived troops were seen concentrated in and about the Russian works, apprehensions were entertained that they might attempt the positions before Sebastopol.

Several deserters came in on the 15th, and spoke with the utmost certainty of an intended attack on the Tchernaya; but no particular attention was paid to their reports, and no special orders were given to the troops, except 'to be prepared'; and this had been so often repeated that it made no impression. In Baidar, whence the English cavalry had been withdrawn, two regiments of heavy French cavalry, and detachments of Chasseurs and Zouaves, were stationed. On the 15th, General d'Allonville sent word by semaphore, that large numbers of Russian troops were concentrated on the heights, and that he expected to be attacked. Late in the evening, notice of this message was sent to General Della Marmora and Osman Pasha. No additional precautions were taken on the Tchernaya line, and the advance was scarcely less a surprise than that of Inkerman. The first news of the attack was brought about daybreak by some

Chasseurs forming part of a patrol who fell into an ambuscade and escaped, while their comrades were taken prisoners. Soon afterwards the outposts across the Tchernaya were driven in, and at daybreak the cannonade began.

The Tchernaya, issuing from the narrow gorge in which it runs after leaving the Valley of Baidar, at the Tower of Karlovka, flows between a succession of hillocks, which formed the basis of the position of the allied armies. On the extreme right, the Turks were stationed. They occupied two hillocks, between which are two roads leading from Higher Tchorgoun and the Tower of Karlovka into the Woronzoff Road. The Sardinians leant on the little mountain stream which limited the Turkish position to the left, and on the large hillock above the road from Balaklava to Tchorgoun, and occupied a position of the utmost importance in the defence of the line of the Tchernaya. In front, and divided from it by the aqueduct, was another hillock, smaller but equally steep, accessible from the first by a stone bridge on which the Sardinians had a small *épaulement*. They had outposts at the other side of the Tchernaya, on the hillock near the Mackenzie Road. The French occupied three hillocks to the left of the Sardinians, and guarded the road leading to Balaklava over the Traktir Bridge from Mackenzie's Farm. The first of these, to the right, was separated from the others by the road to the bridge; and the third, on the left, was protected by the basin of the aqueduct. In front of the bridge there was an *épaulement*, beyond which were the outposts.

The first attack of the Russians was against the outposts of the Sardinians. Corresponding to the hillocks on the south side of the Tchernaya were three plateaux from which their guns could command not only the ground opposite occupied by the Sardinians and Turks, but the plain which opens towards the French position. A company of infantry, and a company of bersaglieri, formed the Sardinian outposts. They were attacked at dawn. As the troops were not under arms, it was necessary to hold this position for a while, and General Della Marmora sent Major Govone, of the Etat-Major, with a company of bersaglieri, to reinforce the companies. They crossed the aqueduct and the river, and went up the plateau;

but, when they arrived on the crest, the two companies had just left the *épaulement*, which had become untenable, as it was swept by the guns which the Russians had brought up on the plateaux, and was exposed to be taken in the rear. The Sardinians retired in good order across the river, and went to reinforce the post which occupied the second hillock on the aqueduct.

The cannonade on both sides commenced. Scarcely had the cannonade opened when three compact columns of infantry advanced towards the French position, and attacked the bridge and the hillock to the right.

The French outpost beyond the bridge consisted of a company of the 2nd regiment of Zouaves. The other *avant postes*, to the right of the Zouaves up to the Sardinian outposts, were furnished by the 20th *léger* and the 22nd of the line. The *réveillée* had not yet gone in camp, when the sentinels were alarmed by hearing the tramp of men, whose forms were yet invisible in the darkness. The posts had not time to stand to their arms ere they were driven across the river; but the desultory firing had given timely warning to the main guards and to the camps, and the men turned out just as a storm of round shot began to rush over the ground.

The Russian columns, protected by the fire of their artillery, moved in excellent order down to the river side, notwithstanding the heavy fire of artillery which greeted them in front from the French, and in flank from the Sardinians. At the river the first column detached itself from the rest, and dividing into two parts crossed the river, which is easily fordable in summer.

Before the troops were properly under arms the Russians were at the bridge and at the foot of the hillock. The 20th *léger* and the 2nd battalion of Zouaves had to stand the first shock, and they certainly stood it gallantly. The Russians, without losing time in firing, advanced with an *élan* scarcely ever seen in Russian troops. They were new troops, belonging, according to the prisoners and wounded, to the 5th division of the 2nd *corps d'armée*, lately arrived from Poland.

The aqueduct which ran close to the foot of the hillock, formed the chief defence of the French. About 9 or 10 feet wide and several feet deep, it skirts the steep hills so close, that it is nearly in all places supported by a high embankment, offering considerable difficulties for an advancing force, and exposing them as soon as they reach the top of the embankment, to commanding musketry fire. Notwithstanding this, the Russians crossed it on the right, and were beginning to scale the heights, when, taken in flank by the Sardinian batteries, which fired with admirable precision, they were swept down wholesale and rolled into the aqueduct.

This first rush did not last ten minutes. The Russians fell back. Scarcely had they gone a few hundred yards when they were met by a second column, which was advancing at the *pas de charge*, and both united and again rushed forward. This second attempt was more successful than the first. They forded the river on the right and left, at the bridge, and forced its defenders to fall back. The moment the bridge was free two guns of the 5th Light Brigade of Artillery crossed it and took position between two of the hillocks on the road which leads to the plain of Balaklava. A third gun crossed the river by a ford, and all three began to sweep the road and the heights. The infantry, without waiting for the portable bridges, the greater part of which had been thrown away during the advance, rushed breast-deep into the water, climbed up the embankment, and began to scale the heights. They succeeded in getting up more than one-half of the ascent, where the dead and wounded afterwards showed clearly the mark they reached; but by this time the French met them in the most gallant style. The Russians were by degrees forced back, and driven across the bridge, carrying away their guns.

While this conflict took place on the bridge, the other column attacked the French right in such a swarm that they could neither be kept back by the aqueduct, nor cowed by the Sardinian guns, which were ploughing long lanes through their ranks. On they came, as it seemed, irresistible, and rushed up the steep hill with such fury that the Zouaves, who lined the sides of it, were obliged to fall back. The officers might be seen leading the way and animating their soldiers. This furious rush brought the advancing column to the crest of the hillock, where it stopped to form. But the French had not been idle. Scarcely did the column of the enemy show its head, ere the guns opened upon it with grape, and a murderous fire was poured in by the French infantry. The column began to waver; but the impetus from those behind was so powerful that the head was pushed forward a few yards more, when the French, giving one mighty cheer, rushed upon the enemy, who, shaken already, immediately turned round and ran. But the mass was so great that all the hurry could not save them, and more than 200 prisoners were taken, the banks of the aqueduct, the aqueduct itself, and the river side were covered and filled with the dead and the wounded. The Sardinian and French artillery poured a murderous cross-fire into the scattered remains of the column. It was a complete rout. The French drove them far across the plain. This defeat completely depressed them; nothing more was attempted against this side.

Not so on the bridge. Notwithstanding the heavy loss suffered in the second attack, the Russians collected the scattered remains of the column which had been routed on the right of the French, and brought up all their reserves. They crossed the river, and the aqueduct too, but the French were now thoroughly prepared, and the tenacity of the Russians only served to augment their losses. This last failure was decisive, and immediately the advance of the artillery – the usual Russian preparation for retreat – showed they were on the point of retiring. Three batteries, each of twelve guns, began to open fire, while the remains of the infantry rallied behind a rising ground leading up towards the plateau of Ayker, or Mackenzie's Height.

The Sardinians, who, with the exception of the little outpost fight on the opposite side of the Tchernaya, had only supported the French by their artillery, began to move across the aqueduct. The Russian riflemen, after the last defeat on the right, had retired behind the banks of the Tchernaya. A battalion of Piedmontese, preceded by a company of bersaglieri, advanced in beautiful order as if on parade, and soon drove these riflemen from their position. It even advanced some way, but it was not intended to force the heights. The French brought up a new division (Dulac's). The English and French cavalry were in readiness on the ground of the Light Cavalry charge, to receive the enemy if they should debouch on the plain. But General Morris would not risk the cavalry on the plain, intersected as it was by the branches of the river, and defended, as it was still, by the Russian guns on the height; so only two squadrons of Chasseurs d'Afrique followed the retreating enemy.

The guns which the Russians had brought up to cover their retreat suffered so much by the fire, which from our side was increased by Captain Mowbray's battery from the open ground between the Sardinian and the French positions, that they made off. As the guns retired, a brilliant line of cavalry appeared from behind the rising ground. I could distinguish five regiments – three in line and two other regiments in second line. They advanced at a gallop, and wheeling round, allowed twelve guns to pass, which again opened fire, but at half-past nine or ten o'clock black lines moving off, through clouds of the dust on the Mackenzie Road, were the only traces which remained of the so long threatened attack of the Russians.

Although not quite so obstinate and sanguinary as the Battle of Inkerman, this affair resembled it in many points. The Russians gave up manoeuvring, and confided entirely in the valour of their troops. The difference was in the manner of fighting. At Inkerman the Russians fell under file firing; on the Tchernaya it was the artillery which did the greatest execution. On the banks of the aqueduct particularly, the sight was appalling; the Russians, when scaling the embankment of the aqueduct, were taken in flank by the Sardinian batteries, and the dead and wounded rolled down the embankment, sometimes more than 20 feet in height.

According to the account of the prisoners, and judging from the straps on the shoulders of the wounded and dead, three divisions were engaged in the actual attack – the 5th of the 2nd *corps d'armée* (of General Paniutin), then lately arrived from Poland, under the command of General Wrangel; the 12th division of the 4th *corps d'armée* (Osten Sacken's), formerly under the command of General Liprandi, afterwards under General Martinolep; and the 17th division of the 6th *corps d'armée* (Liprandi's), under Major-General Wassielkosky. Before the attack began, General Gortschakoff, who commanded in person, read a letter from the

Emperor before them, in which he expressed a hope that they would prove as valorous as last year when they took the heights of Balaklava; and then there was a large distribution of brandy. Besides the three divisions which attacked, the 7th occupied Tchorgoun and the heights, but was not engaged except in the small outpost affair of the Sardinians.

The French had three divisions engaged – the Division Faucheux to the right, the Division d'Herbillon in the centre, and the Division (Camou) on the left of the bridge; their loss was about 1,000 in killed and wounded. The Sardinians had only one division engaged (the Division Trotti), and lost but a few hundred men; they had to regret the loss of a distinguished general officer, the Brigadier-General Count de Montevecchio, who died of his wounds; but they gained great confidence from the day, and were proud of holding their own so well under the eyes of their allies.

The battle had been raging for an hour ere I reached the line of the French works at Fedukhine. From the high grounds over which I had to ride, the whole of the battle-field was marked out by rolling columns of smoke, and the irregular thick puffs of the artillery. All our cavalry camps were deserted; but the sun played on the helmets and sabres of the solid squadrons, which were drawn up about 2 miles in advance of Kadikoi, and just in rear of the line of hills which the French and Sardinians were defending, so as to be ready to charge the Russians should they force the position. The French cavalry, chasseurs, hussars, and two regiments of dragoons, were on our left. Our light and our heavy cavalry brigades were formed in two heavy masses, supported by artillery in the plain behind the second Fedukhine hillock, and seemed in splendid case, and 'eager for the fray'. The Allies had, in fact, not less than 6,000 very fine cavalry that day in the field; but they were held in check, 'for fear' of the artillery, which there is no doubt they could have captured, in addition to many thousands of prisoners, if handled by a Seidlitz or a Murat. But the French General would not permit a charge to be executed, though French and English cavalry leaders were alike eager for it, and so this noble force was rendered ineffective.

Having passed by the left of the cavalry, I gained the side of the hill just as a large body of French troops crowned it at the *pas double*, deployed, and at once charged down towards the aqueduct, where a strong column of Russians, protected by a heavy fire of artillery on the crest of the ridge, were making good their ground against the exhausted French. This new regiment attacking them with extraordinary impetuosity on the flank, literally swept the Russians like flies into the aqueduct, or rolled them headlong down its steep banks; and at the same moment a French battery on my right, belonging, I think, to the Imperial Guards, opened on the shattered crowd with grape, and tore them into atoms. This column was the head, so to speak, of the second attack on the lines, and emerging through the flying mass, another body of Russian infantry, with levelled bayonets, advanced with great steadiness towards the aqueduct once more. As far as the eye could see towards the right, the flat caps and grey coats were marching towards the Allied position, or detaching themselves from the distant reserves, which were visible here and there concealed amid the hills. As the French battery opened, a Russian battery was detached to answer it, and to draw off their fire; but our gallant Allies took their pounding with great gallantry and coolness, and were not diverted for a moment from their business of dealing with the infantry column, the head of which was completely knocked to pieces in two minutes. Then the officers halted it, and tried in vain to deploy them – the column, wavering and wriggling like a great serpent, began to spread out from the further extremity like a fan, and to retreat towards the rear. Another crashing volley of grape, and they are retreating over the plain.

And now there breaks high over all the roar of battle, heavier thunder. Those are the deep, angry voices of the great English heavy battery of 18-pounders and 32-pounder howitzers, under Mowbray, which search out the reserves. These guns were placed far away on my right, near the Sardinians, and it is acknowledged by all that they did good service upon this eventful day. The advance I had just witnessed was the last effort of the enemy. Their infantry rolled in confused masses over the plain on the other side of the Tchernaya, were pursued by the whole fire of the French batteries and of the 8-inch English howitzers in the Sardinian redoubt, and by a continuous and well-directed fusillade, till they were out of range. Their defeat was announced by the advance of their cavalry, and by the angry volleys of their artillery against the positions of the Allies. Their cavalry, keeping out of range, made a very fair show, with lances and standards, and sabres shining brightly; but beyond that they did nothing – and, indeed, they could do nothing, as we did not give them a chance of action. The Russians were supported by guns, but they did not seem well placed, nor did they occupy a good position at any time of the fight. The infantry formed in square blocks in the rear of this force, and then began to file off towards the Mackenzie Road, and the French rocket battery opened on them from the plateau, and, strange to say, reached them several times. It was about eight o'clock when their regular retreat commenced, and the English cavalry and artillery began to retire also at that hour to their camps, much discontented, because they had had no larger share in the honours of the day.

The march of the Russians continued till late in the day – their last column gained the plateau about two o'clock. It must have been a terrible march for them – not a drop of water to be had; and even when they gained their arid camp, it is only too probable that they had nothing to drink; indeed, the prisoners told us the men were encouraged to the attack by being told that if they gained the Tchernaya they would have abundance of water – the greatest inducement that could be held out to them. I rode down towards the *tête-du-pont*. In order to get a good view of the retreat, I descended to the bridge, which was covered with wounded men. Just as I gained the centre of it, a volley of shells was pitched right upon it, and amid the French, who, with their usual humanity, were helping the wounded. Some burst in the shallow stream, the sides of which were crowded with wounded men; others killed poor wretches who were crawling towards the water – one in particular, to whom I had just an instant before thrown a sandwich; others knocked pieces out of the bridge, or tore up the causeway. As the road was right in the line of fire, I at once turned off the bridge, and pulling sharp round, dashed under an arch just as the battery opened on us a second time, and there I remained for about ten minutes, when the Russians seemed ashamed of themselves, and gave us a respite for a few moments. The next time they fired was with round shot; and as I retreated up the road, to obtain shelter behind the hills, one of these knocked a wounded Zouave to pieces before my eyes. In the rear of the hill, there was a party of about 500 Russian prisoners *en bivouac*. Many of them were wounded; all were war-worn, dirty, ill-clad – some in rags, others almost bootless. The French sentries who guarded them seemed to commiserate the poor fellows; but two or three of their own officers, who sat apart, did not look at them, but smoked their cigars with great nonchalance, or talked glibly to the French officers of the fortune of war, &c.

In a short time I returned to the front, and saw General Simpson and a few staff-officers descending from the Sardinian position, whence they had watched the battle. They were on their way back to head-quarters; but Captain Colville, aide-de-camp to the General, a young officer of ability and promise, and always of an inquiring turn of mind, turned back with me, and we rode over the bridge. The French were, however, obdurate, and would not let us cross the *tête-du-pont*, as we were *en pleine portée* of the guns posted behind a white scarp on a hillock on the opposite side. We could see that the Sardinians had recovered their old ground, and occupied the height from which their advanced posts were driven early in the day. Further, we could see the Russian cavalry, but the great mass of infantry was in full retreat; and at nine o'clock the road to Mackenzie's Farm was thronged with a close column of thirsty, footsore, beaten Russians. The aspect of the field, of the aqueduct, and of the river, was horrible beyond description – the bodies were closely packed in parties, and lay in files two or three deep, where the grape had torn through the columns. For two days the bodies rotted on the ground which lay beyond the French lines, and the first Russian burying party did not come down till the 18th, when the stench was so very great that the men could scarcely perform their loathsome task. General Read was killed early in the battle; and the Russians lost every officer in command of an attacking column. Their total loss was, we estimated, at from 12,000 to 15,000 men.

9

The Fall of Sebastopol

All the latter part of August passed quietly away: the Russians on the alert to resist an assault – we prepared to meet the rumoured attack upon our lines. After the failure of June 18, our cannonade languished. We talked of it as slackening, and considered it extinct Prince Gortschakoff assured the world that it was a mere squib a feeble firework, which did those tough Russians no harm, and caused their troops no inconvenience; and yet, somehow or other between the 18th of June and 18th of July, not less than 8,000 pretty little globules of iron, 8, 10, and 13 inches in diameter and falling with a weight equivalent to 50 and to 90 tons, were deposited inside the lines of Sebastopol, and every one that burst sent forth some six or eight fragments, of several pounds weight each, a distance of 200 or 300 yards, unless they were stopped in transitu by traverse or sinew.

There were rumours that the garrison of Sebastopol was in an extremely disorganized state. The losses in the town were frightful and notwithstanding their official and non-official declarations the Russians suffered from want of water and of spirits. Indeed, it was confidently affirmed that, owing to the deficiency of forage their cavalry had been compelled to fall back on the road to Bakschiserai.

They threw up another battery, close to the Spur Battery commanding a small path from the Tchernaya. The French constructed strong redoubts on the site of the old redoubts in the plain. These works were in connection with the outer line of defence from Kamara, Traktir, and Tchorgoun, and the Sardinian and Turkish batteries towards Baidar, and behind them were the old batteries defending Balaklava, which became one of the strongest positions in the world. Our allies were losing heavily, in the White Works, which they captured on the 7th of June, where they lost one-half of the men who went into it every day. The twelve-gun battery on the north side took them in flank and reverse, the Malakoff enfiladed them on the other side, and they were exposed to the direct fire of the shipping in front. They called the place '*l'Abattoir*'. Our own losses were very heavy, but still the army were full of hope and courage.

There was a sortie early on the morning of the 1st of September on the advanced trenches of our right attack, and the Russians kept up a very heavy fire upon our working parties. As the crisis of the siege approached, it was affirmed that the enemy were about to try the chances of war once more, in one grand attack, at three or four points between Baidar and the gorge of Inkerman, and to make a sortie in force on our works. Prince Gortschakoff, Generals Liprandi, Paniutin, and Osten-Sacken were mentioned as the generals of the attacking columns. The mass was concentrated on the plateau between Kamishli and Kalankoi, on the south side of the Belbek, supported by divisions echeloned on the road to Bakschiserai. Near Kalankoi a bad and difficult mountain road to Balaklava crosses the Belbek; strikes off to the right to Mackenzie's Farm ; descending thence from the plateau, crosses the Tchernaya at the bridge of the Traktir, and sweeps across the plain of Balaklava, intersecting in its course the Woronzoff Road. Several paths or indifferent roads branch from this grand causeway ere it descends the plateau of Mackenzie's Farm, leading by Chuliou and Ozenbasch towards Baidar, and it was thought that the Russians might have put these in tolerable condition, and rendered them available for the passage of troops and artillery. The Russians concentrated considerable masses in and about Upu, Ozenbasch, and Chuliou, and Prince Gortschakoff visited the army destined to operate against the Turks, French, and Sardinians on the rear, and was prodigal of promises and encouragement.

The intelligence received by the English, French, and Turkish Generals coincided on these points, and was believed to be entirely trustworthy. It seemed incredible that any General would trust his army among those defiles and mountain-passes, because a failure on the part of the corps on his right to seize Tchorgoun and Kamara would have left him without support, and an active enemy could have easily pursued and crushed him before he could have possibly gained the plateau from which he had descended. Nothing would have given such universal satisfaction to the whole army as another attempt by the enemy to force our position. If the Russians descended into the plain we were sure of success, and the prospect of a sanguinary engagement gave positive pleasure to both officers and men, alike weary of the undistinguished, if not inglorious, service of the trenches.

On the 3rd of September, at 9.15 p.m., a heavy fire of musketry to the left of the Malakoff showed that the enemy were attacking. The night was dark, but clear, and for half an hour our lines were a blaze of quick, intermittent light. The musketry rattled incessantly. Chapman's and Gordon's Batteries opened with all their voices, and the Redan, Malakoff, Garden, and Barrack Batteries replied with roars of ordnance. When the musketry fire flickered and died out commenced for a quarter of an hour a general whirling of shells, so that the light of the very stars was eclipsed, and their dominion usurped by the wandering flight of these iron orbs. Twenty or thirty of these curves of fire tearing the air asunder and uttering their shrill 'tu whit! tu whit! tu whit !' as they described their angry flight in the sky, could be counted and heard at once. While it lasted, it was one of the hottest affairs we have yet experienced.

A party of the 97th, under Captain Plutton, was posted in the advanced trench of the left of the Right Attack. The Russians attacked our working party and drove it in. Lieutenant Brinkley and Lieutenant Preston, with 100 of the 97th, were ordered to proceed to the right of the new sap. On arriving at the trench they found it crowded with the 23rd, that it was impossible to keep the party of the 97th together. This crowded state of the trench is said to have arisen from the 23rd not having recommenced working and remaining in the trench with the covering party of the 77th when the firing ceased. At 12.30 Lieutenant-Colonel Legh, 97th was ordered to take his men to Colonel Bunbury, 23rd, who was in advance of the new sap. He collected forty-five rank and file, and telling Lieutenant Preston to advance with the rest, proceeded to the head of the sap. Here Lieutenant Preston was hit, and one man killed. About 15 yards in front of the sap were stationed Colonel Bunbury and a party of the 77th, under Captain Pechell.

That party having been relieved by the 97th, Colonel Legh placed his men in cover, sending out two parties under Sergeants Coleman and O'Grady in advance. The Russians all of a sudden gave a loud cheer, and the 97th stood up, expecting a rush. When the Russians saw the effect of their ruse, they fired a volley. Lieutenant Preston, in front of Colonel Legh, was mortally wounded, and carried to the rear by Sergeant Coleman; Sergeant O'Grady fell dead just as he had demanded permission to take the enemy's rifle-pits. Lieutenants Ware and Whitehead were sent down to assist. Ware was wounded; but Lieutenant Whitehead succeeded in bringing in all the wounded, except Corporal Macks, who was lying close to the rifle-pit with two legs broken. Lieutenant Brinkley came up in support. The Russians retired from the pits before dawn, having put three officers and twenty-four men *hors de combat*. The Russians lost at least 600 men. The French loss was upwards of 300 men *hors de combat*.

At last, on the morning of the 5th of September, the Allied batteries opened fire for the sixth time, and the last bombardment commenced. A gentle breeze from the south-east, which continued all day, drifted over the steppe, and blew gently into Sebastopol. The sun shone serenely through the vapours of early morning and wreaths of snowy clouds, on the long lines of white houses inside those rugged defences of earth and gabionnade which have so long kept our armies gazing in vain on this 'august city'. The ships floated on the waters of the roads, which were smooth as a mirror, and reflected the forms of these 'monarchs of the main'. Outside our own fleet and that of the French were reposing between Kasatch and Constantino as idly as though they were 'painted ships upon a painted ocean'.

Suddenly, close to the Bastion du Mât, along the earthen curtain between Nos. 7 and 8 Bastions, three jets of flame sprang up into the air and hurled up as many pillars of earth and dust, 100 feet high, which were warmed into ruddy hues by the horizontal rays of the sun. The French had exploded three fougasses to blow in the counterscarp, and to serve as a signal to their men. In a moment, from the sea to the Dockyard Creek, a stream of fire 3 miles in length seemed to run like a train from battery to battery, and fleecy, curling, rich white smoke ascended, as though the earth had suddenly been rent in the throes of an earthquake, and was vomiting forth the material of her volcanoes. The lines of the French trenches were at once covered as though the very clouds of heaven had settled down upon them, and were whirled about in spiral jets, in festoons, in clustering bunches, in columns and in sheets, all commingled, involved together, and uniting as it were by the vehement flames beneath. The crash of such a tremendous fire must have been appalling, but the wind and the peculiar condition of the atmosphere did not permit the sound to produce any great effect in our camp; in the city, for the same reason, the noise must have been terrific and horrible. The iron storm tore over the Russian lines, tossing up, as if in sport, jets of earth and dust, rending asunder gabions, and 'squelching' the parapets, or dashing in amongst the houses and ruins in their rear. The terrible files of this flying army, extending about 4 miles in front, rushed across the plain, carrying death and terror in their train, swept with heavy and irresistible wings the Russian flanks, and searched their centre to the core. A volley so startling, simultaneous, and tremendously powerful, was probably never before discharged since cannon were introduced.

The Russians seemed for a while utterly paralysed. Their batteries were not manned with strength enough to enable them to reply to such an overlapping and crushing fire; but the French, leaping to their guns with astounding energy, rapidity, and vigour, kept on filling the very air with the hurling storm, and sent it in unbroken fury against their enemies. More than 200 pieces of artillery of large calibre, admirably served and well directed, played incessantly upon the hostile lines. In a few moments a great veil of smoke – 'a war-cloud rolling dun' – spread from the guns on the left of Sebastopol; but the roar of the shot did not cease, and the cannonade now pealed forth in great irregular bursts, now died away into hoarse murmurs, again swelled up into tumult, or rattled from one extremity to the other of the line like the file-fire of infantry. Stone walls at once went down before the discharge, but the earthworks yawned to receive shot and shell alike. However, so swift and incessant was the passage of these missiles through the embrasures and along the top of the parapets, that the enemy had to lie close, and scarcely dare show themselves in the front line of their defences. For a few minutes the French had it all their own way, and appeared to be on the point of sweeping away the place without resistance. This did not last long, as after, they had fired a few rounds from each of their numerous guns, the Russian artillerymen got to work, and began to return the fire. They made good practice, but fired slowly and with precision, as if they could not afford to throw away an ounce of powder. The French were stimulated rather than restrained by such a reply to their astonishing volleys, and sent their shot with greater rapidity along the line of the defences, and among the houses of the town. Our Naval Brigade and siege train maintained their usual destructive and solid 'hammering' away at the faces of the Redan and of the Malakoff, and aided our Allies by shell practice on the batteries from the Creek to the Redan. Now two or three mortars from Gordon's, then two or three mortars from Chapman's, hurled 10- and 13-inch shells behind the enemy's works, and connected the discharges by rounds from long 32s or 68s.

Our Quarry Battery, armed with two mortars and eight cohorns, just 400 yards below the Redan, plied the suburb in the rear of the Malakoff vigorously with bombs, and kept the top of the Redan clear with round shot and grape. Redan and Malakoff were alike silent, ragged, and torn. At most the Redan fired three guns, and the adjoining batteries were equally parsimonious. The parapets were all pitted with shot and shell, and the sides of the embrasures greatly injured, so that the gabions were sticking out, and dislodged in all directions. There was no more of that fine polishing and of that cabinet-maker's work which the Russians bestowed on their batteries; our constant fire by night, the efforts of our riflemen, and incessant shelling, having rather checked their assiduous anxiety as to external appearance.

After two hours and a half of furious firing, the artillerymen of our Allies suddenly ceased, in order to let their guns cool and to rest themselves. The Russians crept out to repair damages to their works, and shook sandbags full of earth from the banquette over the outside of their parapets. Their gunners also took advantage of the sudden cessation to open on our Sailors' Batteries in the Left Attack, and caused us some little annoyance from the 'Crow's Nest'. At ten o'clock, however, having previously exploded some fougasses, as before, the French reopened a fire if possible more rapid and tremendous than their first, and continued to keep it up with the utmost vigour till twelve o'clock at noon, by which time the Russians had only a few guns in the Flagstaff Road and Garden Batteries in a position to reply. We could see them in great agitation sending men and carts to and fro across the bridge, and at nine o'clock a powerful column of infantry crossed over to resist our assault, while a movement towards Inkerman was made by the army of the Belbek. Soon after our fire began, the working parties which go over to the north side every morning were recalled, and marched back again across the bridge to the south, no doubt to be in readiness for our expected assault.

From twelve to five o'clock p.m. the firing was slack; the French then resumed their cannonade with the same vigour as at dawn and at ten o'clock, and never ceased their volleys of shot and shell against the place till half-past seven, when darkness set in, whereupon all the mortars and heavy guns, English as well as French, opened with shell against the whole line of defences. A description of this scene is impossible. There was not one instant in which the shells did not whistle through the air; not a moment in which the sky was not seamed by their fiery curves or illuminated by their explosion. Every shell burst as it ought, and the lines of the Russian earthworks of the Redan, Malakoff, and of all their batteries, were rendered plainly visible by the constant light of the innumerable explosions. The Russians scarcely attempted a reply

At five o'clock it was observed that a frigate in the second line, near the north side, was smoking, and, as it grew darker, flames were seen to issue from her sides. Men and officers rushed to the front in the greatest delight and excitement, and, as night came on, the whole vessel was enveloped in one grand blaze from stem to stern. The delight of the crowd upon Cathcart's Hill was intense. 'Well, this is indeed a sight! To see one of those confounded ships touched at last!' These, and many different and stronger expressions, were audible on all sides, but there were some wise people who thought the Russians had set the ship on fire, or that incendiaries and malcontents were at work, and one gentleman even went so far as to say that he 'thought it was merely a signal maybe to recall their cavalry from Eupatoria!'

It is not known precisely how the thing was done. Some said it was done by the French; others, by ourselves; and bombs, redhot shot, and rockets were variously named as the means by which the vessel was set on fire. In spite of the efforts of the Russians, the flames spread, and soon issued from the ports and quartergallery. At eight o'clock the light was so great that the houses of the city and the forts on the other side could be distinguished without difficulty. The masts stood long, towering aloft like great pillars of fire; but one after the other they came down; the decks fell in about ten o'clock, and at midnight the frigate had burnt to the water's edge.

At night a steady fire was kept up with the view of preventing the Russians repairing damages. At 10 p.m. orders were sent to our batteries to open the following morning, as soon as there was a good light, but they were limited to fifty rounds each gun. At 5.30 a.m. the whole of the batteries from Quarantine to Inkerman began their fire with a grand crash. There were three breaks or lulls in the tempest; one from half-past eight till ten; another from twelve till five; and the third from half-past six till seven – during these intervals the fire was comparatively slack.

The agitation in the town was considerable throughout the day; and the enemy seemed to be greatly distressed. They were strengthening their position on the north side – throwing up batteries, dragging guns into position, and preparing to defend themselves should they be obliged to leave the city. They evinced a disposition to rely upon the north side, and were removing their stores by the large bridge of pontoons, and by the second and smaller bridge of boats to the Karabalnayia. Notwithstanding the large number of men in the town, the enemy showed in strength from Inkerman to Mackenzie; and General Pelissier and General Simpson received intelligence which led them to believe that the enemy meditated another attack on the line of the Tchemaya as the only means of averting the fall of the place.

The bombardment was renewed on Thursday night at sunset, and continued without intermission till an hour before daybreak on Friday. The trench guards were ordered to keep up a perpetual fusillade on the face of the Russian works, and about 150,000 rounds were expended each night after the opening of the bombardment.

At daybreak on Friday, the cannonade was reopened, and continued as before – the Russians made no reply on the centre, but their Inkerman Batteries fired on the French Right Attack. A strong wind from the north blew clouds of dust from the town, and carried back the smoke of the batteries, so that it was very difficult to ascertain the effect of the fire; but now and then the veil opened, and at each interval the amount of destruction disclosed was more evident.

A bright flame broke out in the rear of the Redan in the afternoon, and another fire was visible in the town over the Woronzoff Road at a later period of the evening. At 11 p.m. a tremendous explosion took place in the town, but it could not be ascertained exactly where or how it occurred. At dusk, the cannonade ceased, and the bombardment recommenced – the thunder of the bombs bursting from the sea-shore to the Tchernaya sounded like the roll of giant musketry. The Russians replied feebly, threw bouquets into the French trenches, and showers of vertical grape into ours, and lighted up the works now and then with fire-balls and carcasses. Captain John Buckley, Scots Fusileer Guards, was killed in the evening as he was posting his sentries in the ravine between the Malakoff and the Redan in front of our advanced trench of the Right Attack. Major M'Gowan, 93rd Regiment, was taken prisoner, and Captain Drummond was killed soon afterwards at this spot. Captain Buckley was a young officer of zeal and promise. He was devoted to his profession, and although he was wounded so severely at the Alma that he could have had every excuse and right to go home, he refused to do so, and as soon as he came out of hospital, on board a man-of-war, in which he was present when the attack of the 17th October was made, he returned to his regiment and shared its privations during the winter of '54–5. In twenty-four hours, we lost one officer, eleven rank and file killed, and forty-eight rank and file wounded.

In addition to the burning ship and the fires in the town, a bright light was observed at the head of the great shears of the Dockyard about four o'clock in the afternoon, and it continued to burn fiercely throughout the night. It was probably intended to light up the Dockyard below, or to serve as a signal, but it was for some time imagined that the shears had been set on fire by a shell. The night was passed in a fever of expectation and anxiety amid the roar of the bombardment, which the wind blew in deafening bursts back on the Allied camp.

The contest on which the eyes of Europe had been turned so long – the event on which the hopes of so many mighty empires depended, was all but determined. On the 9th September, Sebastopol was in flames! The fleet, the object of so much diplomatic controversy and of so many bloody struggles, had disappeared in the deep! One more great act of carnage was added to the tremendous but glorious tragedy, of which the whole world, from the most civilized nations down to the most barbarous hordes of the East, was the anxious and excited audience.

The weather changed suddenly on the 7th September, and on the morning of the 8th it became bitterly cold. A biting wind right from the north side of Sebastopol blew intolerable clouds of harsh dust into our faces. The sun was obscured; and the sky became of a leaden wintry grey. The cannonade languished purposely towards noon; but the Russians, catching sight of the cavalry and troops in front, began to shell Cathcart's Hill and the heights, and the bombs and long ranges disturbed the equanimity of some of the spectators by bursting with loud 'thuds' right over their heads, and sending 'the gunners' pieces' sharply about them.

After hours of suspense, the moment came at last. At five minutes before twelve o'clock, the French issued forth from the trenches close to the Malakoff, crossed the 7 metres of ground which separated them from the enemy at a few bounds – scrambled up its face, and were through the embrasures in the twinkling of an eye. They drifted as lightly and quickly as autumn leaves before the wind, battalion after battalion, and in a minute after the head of their column issued from the ditch the tricolour was floating over the Korniloff Bastion. Our Allies took the Russians by surprise, very few of the latter were in the Malakoff; but they soon recovered themselves, from twelve o'clock till past seven in the evening the French had to meet repeated attempts to regain the work: then, weary of the fearful slaughter, despairing of success, the Muscovite General withdrew his exhausted legions, and prepared, with admirable skill, to evacuate the place. As soon as the tricolour was observed waving through the smoke and dust over the parapet of the Malakoff, four rockets were sent up from Chapman's attack one after another, as a signal for our assault upon the Redan. They were almost borne back by the violence of the wind, and the silvery jets of sparks they threw out on exploding were scarcely visible against the raw grey sky.

Now, it will be observed that, while we attacked the Redan with two divisions only, a portion of each being virtually in reserve and not engaged in the affair at all, the French made their assault on the Malakoff with four divisions of the 2nd Corps d'Armée, the first and fourth divisions forming the storming columns, and the third and fifth being the support, with reserves of 10,000 men.

It was a few minutes after twelve when our men left the fifth parallel. In less than five minutes the troops, passing over about 230 yards from the approach to the parapet of the Redan, had lost a large proportion of their officers. The Riflemen behaved, as usual, admirably; but could not do much to reduce the fire of the guns on the flanks and below the re-entering angles. As they came nearer, the fire became less fatal. They crossed the abattis without difficulty; it was torn to pieces and destroyed by our shot, and the men stepped over and through it with ease. The Light Division made straight for the salient and projecting angle of the Redan, and came to the ditch, at this place about 15 feet deep. The men, led by their officers, leaped into the ditch, and scrambled up the other side, whence they scaled the parapet almost without opposition; for the few Russians who were in front ran back and got behind their traverses and breastworks, and opened fire upon them as soon as they saw our men on the top.

As the Light Division rushed out into the open, the guns of the Barrack Battery, and on the proper right of the Redan, loaded with grape, caused considerable loss ere they reached the salient. One officer told me the Russians visible in the Redan when we got into it did not exceed 150 men, that we could have carried the breastworks at the base with the greatest ease, if we had only made a rush for it. He expressed his belief that they had no fieldpieces from one re-entering angle to the other. Another officer positively assured me that when he got on the top of the parapet he saw, about 100 yards in advance, a breastwork with gaps, through which were the muzzles of field-pieces, and that in rear of it were compact masses of infantry, the front rank kneeling with fixed bayonets as if prepared to receive a charge of cavalry, while the rear ranks kept up a sharp and destructive fire. The only way to reconcile these discrepancies is to suppose that the first spoke of the earliest stage of the assault, and that the latter referred to a later period, when the Russians, having been reinforced by the fugitives from the Malakoff, and by the troops behind the barracks in the rear, may have opened embrasures in the breastwork. Lamentable as it no doubt is, and incredible almost to those who know how well the British soldier generally behaves in presence of the enemy, the men, when they reached the parapet, were seized by some strange infatuation, and began firing, instead of following their officers, who were now falling fast. Most men stand fire much better than the bayonet – they will keep up a fusillade a few paces off much sooner than they will close with an enemy. It is difficult enough sometimes to get cavalry to charge, if they can find any decent excuse to lay by their swords and take to pistol and carabine, with which they are content to pop away for ever; and when cover of any kind is near, a trench-bred infantry-man finds the charms of the cartridge quite irresistible.

The 77th Regiment furnished 160 men for the ladder party, and 200 for the storming party. The former, under the command of Major Welsford, were to proceed to the advanced parallel, and the latter, under the command of Lieutenant-Colonel Handcock, were to be in the fifth parallel. At 5 a.m. the regiment paraded and marched off. Eight men were told off to each ladder, and they had orders to leave the trench when the appointed signal was made from the Malakoff. They were to be preceded by 100 of the Rifle Brigade, and by some Sappers and Miners to cut down the abattis, and they were to be followed by 160 of the 3rd Buffs, with twenty ladders also. The storming party was to follow the ladder party. A few minutes after twelve, Major Welsford, seeing the signal flying from the Malakoff, gave the word: 'Ladders to the front!' The men instantly ran out of the parallel towards the salient of the Redan, and at the same time, Colonel Handcock, with his 200 stormers of the 97th, and 100 of the 90th, left the parallel. The ladders were managed with difficulty, but on entering the place there was little or no resistance. However, the Russians were soon roused out of their casemates, and flocked to the traverses, from which they kept up a heavy fire on the men getting over the parapet or through the embrasures. By a rapidly increasing flanking and direct fire, converging on the salient, the Russians diminished our force; and as we were weakened they were strengthened by parties from both re-entering angles. The leader of the ladder party was killed by a gun fired as he entered the embrasure; Captain Sibthorpe was hit in two places; Lieutenant Fitzgerald and Ensign Hill were wounded; Lieutenant-Colonel Handcock was mortally wounded; M'Gregor fell inside the Redan; Captain Lumley was badly wounded; Lieutenant Goodenough died of his wounds; Captain Woods and Lieutenant Browne were also hit, so that the 97th Regiment had five officers killed and six wounded, out of a complement of thirteen engaged; and 201 noncommissioned officers and men out of 360. Those officers of the regiment who saw Colonel Windham in the Redan say they were in ten minutes before they observed him. The 3rd Buffs and 41st came in through the embrasures immediately after the 97th and 90th, then the enemy made their rush, and drove the English into the angle, and finally over the parapet to the exterior slope, where men of different regiments of the Light and Second Divisions were packed together firing into the Redan. One hour and a half had elapsed. The Russians had cleared the Redan, but were not in possession of the parapets, when they made a second charge with bayonets under a heavy fire of musketry from the rear, and throwing quantities of stones, grape and round-shot, drove those in front back on the men in the rear, who were precipitated into the ditch. The gabions in the parapets gave way, and rolled down with those upon them; the men in the rear retired precipitately into the fifth parallel. A party of the 30th advanced from this parallel just as Colonel Windham was asking for reinforcements, and ran up to the salient of the Redan, where they suffered severe loss. Captain Rowlands, 41st, made a gallant attempt with a few men, but they were nearly all killed or wounded, and he was obliged to retire. Colonel Legh, Lieutenant Whitehead, Captain Sibthorpe, Lieutenants Browne and Fitzgerald, remained, till only three privates were left in the angle.

The storming columns of the Second Division issuing out of the fifth parallel rushed up immediately after the Light Division; but when they came close to the apex, Colonel Windham brought them to the right flank of the Light Division, so as to come on the slope of the proper left face of the Redan. The first embrasure to which they came was in flames, but, moving on to the next, the men leaped into the ditch, and, with the aid of ladders and of each other's hands, scrambled up on the other side, climbed the parapet, or poured in through the embrasure, which was undefended. Colonel Windham was the first or one of the first men to enter, and with him, Pat Mahony, a great grenadier of the 41st, Kennelly and Cornellis, privates of the same regiment. As Mahony entered with a cheer, he was shot through the head by a Russian rifleman, and fell dead; at the same moment Kennelly and Cornellis were wounded. (The latter claimed the reward of *5l* offered by Colonel Herbert to the first man of his division who entered the Redan.) Running parallel to the faces of the Redan there was an inner parapet, intended to shield the gunners at the embrasures from the splinters of shell. Cuts in the rear enabled the men to retire, and strong and high traverses ran along the sides.

At the base of the Redan, before the re-entering angles, was a breastwork, or, rather, a parapet with an irregular curve, which ran in front of the body of the place to the height of a man's neck. As our men entered through the embrasures, the few Russians who were between the salient and this breastwork retreated behind the latter, or got behind the traverses for protection. From these they poured in a quick fire on the parapet of the salient, which was crowded by the men of the Second and Light Divisions; and they began to return the fire without advancing or charging. There were riflemen behind the lower traverses near the base of the Redan, who kept up a galling fire. The Russians were encouraged to maintain their ground by the immobility of our soldiers and the weakness of a fusillade from the effects of which the enemy were well protected. In vain the officers, by voice and example, urged our soldiers to clear the work. The men, most of whom belonged to regiments which had suffered in the trenches, and were acquainted with the traditions of June 18th, had an impression that the Redan was extensively mined, and that if they advanced they would all be blown up. The officers fell, singled out as a mark for the enemy by their courage. The men of the different regiments got mingled together in inextricable confusion. All the Brigadiers, save Colonel Windham, were wounded, or rendered unfit for the guidance of the attack.

This was going on at the proper left face of the Redan, while nearly the same scene was being repeated at the salient. Every moment our men were diminishing in numbers, while the Russians were arriving from the town, and from the Malakoff, which had been occupied by the French. Thrice did Colonel Windham despatch officers to Sir W. Codrington, who was in the fifth parallel, to entreat him to send up supports in formation; all these three officers were wounded as they passed from the ditch of the Redan to the rear. Supports were, indeed, sent up, but they advanced in disorder, and in driblets, only to increase the confusion and the carnage. The narrow neck of the salient was too close to allow of any formation; and the more the men crowded into it, the worse was the disorder, and the more they suffered from the enemy's fire. This miserable work lasted for an hour. Colonel Windham resolved to go to General Codrington himself. Seeing Captain Crealock, of the 90th, he said, 'I must go to the General for supports. Now, mind, let it be known, in case I am killed, why I went away.' He succeeded in gaining the fifth parallel, through a storm of grape and bullets, and standing on the top of the parapet he again asked for support. Sir W. Codrington asked him if he thought he really could do anything with such supports as he could afford, and said, if he thought so, 'he might take the Royals,' who were then in the parallel. 'Let the officers come out in front – let us advance in order, and if the men keep their formation the Redan is ours,' was the Colonel's reply. But at that moment our men were seen leaping into the ditch, or running down the parapet of the salient, and through the embrasures out of the work into the ditch, the Russians following them with the bayonet, musketry, and throwing stones and grape-shot at them as they lay in the ditch.

But the solid weight of the advancing mass, urged on and fed each moment from the rear by company after company, and battalion after battalion, prevailed at last against the isolated and disjointed band, which had abandoned that protection which unanimity of courage affords, and had lost the advantages of discipline and obedience. As though some giant rock advanced into the sea, and forced back the agitated waters that buffeted it, so did the Russian columns press down against the spray of soldiery which fretted their edge with fire and steel, and contended in vain against their weight. The struggling band was forced back by the enemy, who moved on, crushing friend and foe beneath their solid tramp. Bleeding, panting, and exhausted, our men lay in heaps in the ditch beneath the parapet, sheltered themselves behind stones and in bomb craters in the external slope of the work, or tried to pass back to our advanced parallel and sap, having to run the gauntlet of a tremendous fire.

The scene in the ditch was appalling, although some of the officers assured me that they and the men were laughing at the precipitation with which many fellows plunged headlong upon the mass of bayonets, muskets, and sprawling soldiers, the ladders were all knocked down or broken, so that it was difficult for the men to scale the other side, and the dead, the dying, the wounded, and the uninjured, were all lying in piles together.

General Pelissier observed the failure of our attack from the rear of the Malakoff, and sent over to General Simpson to ask if he intended to renew it. The English Commander-in-Chief did not feel in a condition to do so. The Guards and Highlanders, the Third and Fourth Divisions, and most of the reserves, had not been engaged. As soon as we abandoned the assault, the firing slackened along our front; but in the rear of the Malakoff there was a fierce contest going on between masses of Russians, released from the Redan, or drawn from the town, and the French inside the work; and the fight for the Little Redan, on the proper left of the Malakoff, was raging furiously. Clouds of smoke and dust obstructed the view, but the rattle of musketry was incessant, and betokened the severe nature of the struggle below. Through the breaks in the smoke there could be seen now and then a tricolour, surmounted by an eagle, fluttering bravely over the inner parapet of the Malakoff. The storm of battle rolled fiercely round it, and beat against it; but it was sustained by strong arms and stout hearts, and all the assaults of the enemy were vain against it. It would be untrue to say that the result of our assault was not the source of deep grief and mortification to us, which all the glorious successes of our Allies could not wholly alleviate. Even those who thought any attack on the Redan useless and unwise, inasmuch as the possession of the Malakoff would, in their opinion, render the Redan untenable, could not but regret bitterly that, having undertaken the assault, we had not achieved a decisive triumph, and that so much blood had been, if not ingloriously, at least fruitlessly, poured forth.

The French, indeed, were generous enough to say that our troops behaved with great bravery, and that they wondered how we kept the Redan so long under such a tremendous fire; but British soldiers are rather accustomed to the *nil admirari* under such circumstances, and praise like that gives pain as well as pleasure. Many soldiers, entertaining the opinion to which I have alluded, think that we should at once have renewed the attempt. It is but small consolation to them to know that General Simpson intended to attack the Redan the following morning, inasmuch as the Russians by their retreat deprived us of the chance of retrieving our reputation, and at the same time acknowledged the completeness of the success achieved by our Allies, and the tremendous superiority of the fire directed against them.

The Second Brigade, Light Division, stormed at noon. The 97th and 90th, 300 of each, commanded, the former by Major Welsford (whose head was blown off as he was mounting an embrasure – the gun was fired by a Russian officer, who immediately gave himself up as a prisoner to a sergeant of the 97th, that entered the moment after, throwing down his sword and saying, 'I am a prisoner of war'), the latter by Captain Grove, the senior officer of the regiment present with the service companies. The salient was carried at once, and the men entered the stronghold, which is a work traced on a most obtuse angle, requiring a large mass of men to assault it, not only at the salient, but at the same moment on both flanks, so as to turn them, and to enable the salient storming party to advance down the interior space of the works at once, taking the defenders in front and flank, and indeed in rear, at the same moment. In consequence of attacking the salient only, no front could be formed, on account of the small interior space at that point; the men were forced to advance by driblets, and at the same moment fired on from traverses on either flank, where they could not see their assailants, an evil at once obviated had the attack on the flanks and salient been simultaneous.

The handful of men who assaulted and took the salient most gallantly held it against far superior numbers for a considerable time, until their ammunition being nearly expended, and receiving no flank support, which could alone assist them to any purpose, and being rushed on from these flanks by a vastly superior force, they retreated to the extreme side of the parapet, where they remained, and, being reinforced by some fresh men, kept up a heavy and continuous fire on the Russians in the interior of the work. They held their ground on this fast sinking parapet of loose earth, stones and broken gabions, under a most galling fire from both flanks and in front, and continuous showers of vertical grape, from inside the work, for an hour and a half at least, when a sudden rush, made by the enemy, who had crept up the faces by the traverses, obliged the troops to give way, and step by step, pelting each other with huge stones, they retired, slipping and tumbling into the ditch, where many poor fellows were buried alive, from the scarps giving way. Then came the fearful run for life or death, with men rolling over like rabbits, then tumbling into the English trench, where the men lay four deep on each other. The men once in manned the parapet, and kept up a heavy and continuous fire on the enemy on the parapets of the Redan.

The rest you know. The Rifles behaved nobly, and where they had tried to creep up the ditch to pick off the Russians on the flanks, they lay four and five deep, all together. Colonel Lysons, of the 23rd, as usual, was all energy, and, though severely wounded through the thigh and unable to stand, remained on the ground cheering on the men. Colonel Handcock, of the 97th, was shot through the head on the crest of the Redan, and died soon after arriving in camp. Captain Preston, and Lieutenants Swift and Wilmer, of the 90th, were all killed inside, where their bodies were found the next morning. Captain Vaughan, of the 90th, was shot in both legs, and taken prisoner when we left the place, it being impossible to get him over the ditch. He was found in a Russian hospital and brought to camp to die. Lieutenant and Adjutant Dyneley, of the 23rd Fusileers, was mortally wounded. Individual deeds of daring were too frequent to particularize. The first dead

Russian on the extreme salient was a Russian officer shot through the mouth – a singularly handsome man, with hands and feet white and delicate as a woman's.

The 41st, which followed the Light Division storming party, whose position in advance was determined, as I have already stated by Colonel Windham and Colonel Unett 'tossing up for choice', got into the Redan nearly as soon as the 90th and 97th, who formed the leading column of attack on the salient, and the parties of each division were soon inextricably mixed. I do not know the names of the first soldiers of the 90th and 97th who got in, but several soldiers of these regiments lay dead and wounded in advance near the Russian breastwork on the morning of the 9th. The men of the 41st who rushed into the Redan with Colonel Windham, were, Hartnardy, Kennelly, Cornellis, and Pat Mahony the last, a fine tall grenadier, fell dead in the embrasure by Colonel Windham's side, shot through the heart as he was shouting, 'Come on, boys – come on!' His blood spouted over those near him, but the men rushed on till they became confused among the traverses, and then the scene took place which I have tried to describe. The salient, however favourable to the assailants in one sense, was extremely disadvantageous to them in another, inasmuch as it prevented them getting into any kind of formation. It was, of course, the apex of the triangle, and was very narrow, while the enemy firing from the base poured a concentrated fire upon the point, and felled every man who showed boldly from behind the traverses, and the parapet upon which our soldiers were crowded. At the first rush, had Colonel Windham been able to get a handful of men together to charge at the breastwork, the few Russians there must have been routed, and by the time their reinforcements came up our men would have been able to reverse the face of the breastwork, and to close the Redan to their assailants. But seconds of time generate great events in war. Our delay gave the enemy time both to recover from their panic when they were driven from the salient, and to send up strong bodies of men from their bomb-proofs and the cover at the back of the Redan; and by degrees this accumulating mass, advancing from the angles of the breastwork, moved up along the traverses parallel with the parapets of the Redan, and drove our men into the salient, where, by feeble driblets and incapable of formation, they were shot down in spite of the devotion and courage of their leader and the example of their officers. The salient was held by our men for one hour and fifty-six minutes!

While General Codrington, who seemed (in the opinion of those around him) to have lost for the time the coolness which characterized him, was hesitating about sending up more men, or was unable to send them up in any formation so as to form a nucleus of resistance and attack, the Redan was lost, and our men, pressed by the bayonet, by heavy fusillades, and by some field guns which the enemy had now brought up, were forced over the parapet into the ditch. Colonel Eman, one of the very best officers in the army – a man of singular calmness and bravery, who was beloved by his regiment, his officers and men, and whose loss was lamented by all who knew him – was shot through the lungs as he was getting his men into order. His sword arm was uplifted over his head at the time, and it was thought his lungs were uninjured. The surgeon, when he was carried back, told him so, but he knew too well such hopes were vain. 'I feel I am bleeding internally,' he said, with a sad smile. He died that night. Two Captains of the same regiment fell beside him – Corry and Lockhart. Captain Rowlands, who very much distinguished himself, had the most extraordinary escapes, and was only slightly wounded, though hit in two places. This detachment lost 184 officers and men. The 49th, who were in reserve, lost one officer killed, two wounded, two privates killed, and twenty-three wounded. For the last thirty minutes of this contest the English, having exhausted their ammunition, threw stones at their opponents, but the Russians retaliated with terrible effect by 'handgrape' and small cannon-shot, which they hurled at our men. Captain Rowlands was knocked down and stunned by one of these missiles, which hit him right on the eye. As soon as he recovered and got up, he was struck by another grape-shot in the very same place, and knocked down again.

The 30th Regiment was formed in the fourth parallel, left in front, on the right of the 55th; and when the storming party moved out of the fifth parallel the supports occupied it, and were immediately ordered to advance on the salient angle of the Redan, by three companies at a time, from the left. The distance from the place in which they were posted up to the salient considerably exceeded 200 yards; and as the men had to cut across as quickly as they could in order to escape the raking fire of grape, and to support the regiments in front, they were breathless when they arrived at the ditch. When they arrived, all blown by this double, they found only two scaling-ladders at the scarp, and two more at the other side, to climb up to the parapet. They got over, however, and ascended the face of the Redan. By the time the supports got up, the Russians were pushing up their reserves in great force, and had already got some field-pieces up to the breastwork; and the regiment falling into the train of all around them, instead of advancing, began to fire from the parapet and upper traverses till all their ammunition was exhausted, when they commenced pelting the Russians with stones. In this condition no attempts were made to remove the reserves whatever, while the Russians accumulated mass after mass upon them from the open ground in rear of the Redan, and deployed their columns on the breastwork, whence they delivered a severe fire upon us. The whole garrison of the Malakoff and their supports also came down on the left flank of the Redan and added to our assailants; and indeed there was reason to fight, for the possession of the Redan would have destroyed the enemy's chance of escape. In this gallant regiment there were 16 officers, 23 sergeants, &c., and 384 privates. On marching down to the trenches, 1 officer was killed and 10 were wounded, 6 sergeants were wounded, 41 privates were killed and 101 privates were wounded, and 2 officers and 6 privates died of their wounds.

The 55th Regiment was the support along with the 30th, and was stationed in the fourth parallel till the assaulting columns had cleared out of the fifth parallel, which it then occupied, and left soon afterwards to mingle in the melee at the salient of the Redan. Poor Lt-Col. Cuddy, who assumed the command when Lt-Col.

Cure was wounded in the right arm, was killed as he led his men up the open to the face of the Redan; and of the remaining ten officers who went out with the regiment, Captain Morgan, Captain Hume, Lieutenant J. R. Hume, and Lieutenant Johnson were wounded. The regiment went out less than 400 strong, and suffered a loss of 140 officers and men killed and wounded.

Our attack lasted about an hour and three-quarters, and in that time we lost more men than at Inkerman, where the fighting lasted for seven hours. At 1.48 p.m., which was about the time we retired, there was an explosion either of a tumbrel or of a fougasse between the Mamelon and the Malakoff, to the right, which seemed to blow up several Frenchmen, and soon afterwards the artillery of the Imperial Guard swept across from the rear towards the Little Redan, and gave us indication that our Allies had gained a position from which they could operate against the enemy with their fieldpieces. From the opening of the attack the French batteries over Careening Bay had not ceased to thunder against the Russian fleet, which lay silently at anchor below; and a lively cannonade was kept up between them and the Inkerman batteries till the evening, which was interrupted every now and then by the intervention of the English redoubt, and the late Selinghinsk and Volhynia redoubts, which engaged the Russian batteries at the extremity of the harbour. At one o'clock wounded men began to crawl up from the batteries to the camp; they could tell us little or nothing, 'Are we in the Redan?' 'Oh, yes; but a lot of us is killed, and the Russians are mighty strong.' Some were cheerful, others desponding; all seemed proud of their wounds. Half an hour more, and the number of wounded increased; they came up by twos and threes, and – what I had observed before as a bad sign – the number of stragglers accompanying them, under the pretence of rendering assistance, became greater also. Then the ambulances and the cacolets (or mule litters) came in sight along the Woronzoff Road filled with wounded. Every ten minutes added to their numbers, and we could see that every effort was made to hurry them down to the front as soon as they were ready for a fresh load. The litter-bearers now added to the length of the melancholy train. We heard that the temporary hospitals in front were full, and that the surgeons were beginning to get anxious about the extent of their accommodation for the wounded.

Another bad sign was, that the enemy never ceased throwing up shell to the front, many of which burst high in the air, over our heads, while the pieces flew with a most unpleasant whir around us. These shells were intended for our reserves; and, although the fusees did not burn long enough for such a range, and they all burst at a considerable elevation, they caused some little injury and annoyance to the troops in the rear, and hit some of our men. The rapidly increasing swarms of wounded men, some of whom had left their arms behind them, at last gave rise to suspicions of the truth; but their answers to many eager questioners were not very decisive or intelligible, and some of them did not even know what they had been attacking. One poor young fellow, who was stumping stiffly up with a broken arm and a ball through his shoulder, carried off his firelock with him, but he made a *naïve* confession that he had 'never fired it off, for he could not'. The piece turned out to be in excellent order. It struck one that such men as these, however brave, were scarcely a fit match for the well-drilled soldiers of Russia; and yet we were trusting the honour, reputation, and glory of Great Britain to undisciplined lads from the plough, or the lanes of our towns and villages! As one example of the sort of recruits we received, I may mention that there was a considerable number of men in draughts, which came out to regiments in the Fourth Division, who had only been enlisted a few days, and who had never fired a rifle in their lives!

There was a feeling of deep depression in camp. We knew the French were in the Malakoff only, and we were painfully aware that our attack had failed. It was an eventful night. The camp was full of wounded men; the hospitals were crowded; sad stories ran from mouth to mouth respecting the losses of the officers and the behaviour of the men.

Fatigued and worn out, I lay down to rest, but scarcely to sleep. At my last walk to the front after sunset, nothing was remarkable except the silence of the batteries on both sides. About seven o'clock, an artillery officer in the Quarries observed the enemy pouring across the bridge to the north side, and sent word to that effect to General Simpson. About eleven o'clock my hut was shaken by a violent shock as of an earthquake, but I was so thoroughly tired, that it did not rouse me for more than an instant; having persuaded myself it was 'only a magazine', I was asleep again. In another hour these shocks were repeated in quick succession, so that Morpheus himself could not have slumbered on, and I walked up to Cathcart's Hill. Fires blazed in Sebastopol, but they were obscured with smoke, and by the dust which still blew through the night air. As the night wore on, these fires grew and spread, fed at intervals by tremendous explosions. The Russians were abandoning the city they had defended so gallantly and so long. Their fleet beneath the waters. A continuous stream of soldiery could be seen marching across the bridge to the north side. And what were we doing? Just looking on.

At 8 o'clock the night before, the Russians began to withdraw from the town, in which they had stored up combustibles, to render Sebastopol a second Moscow. The general kept up a fire of musketry from his advanced posts, as though he intended to renew his efforts to regain the Malakoff. About 12.30 a.m. the Highland Division on duty in the trenches, surprised at the silence in the Redan, sent some volunteers to creep into it. Nothing could they hear but the breathing and groans of the wounded and dying, who, with the dead, were the sole occupants of the place. As it was thought the Redan was mined, the men came back. By two o'clock a.m. the fleet, with the exception of the steamers, had been scuttled and sunk. Flames were observed to break out in different parts of the town. They spread gradually over the principal buildings. At four o'clock a.m. a terrible explosion behind the Redan shook the whole camp; it was followed by four other explosions equally startling. The city was enveloped in fire and smoke, and torn asunder by the tremendous shocks of these volcanoes. At 4.45 a.m. the magazine of the Flagstaff and Garden Batteries blew up. At 5.30 a.m. two of the southern forts, the Quarantine and Alexander, went up into the air, and a great number of live shell followed, and burst in all directions. While this was going on, a steady current of infantry was passing to the north side over the bridge. At 6.45 a.m. the last battalion had passed, and the hill-sides opposite the city were alive with Russian troops. At 7.10 a.m. several small explosions took place inside the town. At 7.12 a.m. columns of black smoke began to rise from a steamer in one of the docks. At 7.15 a.m. the connection of the floating-bridge with the south side was severed. At 7.16 a.m. flames began to ascend from Fort Nicholas. At 8.17 a.m. the last part of the bridge was floated off in portions to the north side. At 9 a.m. several violent explosions took place in the works on our left, opposite the French. At 10 a.m. the town was a mass of flames, and the pillar of velvety fat smoke ascending from it seemed to support the very heavens. The French continued to fire, probably to keep out stragglers; but, ere the Russians left the place, the Zouaves and sailors were engaged in plundering. Not a shot was fired to the front and centre. The Russian steamers were very busy towing boats and stores across. His steamers towed his boats across at their leisure, and when every man had been placed in safety, and not till then, the Russians began to dislocate and float off the different portions of their bridge, and to pull it over to the north side.

This Redan cost us more lives than the capture of Badajoz, without including these who fell in its trenches and approaches and, although the enemy evacuated it, we could scarcely claim the credit of having caused them such loss that they retired owing to their dread of a renewed assault. On the contrary, we must, in fairness, admit that the Russians maintained their hold of the place till the French were established in the Malakoff and the key of the position was torn from their grasp. They might, indeed, have remained in the place longer than they did, as the French were scarcely in a condition to molest them from the Malakoff with artillery; but the Russian general possessed too much genius and experience as a soldier to lose men in defending an untenable position, and his retreat was effected with masterly skill and with perfect ease in the face of a victorious enemy. Covering his rear by the flames of the burning city, and by tremendous explosions, which spoke in tones of portentous warning to those who might have wished to cut off his retreat, he led his battalions in narrow files across a deep arm of the sea, which ought to have been commanded by our guns, and in the face of a most powerful fleet, he actually paraded them in our sight as they crossed, and carried off all his most useful stores and munitions of war. He left us few trophies, and many bitter memories. He sank his ships and blew up his forts without molestation; nothing was done to harass him in his retreat, with the exception of some paltry efforts to break down the bridge by cannon-shot, or to shell the troops as they marched over.

The surprise throughout the camp on the Sunday morning was beyond description when the news spread that Sebastopol was on fire, and that the enemy were retreating. The tremendous explosions, which shook the very ground like so many earthquakes, failed to disturb many of our wearied soldiers. As the rush from camp became very great, and every one sought to visit the Malakoff and the Redan, which were filled with dead and dying men, a line of English cavalry was posted across the front from our extreme left to the French right. They were stationed in all the ravines and roads to the town and trenches, with orders to keep back all persons except the Generals and Staff, and officers and men on duty, and to stop all our men returning with plunder from the town, and to take it from them. As they did not stop the French, or Turks, or Sardinians, this order gave rise to a good deal of grumbling, particularly when a man, after dragging a heavy chair several miles, or a table, or some such article, was deprived of it by our sentries.

Mingled with the plunderers from the front were many wounded men. The ambulances never ceased – now moving heavily and slowly with their burdens, again rattling at a trot to the front for a fresh cargo – and the ground between the trenches and the camp was studded with cacolets or mule litters. Already the funeral parties had commenced their labours. The Russians all this time were swarming on the north side, and evinced the liveliest interest in the progress of the explosions and conflagrations. They took up ground in their old camps, and spread all over the face of the hills behind the northern forts. Their steamers cast anchor, or were moored close to the shore among the creeks, on the north side, near Fort Catherine. By degrees the Generals, French and English, and the Staff officers, edged down upon the town, but Fort Paul had not yet gone up, and Fort Nicholas was burning, and our engineers declared the place would be unsafe for forty-eight hours. Moving down, however, on the right flank of our cavalry pickets, a small party of us managed to turn them cleverly, and to get out among the French works between the Mamelon and Malakoff.

The ground was here literally paved with shot and shell, and the surface was deeply honeycombed by the explosions of the bombs at every square yard. The road was crowded by Frenchmen returning with paltry plunder from Sebastopol, and with files of Russian prisoners, many of them wounded, and all dejected, with the exception of a fine little boy, in a Cossack's cap and a tiny uniform greatcoat, who seemed rather pleased with his kind captors. There was also one stout Russian soldier, who had evidently been indulging in the popularly credited sources of Dutch courage, and who danced all the way into the camp with a Zouave.

There were ghastly sights on the way, too – Russians who had died, or were dying as they lay, brought so far towards the hospitals from the fatal Malakoff. Passing through a maze of trenches, of gabionades, and of zigzags and parallels, by which the French had worked their sure and deadly way close to the heart of the Russian defence, and treading gently among the heaps of dead, where the ground bore full tokens of the bloody fray, we came at last to the head of the French sap. It was barely 10 yards from that to the base of the huge sloping mound of earth which rose full 20 feet in height above the level, and showed in every direction the grinning muzzles of its guns. The tricolour waved placidly from its highest point, and the French were busy constructing a semaphore on the top. There was a ditch at one's feet, some 20 or 22 feet deep, and 10 feet broad. That was the place where the French crossed – there was their bridge of planks, and here they swarmed in upon the unsuspecting defenders of the Malakoff. They had not 10 yards to go. We had 200, and the men were then out of breath. Were not planks better than scaling-ladders?

Inside the sight was too terrible to dwell upon. The French were carrying away their own and the Russian wounded, and four distinct piles of dead were formed to clear the way. The ground was marked by pools of blood, and the smell was noisome; swarms of flies settled on dead and dying; broken muskets, torn clothes, caps, shakos, swords, bayonets, bags of bread, canteens, and haversacks, were lying in indescribable confusion all over the place, mingled with heaps of shot of grape, bits of shell, cartridges, case and canister, loose powder, official papers, and cooking tins. The traverses were so high and deep that it was almost impossible to get a view of the whole of the Malakoff from any one spot, and there was a high mound of earth in the middle of the work, either intended as a kind of shell proof, or the remains of the old White Tower. The guns, which to the number of sixty were found in the work, were all ships' guns, and mounted on ships' carriages, and worked in the same way as ships' guns. There were a few old-fashioned, oddly-shaped mortars. On looking around the work, one might see that the strength of the Russian was his weakness – he fell into his own bomb-proofs. In the parapet of the work might be observed several entrances – very narrow outside, but descending and enlarging downwards, and opening into rooms some 4 or 5 feet high, and 8 or 10 square. These were only lighted from the outside by day, and must have been pitch dark at night, unless the men were allowed lanterns. Here the garrison retired when exposed to a heavy bombardment. The odour of these narrow chambers was villanous, and the air reeked with blood and abominations unutterable. There were several of these places, and they might bid defiance to the heaviest mortars in the world: over the roof was a layer of ships' masts, cut into junks, and deposited carefully; then there was over them a solid layer of earth, and above that a layer of gabions, and above that a pile of earth again.

In one of these dungeons, excavated in the solid rock, and which was probably underneath the old White Tower, the officer commanding seems to have lived. It must have been a dreary residence. The floor and the entrance were littered a foot deep with reports, returns, and perhaps despatches assuring the Czar that the place had sustained no damage.

Descending from the Malakoff, we came upon a suburb of ruined houses open to the sea – it was filled with dead. The Russians had crept away into holes and corners in every house, to die like poisoned rats; artillery horses, with their entrails torn open by shot, were stretched all over the space at the back of the Malakoff, marking the place where the Russians moved up their last column to retake it under the cover of a heavy field battery. Every house, the church, some public buildings, sentry-boxes – all alike were broken and riddled by cannon and mortar. Turning to the left, we proceeded by a very tall snow-white wall of great length to the dockyard gateway. This wall was pierced and broken through and through with cannon. Inside were the docks, which, naval men say, were unequalled in the world. The steamer was blazing merrily in one of them. Gates and store sides were splintered and pierced by shot. There were the stately dockyard buildings on the right, which used to look so clean and white and spruce. Parts of them were knocked to atoms, and hung together in such shreds and patches that it was only wonderful they cohered. The soft white stone of which they and the walls were made was readily knocked to pieces by a cannon-shot.

Of all the pictures of the horrors of war which have ever been presented to the world, the hospital of Sebastopol offered the most horrible, heartrending, and revolting. How the poor human body could be mutilated, and yet hold its soul within it, when every limb is shattered, and every vein and artery is pouring out the life-stream, one might study there at every step, and at the same time wonder how little will kill! The building used as an hospital was one of the noble piles inside the dockyard wall, and was situated in the centre of the row, at right angles to the line of the Redan. The whole row was peculiarly exposed to the action of shot and shell bounding over the Redan, and to the missiles directed at the Barrack Battery; and it bore in sides, roof, windows, and doors, frequent and distinctive proofs of the severity of the cannonade.

Entering one of these doors, I beheld such a sight as few men, thank God, have ever witnessed. In a long, low room, supported by square pillars arched at the top, and dimly lighted through shattered and unglazed window-frames, lay the wounded Russians, who had been abandoned to our mercies by their General. In the midst of one of these 'chambers of horrors' – for there were many of them

– were found some dead and some living English soldiers, and among them poor Captain Vaughan, of the 90th, who afterwards died of his wounds. I confess it was impossible for me to stand the sight, which horrified our most experienced surgeons.

The Great Redan was next visited. Such a scene of wreck and ruin! – all the houses behind it a mass of broken stones – a clock turret, with a shot right through the clock; a pagoda in ruins; another clock tower, with all the clock destroyed save the dial, with the words, 'Barwise, London', thereon; cook-houses, where human blood was running among the utensils; in one place a shell had lodged in the boiler, and blown it and its contents, and probably its attendants, to pieces. Everywhere wreck and destruction. This evidently was a *beau quartier* once. The oldest inhabitant could not have recognized it on that fatal day. Climbing up to the Redan, which was fearfully cumbered with the dead, we witnessed the scene of the desperate attack and defence, which cost both sides so much blood. The ditch outside made one sick – it was piled up with English dead, some of them scorched and blackened by the explosion, and others lacerated beyond recognition. The quantity of broken gabions and gun-carriages here was extraordinary; the ground was covered with them. The bomb-proofs were the same as in the Malakoff, and in one of them a music-book was found, with a woman's name in it, and a canary bird and a vase of flowers were outside the entrance.

In one year we stormed the heights of the Alma, sustained the glorious disaster of Balaklava, fought the great fight of Inkerman, swept the sea of Azoff and its seaboard, wasted Kertch and seized upon Yenikale, witnessed the Battle of the Tchernaya, opened seven bombardments upon Sebastopol, held in check every general and every soldier that Russia could spare; and, after the endurance of every ill that an enemy at home and abroad could inflict upon us – after passing through the summer's heat and winter's frost – after being purged in the fire of sickness and death, repulse and disaster, and, above all, in the glow of victory, the British standard floated over Sebastopol!